TURNING POINTS IN ECONOMIC DEVELOPMENT

STUDIES IN THE SOCIAL SCIENCES

edited by C. A. O. van Nieuwenhuijze

4

TURNING POINTS IN ECONOMIC DEVELOPMENT

by

RUDOLF BIĆANIĆ

1972
MOUTON
THE HAGUE · PARIS

LIBRARY OF CONGRESS CATALOG CARD NUMBER: 71-123128

Printed in The Netherlands by Mouton & Co., Printers, The Hague.

EDITORIAL PREFACE

The intensely sad fact about this book is that it appears at a moment when its author is no longer with us. To those who have known him, whether personally or from his writings, it is some consolation to realize that his work remains, not merely as a memorial but indeed as a stimulus and a guideline for their own continued efforts.

It is appropriate, at this point, to evoke the memory of Professor Rudolf Bićanić in the words of two of his *collegae proximi*, as especially translated for this purpose.

Professor Stanko Pintarić has written as follows:

Professor Bićanić's life was extraordinarily rich and varied both before he joined the faculty and afterwards.

He was born in Bjelovar, June 5, 1905 and he graduated from secondary school there in 1924. According to the custom of that time, and like so many of his contemporaries, he went to Paris for one year of study at the "Ecole des Hautes Etudes Commerciales", and in 1925 got his Certificat d'Etudes, coming second in his whole year. The same year he enrolled at the Zagreb Faculty of Law, and in 1931 graduated as a Doctor of Law. While he was studying he worked in the solicitor's office of Frank Winter in Bjelovar, and from 1929-30 in the Merkur Insurance Society. 1930-32 he was secretary to the General Consul of the Republic of Peru at Zagreb. In 1933 he was sent to prison for three years for offences against the state security. On coming out of prison he became secretary for the Committee for Aid to the Underdeveloped Regions of Yugoslavia, and not long afterwards joined Gospodarska sloga (the economic sector of the Peasant Party) and became its first director. It was here that he founded his Institute for Study of the Peasant and National Economy and began to publish and edit *Politicki vjesnik* [Political Herald]. In 1940 he was called to Belgrade and given the post of Director of Foreign Trade, which post he held when Yugoslavia was occupied. In 1941 he left the country and went with the Yugoslav government to England and from April 1941 he continued to carry out the duties of Deputy Director of the

Yugoslav National Bank. In autumn 1941 he was named member of the National Committee for Reconstruction and Yugoslav representative in the U.N.R.R.A. Committee in London.

Professor Bićanić's life in emigration was rich with many kinds of work with various groups of scholars and well-known research institutes in London, such as: the Royal Institute of International Affairs, the Royal Geographic Society, the Royal Statistical Society, the School of Slavonic Studies, the Fabian Society and the Economic Research Group, and he delivered many lectures on Yugoslav and international economic problems. He became a member of the Presidency of the United Committee of South Slavs in London and president of the economic committee of the All-Slav Committee in London. In 1943 he resigned from the émigré government and in 1944 was authorized by the Committee for the Liberation of Yugoslavia to represent its interests in London. He became the representative of the Yugoslav People's Government in the council of U.N.R.R.A. and head of the delegation at the second session of that council. In February 1945 he returned from emigration to liberated Belgrade and took up his pre-war post of Director of Foreign Trade. The same year he travelled to the U.S.A. as head of the delegation for economic discussions between the two countries, and at the same time took part in the work of our delegation at the San Francisco conference. In autumn 1945 as member of the delegation he took part in the Foreign Ministers Conference in London in connection with Trieste and the Julian Region.

From April 1946 the second phase of his life began. The Council of the Faculty of Law invited him to become professor and he held his lecture courses there for a full 22 years on the economics of Yugoslavia, and on planning. He also gave lecture courses in the economic history of Croatia and the economics of foreign trade.

This phase of Professor Bićanić's life was marked by incredible dynamism and creativity. His first study of human labor had come out when he was only 25. From that time several hundred articles, reviews and polemical discussions followed and more than a score of books, among which were: *How People Live, Life in the Passive Areas, Our Economic Orientation from the World Point of View* (Zagreb, 1939), *The Croatian Economy in the Changeover from Feudalism to Capitalism* (Part I, Zagreb 1951), *Lectures on the Economics of FPRJ* (2 vols., Zagreb, 1953), *Problems of Foreign Trade* (Zagreb, 1954), *The Creation of Capitalism* (Zagreb, 1959), *The Economic Policy of FPRJ* (Zagreb, 1962), *Problems of Planning East and West* (The Hague, 1967). Several of the above works were the subject of fierce polarization in our public life.

In his scholarly and teaching work during his whole life Professor Bićanić worked inductively. He continually pinpointed new problems, analyzed them and worked out approaches in a new and hitherto unexplored field of scholarly work. The whole of his work is lit by the burning desire for discovery which constantly urged him on.

In all his work the first center of interest is the human being, sometimes as a serf, at others as peasant, industrial worker, economist or planner. But his people live in worker's or peasant's families in villages and towns from Zagreb to Rijeka, in Croatia in Yugoslavia. His second circle of interest is in commodities, sectors, times, prices, markets, institutions, social and economic policies, plans, structure, development and complex inter-relationships such as industrial, rural, foreign trade, self-management, social and economic reform. In short his pen was active in writing about everything that was of vital concern to all of us, and in the solutions he offered he was always forward looking.

Because of the plurality of his interests he forced his way ahead parallel on many different lines: especially in statistics, sociology, social policy and econometrics. But nearest to his heart were agricultural economics, foreign trade and sociology and to these he often returned. Unfortunately his last work, one of enormous interest to us today, remained unfinished — a study entitled "Concerning Economic Unity in Yugoslavia". The last subject that he raised in the university teachers council was the employment of the young lawyer. These were the two things that were occupying his mind when his life began to fade.

This country alone was too small for all he had to say. He often travelled and lectured in towns of all five continents and everywhere he went he was remembered for the wit of his spoken or written word. In this way he helped to make our faculty better known from London to Moscow, from Cairo to Johannesburg, from New York to Caracas, from New Delhi to Tokyo, Sydney and New Zealand. He was in personal contact with hundreds of scholars from all over the world.

He developed a very wide field of teaching, delivered lectures, organized post graduate study, held innumerable scholarly and popular lectures all over the country. And in addition to this he used his extra energies by tirelessly writing and thinking, day and night. He was splendid in discussion, and famous for the inexhaustable richness of his ideas. Before he died his hand had become too slow for all he had to say and he turned to modern means such as the tape-recorder and the dictaphone so that his output should be even greater, for he was in a hurry to finish all he had to do. When he worked with young people however his approach was just the opposite, he was unhurried, patient, methodical and optimistic.

Professor Bićanić's life was a truly creative one. Being a great humanist he was universal. To the younger generation he left the quiet message that only through work can a man affirm himself. He showed this by his example. He succeeded because of his great qualities such as: unusual intelligence and courage, enormous knowledge and experience, inexhaustible energy and powers of work, great humanity in his personal relationships, a breadth of spirit, inexhaustable scholarly and cultural curiosity and a continual concern with actual economic and social problems in the world in which he lived and worked.

The death of Professor Bićanić has left a great emptiness which will not easily be filled. He will be our example, and many will follow in the lines he set down but few will reach the place that he did.

As first his student and later his co-worker of many years I wish to express my deep gratitude and that of my colleagues to him, in my own name, and that of 22 generations of students of law to whom he was teacher and who he led on the path of economic culture and understanding.

In his turn, Professor Eugene Pusić has written the following:

It is not easy to write about Rudolf Bićanić. To present him in his full stature seems to me at this moment something that is beyond my powers to do.

What then shall I say? That Rudi Bićanić was, as a man, both loveable and good, without any pretentiousness, that he withstood every kind of force or pressure put upon him, and was at the same time tolerant, disinclined to impose his own views on others, full of varied interests and with boundless intellectual curiosity for the world and for all the problems that the world presents to men, open-minded to everything new, never contented with what he had achieved.

Truly he was all these things, and even more, for it was very rare for anyone to know all the sides of his unusually rich and complex personality. But with people of his order of greatness these attributes attain their true proportions only if we look at them in relationship to the complete man and to the times in which he lived. Only such a view can provide us with a measure of the individual man and his human and humane qualities. This will show us what is great and lasting and will thus remain with us, even though Rudolf Bićanić is with us no longer.

In this wider context of the man and his times the basic thing for an understanding of the character and life of Rudolf Bićanić seems to me to be his utterly sincere, unsentimental, anti-jingoistic and for these reasons truly deep patriotism. He was the real patriot in that he loved his country as it was and worked and fought for it to become what he saw it should be.

The motivating force behind his whole political life was the realization which came very early, that realization which is basic for any realistic concept of Yugoslavia, that the Yugoslav community can only be built up on the basis of equality and respect for the identity of each of the Yugoslav nations, never on any kind of centralism or hegemony.

Parallel with this was his consciousness that a free Yugoslavia can only come into being as a democratic community of the working people of town and village, and never as a court, military, bourgeois, bureaucratic or any other kind of minority group dictatorship, which would inevitably become dependent on one of the great powers and thus jeopardize the independence of the country.

It was these ideas that guided Rudolf Bićanić throughout the whole of his political and scholarly work, from the time he took part in the Yugoslav Youth Movement, his *Economic Basis of the Croatian Question*, his leading position in the left wing of the Croatian Peasant Party, his work in Gospodarska sloga (Economic Research Institute of the Peasant Party), his very interesting attempts to create a form of agrarian syndicalism movement, and his role as representative of the National Committee for the Liberation of Jugoslavia in U.N.R.R.A., right down to the democratic socialism and the theory of polycentric planning of his last and most mature period of intellectual development.

In realizing the fundamental loyalties of his life towards his people and his country, Rudolf Bićanić combined thought with action in a way which is seldom realized. He came relatively early to a very responsible position in political life, and even so was able, when already a mature man, to enter the scholarly world with a vitality and a breath of interest for which many younger men might envy him. He experienced to the full the inescapable, tragic tension between thought and action. In politics he did his utmost to act on the basis of logical and coherently ordered theoretical principles. He refused to allow himself to be attracted by the apparently practical solutions and compromises of what is known as being realistic. On the other hand to his intellectual work he brought the intense activity of the politician, and a dynamism which exhausted him before his time.

It is in the light of such a life and of such a death that Rudolf Bićanić comes to his full stature.

Yes, he was, truly and essentially, a loveable and a good man even though he suffered from years of police persecution, from malicious and unjust attacks, which would have turned someone of less integrity and high morale into an embittered, crabbed, disappointed man imbued with that cynicism which starts as a defense against the world and ends as isolation from it.

His complete lack of arrogance and of any kind of pretentiousness are seen in their true light when we think to what extent these characteristics are so marked in people of lesser size and who have known power of much smaller dimensions than he knew it.

Of special attraction was the freshness of his progressive outlook. It never became tarnished even in the years of his maturity, and it never flagged even when many expected that he would take a conservative stand in politics.

From his deeply progressive outlook upon which his whole life was based, from his constant urge towards the future, from his openness to what is new, grew up his finest contribution to our Faculty. He had the necessary breadth of outlook to see what the future held and was brave enough to fight for what was new, even if he had to fight alone. It is a strange coincidence that this very day we are having the first meeting since this faculty became integrated — the first serious step towards a broad-based modern faculty of the kind that Bićanić advocated all his life.

Rudolf Bićanić is among those graduates of the faculty who later in life taught in it himself but who are at the same time men of national standing. This faculty gave him to the country and both faculty and country can be proud of him.

The final word to say is that he was a man, a true man, and that means not ideal, not without fear and faults. He loved as we love and hoped as we hope. He lived through the fears and anxieties which we must live through too, and if in the ordeals and trials that he had to face he came out strong, and acquitted himself well, we may hope that the memory of Rudolf Bićanić will long remain alive to be a moving force among us.

There is little reason to add to these statements, impressive as they are in their factual, sober eloquence. At The Hague, where these few additional lines are written, the gap that his sudden demise has left is still felt, both at the Institute of Social Studies and in the hearts of the many friends who would always look forward to his next visit.

The Hague, June 1970 *C.A.O.van Nieuwenhuijze*

BIBLIOGRAPHICAL SURVEY

taken from

Zbornik pravnog fakulteta u Zagrebu
(Journal of the Zagreb faculty of Law)
XIX - no. 3-4, 1969

1. BOOKS

a) *In Yugoslavia*

Kako živi narod. Život u pasivnim krajevima [How People Live. Life in the Underdeveloped Regions] (Zagreb, 1936, book I and Zagreb, 1939, book II).

Ekonomska podloga hrvatskog pitanja [The Economic Basis of the Croatian Question] (Zagreb, first ed. 1938, 2nd. ed. 1938).

Gospodarska politika [Economic Policy] (Zagreb, 1939).

Pogled iz svjetske perspektive i naša ekonomska orijentacija [A World View of Our Economic Orientation] (Zagreb, 1939).

Najnužnije narodne potrebe. Prehrana-narodne potrebe- seljačka tržištalokalni disparitet cijena. [The Most Essential National Needs. Food supply, national needs, peasant market, local price disparities] with A. Mihletić and D. Štefek (Zagreb, 1940).

Hrvatska ekonomika na prijelazu iz feudalizma u kapitalizam [The Economy of Croatia During the Changeover from Feudalism to Capitalism], Vol. 1. *Doba manufakture u Hrvatskoj i Slavoniji 1750-1860* [The Period of Manufacture in Croatia and Slavonia 1750-1860] (Yugoslav Academy, Zagreb, 1951).

Počeci kapitalizma u hrvatskoj ekonomici i politici [The Beginnings of Capitalism in Croatian Economics and Politics] (=*Mala historijska knjižnica* No. 6) (Zagreb, 1952).

Ekonomska politika [Economic Policy], 2 vols. (Zagreb, 1953).

Ekonomski razvitak Zagreba i zagrebačkog regiona [The Economic Development of Zagreb and the Zagreb Region] (Zagreb Town Planning Institute, 1953).

Predavanja iz ekonomike FNRJ [Lectures on the Economics of FPRY] 1. Introduction, 2. People's Property (*Školska knjiga*) (Zagreb. 1953).

Trgovina, platežna bilanca i životna razina stanovništva kotara Krapina [Trade, Balance of Payments and Living Standard of the Population of the Krapina Kotar] (Town Planning Institute of Croatia, Zagreb, 1956).

Ekonomska politika FNRJ [Economic Policy FPRY] (script), 1, 2a, 2b (Zagreb, 1960).

Ekonomska politika FNRJ [Economic Policy FPRY], vol. 1 (Zagreb, Birozavod, 1962).

b) *Abroad*

Problems of Planning East and West (Mouton, The Hague, 1967).

Turning Points in Economic Development (Mouton, The Hague, 1970).

2. ARTICLES

a) *In Yugoslavia*

"Ljudski rad kao objekt socijalne politike [People as the Object of Social Policy]", *Radnička zaštita*, 1 (1930).

"Neprekinuti tzv. engleski radni dan [The So-called Unbroken English Workday]", *Radnička zaštita*, 7 (1930).

"Da li postoji kod nas hiperprodukcija inteligencije [Do we have a Hyperproduction of Intelligentsia]", *Nova Evropa*, VII (1931).

"Industrijalizacija i vanjska trgovina Jugoslavije [Industrialization and Yugoslav Foreign Trade]", *Privreda*, 1 (1932).

"Kriza nacionalizma [The Crisis of Nationalism]", *Nova Evropa*, 5 (1932).

"Naša trgovinska bilanca i njezino sezonsko kretanje [Seasonal Fluctuations in our Balance of Trade]", *Financijski arhiv*, 6 (1932).

"Sezonski karakter našeg izvoza [The Seasonal Character of our Exports]", *Privreda*, 3 (1932).

"Uvoz i njegovo sezonsko kretanje [Imports and their Seasonal Movement]", *Privreda*, 7-8 (1932).

"Podignimo cijene stoci [Raising the Price of Cattle]". A report given at a meeting of The Economic Unity Association — "Gospodarska sloga" — Feb. 2, 1936. Suggestions to peasant farmers on how to increase the price of cattle (Zagreb, 1936).

"Strukturne promjene našeg uvoza u pravcu industrijalizacije [Structural Changes in Imports in the Direction of Greater Industrialization]", *Privreda*, 12 (1936).

"Škare agrarno-industrijskih cijena [Agrarian-Industrial Price Scissors]", *Ekonomist*, 2 (1936).
"Što će biti sa ošenicom [What Will Happen to the Wheat]", *Gospodarska sloga* (1936).
"Trebaju li seljaštvu poljoprivredne komore [Do Peasants need an Agricultural Chamber]", *Ekonomist*, 7-8 (1936).
"Tržište i cijene pšenice [The Market and the Price of Wheat]", *Ekonomist*, 6 (1936).
"Agrarna kriza u Hrvatskoj 1873-1895 [The Agrarian Crisis in Croatia 1873-1895]", *Ekonomist*, 3-5 (1937).
"Agrarna prenapučenost V [Agrarian Overpopulation]", *Gospodarska struktura Banovine Hrvatske*, 3 (Zagreb, 1940).
"Ekonomski faktor u porastu stanovništva [The Economic Factor in Population Increase]", *Liječnički vjesnik*, (god.) 62, 11 (Zagreb, 1940).
"Jedan presjek kroz našu društvenu strukturu [A Cross Section of our Social Structure]", *Kolo Matice Hrvatske* (Zagreb, 1946).
"Ekonomska politika [Economic Policy]" (shorthand notes of lectures) (Zagreb, 1946/47), 3 vols.
"Naš petogodišnji plan treba da riješi i temeljne zadatke naše privrede [Our Five Year Plan Ought to Find Solutions to the Basic Problems of our Economy]", *Zadrugar III*, 10 (1947).
"M.Dobb, Study in the development of capitalism (prikaz) [M.Dobb, Study in the Development of Capitalism]", *Historijski Zbornik*, I (1948).
"Druga godina planske privrede u Poljskoj [The Second Year of Poland's Planned Economy]", *Djelo*, 4 (1948).
"Ekonomska struktura nove Poljske [The Economic Structure of New Poland]", *Današnja Poljska* (1948).
"Industrijska revolucija u Hrvatskoj i 1848 godina [The Industrial Revolution in Croatia in 1848]", *Historijski Zbornik* (Zagreb, 1948).
"Narodna imovina u našem planskom gospodarstvu [People's Property in our Planned Economy]", *Zbornik Pravnog fakulteta* (Zagreb, 1948).
"Oslobodenje kmetova u Hrvatskoj 1848 [The Freeing of the Serfs in Croatia 1848]", *Djelo*, 3 (1948).
"Rezultati druge godine IV pjatiljetka u SSSR-u [Results of the Second Year of the Fourth Five Year Plan in SSSR]", *Djelo*, 2 (1948).
"Vučo M. Privredna historija naroda FNRJ do prvog svjetskog rata — prikaz [M. Vučo, The Economic History of the Peoples of Yugoslavia Before the First World War]", *Historijski Zbornik*, 2 (Zagreb, 1949).

"Dva nova rada o periodizaciji ruske povijesti [Two New Works on the Periods of Russian History]", *Historijski Zbornik* (Zagreb, 1950).

"Gorodeckij, S. O. predmetu i sadržaju ekonomskih nauka — O granama narodnog gospodarstva [S. Gorodecki, The Subject and Content of Economic Sciences — Concerning the Branches of the National Economy]", *Ekonomski pregled*, 1 (1950).

"Knjige o ekonomici FNRJ" [Books on the Economics of Yugoslavia]", *Ekonomski pregled*, 5 (1951).

"Mjesto ekonomike FNRJ u sistemu ekonomskih nauka [The Place of Yugoslav Economics in the System of Economic Studies]", *Zbornik Pravnog fakulteta* (Zagreb, 1951).

"Problematika manufakturne periode u sovjetskoj historiografiji [The Problem of Periods of Manufacture in Soviet History]", *Historijski Zbornik* (Zagreb, 1951).

"Začetki kapitalističkih odnosov v Horvatsko-slovenskom kmečkom uporu leta 1572 [The Beginning of Capitalist Relations in the Croatian and Slovenian Peasant Revolts of 1572]", *Ekonomska revija* (Ljubljana, 1951).

"Agrarni odnosi u Slovoniji [Agrarian Relationships in Slovonia]", *Historijski Zbornik V*, 3-4 (1952).

"Suština jednog naučnog spora [The Essence of a Scholarly Disagreement]", *Kolo Matice Hrvatske*, 3 (1952).

"Ekonomska povijest medu ekonomskim i historijskim naukama [Economic History as an Economic and Historical Subject]", *godovinski časopis*, 6-7 (1952-53); "Ljubljana Agrarna prenaseljenost-akutan problem [Agricultural Overpopulation — an Acute Problem]", *Ekonomska politika*, 6. VIII (Belgrade, 1953).

"Diskusija o problemu razvoja poljoprivrede [A Discussion of the Problem of Agricultural Development]", *Ekonomska politika*, 18. IV (Belgrade, 1953).

"Dohodak evropskog agrara [The Income from European Agriculture]", *Ekonomska politika*, 16. IV (Belgrade, 1953).

"Kako trošimo naš dohodak (Odnos visine dohotka i strukture potrošnje) [How we Spend our Income (Relationship between Incomes and Expenditure)]", *Robni promet*, 11-12, year 4 (Zagreb, 1953).

"Metodologija za obračun narodnog dohotka u 1953 [The Method of Calculating the National Income in 1953]", *Savezni Zavod za Statistiku, Zbornik Pravnog fakulteta* (1953).

"Pogovor knjizi Lawrence Ezekiel-Selo i grad [Preface to Lawrence Ezekiel Town and Country]", *Poljoprivredni nakladni zavod* (Zagreb, 1953).

"Pojam sektora u ekonomici [Sectors in Economics]", *Zbornik Pravnog fakulteta* (Zagreb, 1953).
"Primjedbe na desetgodišnji program unapredenja poljoprivrede u Hrvatskoj [Observations on the Croatian Ten Year Plan for Agricultural Improvement]", *Agronomski glasnik*, 10 (1953).
"Stanovništvo FNRJ po nacionalnoj pripadnosti [The Yugoslav Population According to Nationality]", *Hrvatsko kolo* (1953).
"R. Stone, The role of measurement in Economics", *Zbornik Pravnog fakulteta* (1953).
"J. Tinbergen, Econometrics", *Zbornik Pravnog fakulteta* (1953).
"U.N. Special Study on Economic Condition and Development in Self-governing Territories", *Zbornik Pravnog fakulteta* (1953).
"Važnost Rijeke u ekonomskom životu Hrvatske [The Importance of Rijeka in the Economic Life of Croatia]", *Rijeka, Zbornik Matice Hrvatske* (Zagreb 1953).
"Nekoliko misli o Pravnom fakultetu [Some Reflections Concerning the Faculty of Law]", *Naša zakonitost*, 8-0 (1954).
"Ocjena naturalnog dijela narodnog dohotka [An Appraisal of the In-Kind Part of the National Income]", *Statistička revija*, 3-4 (1954).
"Problemi vanjske trgovine [Foreign Trade Problems]", *Trgovinska komora NR Hrvatske* (1954).
"Sirotković J. Novi privredni sistem FNRJ [J. Sirotković the New Economic System of FPRY]", *Zbornik Pravnog fakulteta*, 3-4 (1954).
"Uloga ekonomista i ekonomska nastava [The Role of Economists and Economic Studies]", *Ekonomist*, 5-6 (1954).
"Ekonomska historija i marksizam [Economic History and Marxism]", *Ekonomski pregled* (Zagreb, 1955).
"Još jedna riječ o ekonomskoj povijesti [Another Word about Economic History]", *Zgodovinski časopis* (Ljubljana, 1955).
"Nepoljoprivredna zanimanja u seljačkom gospodarstvu [Non-Agricultural Occupations on Peasant Holdings]", *Statistička revija*, 2 (Belgrade, 1955).
"Pregled ekonomike poljoprivrede u svijetu [A Survey of World Agricultural Economics]", *Poljoprivreda svijeta*, 2 (Zagreb, 1955).
"Zanimanje našeg stanovništva [How our Population Earns a Living]", *Ekonomist*, 5-6 (Belgrade, 1955).
"Dohodak seljačkog gospodarstva u FNRJ i NRH u razdoblju od 1953-1955.g. Analitički pregled [The Income of a Peasant Holding in FPRY and PR Croatia 1953-1955. An Analytical Survey]", *Ekonomski pregled*, 8-9 (1956).

"Kostić C. Seljaci-industrijski radnici [C. Kostić, Peasant-Workers]", *Zbornik Pravnog fakulteta* (Zagreb, 1956).

"Osvrt na predmet Ekonomika FNRJ [Concerning the Study of Yugoslav Economics]", *Zbornik Pravnog fakulteta*, 3-4 (Zagreb, 1956).

"Svjetsko stanovništvo i svjetska proizvodnja [World Population and World Production]", *Zbornik Pravnog fakulteta*, 3-4 (Zagreb, 1956).

"Uzroci i posljedice razvoja stanovništva" [Causes and Results of Population Development]", *Zbornik Pravnog fakulteta*, 3-4 (Zagreb, 1956).

"Bobrowsky, C. La Yugoslavie socialiste (prikaz) [Bobrowsky, La Yugoslavie socialieste (review)]", *Zbornik Pravnog fakulteta*, 2 (Zagreb, 1957).

"Distribucija osobnih dohodaka seljačkih obitelji u FNRJ 1955. g. [Distribution of Income in a Peasant Family in FPRY 1955]", *Statistička revija*, 3 (Belgrade, 1957).

"Dobit privredne organizacije [The Gains of Economic Organizations]", *Privredni vijesnik*, 1. VI (Zagreb, 1957).

"Nekoliko misli o problematici lične potrošnje u FNRJ [Some Thoughts Concerning the Problem of Personal Spending in FPRY]", *Progres* (Ljubljana, 1957).

"Podruštvljenje društvenih funkcija seljačke obitelji [The Socialization of the Functions of the Peasant Family]", *Progres* (Ljubaljana, 1957).

"Primjedbe na zakonski nacrt o raspodjeli ukupnog prihoda privrednih organizacija [Observations Concerning the Draft Law on the Distribution of the Total Income of Economic Organizations]", *Informator*, 23.X, 19.X. i 2.XI. (Zagreb, 1957).

"Produktivnost investicija i brzina ekonomskog rasta [The Productivity of Investment and the Rate of Economic Growth]", *Ekonomska politika*, 267 (Belgrade, 1957).

"Razvoj industrije u Zagrebu [Industrial Development in Zagreb]", *Zbornik iz starog i novog Zagreba* (1957).

"Redukcija obiteljskih funkcija seljačke obitelji u FNRJ [Reduction of Family Functions in the Peasant Family in FPRY]", *Statistička revija* (Belgrade, 1957).

"Riječna plovidba i veza s Jadranskim morem [River Transport and Connections with the Adriatic]", *Pomorska enciklopedija* (Zagreb, 1957), Leksikografski zavod FNRJ.

"Što očekujemo od naše statističke službe [What We Expect from Our Statistical Service]", *Ekonomska politika* (February 1957).

"Vinski I. Investicije na području Hrvatske izmedu dva svjetska rata [I. Vinski, Investment in Croatia Between the Two World Wars]",

Historijski zbornik (1957).
"Zagreb kao multifunkcionalan grad i zanimanja njegovog stanovništva [Zagreb as a Multifunctional City and the Occupations of its Inhabitants]", *Zbornik iz starog novog Zagreba* (1957).
"Ekonomski rast i ekonomski sektori [Economic Growth and Economic Sectors]", *Ekonomski pregled*, 11-12 (1959).
"Ekonomski rast, ekonomski razvoj i planiranje [Economic Growth, Economic Development and Planning]", *Ekonomist*, 1 (Belgrade, 1959).
"Interakcija odluka društvenih planova i odluka privrednih organizacija u FNRJ 1954-1957 [Interaction Between Social Plans and the Decisions of Economic Organizations in FPRY 1954-57]", *Jugoslavensko Statističko društvo* (1959).
"X. Kongres agrarnih ekonomista u Mysore 1959.g. [The Tenth Congress of Agricultural Economists in Mysore 1959]", *Agronomski glasnik* (1959).
"Nastajanje kapitalizma [The Development of Capitalism]", *Školska knjiga* (Zagreb 1959).
"O institucionalnim promjenama u poljoprivredi [Institutional Changes in Agriculture]", *Medunarodni problemi*, 2 (1959).
"Tipovi mješovite seljačko-radničke obitelji s obzirom na raspodjelu dohotka [Types of Mixed Peasant-Worker Families with Reference to Distribution of Income]", *Sociologija*, 1 (Belgrade, 1959).
"Zagrebački velesajam — barometar privredne situacije [Zagreb Fair — Barometer of the Economic Situation]", *Yugoslav Export* (August, 1959).
"Impresije s IV. svjetskog sociološkog kongresa u Stresi 1959 [Impressions of the Fourth World Sociological Congress in Stresa 1959]", *Zbornik Pravnog fakulteta* (1960).
"Industrijska revolucija i naučni rad [Industrial Revolution and the Scholar]", *Univerziteti danas* (Belgrade, 1960).
"Industrijski odnosi kao predmet sveučilišne nastave [Industrial Relations as a University Subject]", *Sveučilišni vjesnik* (1960).
"Matematika u sovjetskoj ekonomici [Mathematics and Soviet Economics]", *Ekonomska politika* (Belgrade, 1960).
"Osnovna sredstva privrednih organizacija u FNRJ po kotarevima [Fixed Capital of Economic Organizations in FPRY by Districts]", *Ekonomski pregled*, 6 (Zagreb, 1960).
"Planiranje i sociologija [Planning and Sociology]", *Ekonomski pregled* (Zagreb, 1960).

"Pola stoljeća narodnog bogatstva i narodnog dohotka [Half a Century of National Wealth and National Income]", *Historijski zbornik* (1960).

"Pravilnosti u promjenama kapitalnog koeficijenta [Regularity in Changes of the Capital Coefficient]", *Savezni zavod za privredno planiranje* (Beograd, 1960).

"Sinhronizacija industrijskih revolucija [Synchronization of Industrial Revolutions]", *Medunarodni problemi*, 3 (Belgrade, 1960).

"Stići i prestići — kvalitet ili kvantitet [To Catch Up or to Overtake — Quality or Quantity]", *Medunarodni problemi*, 3 (Belgrade, 1960).

"Ekonomski razvoj Jugoslavije kroz petgodišnje planove [Yugoslav Economic Development and the Five Year Plans]", *Zbornik Pravnog fakulteta* (Zagreb, 1961).

"Kapitalni koeficijent, tehnički napredak i teorija praga ekonomskog razvoja [Capital Coefficient, Technical Progress and the Theory of the Threshold of Economic Development]", *Ekonomski pregled*, 3 (Zagreb, 1961).

"Valutni tečajevi kao instrument ekonomskog razvoja [Exchange Rates as Instruments of Economic Development]", *Ekonomska fakulteta* (Ljubljana 1961).

"Izbor integracije [Selective Integration]", *Medunarodni problemi* (Belgrade, 1962).

"Promjene u agraru i poljoprivredna statistika [Changes in Agriculture and Agricultural Statistics]", *Jugoslavensko Statističko društvo* (1962).

"Tržište i njegove dimenzije [The Market and its Dimensions]", *Ekonomski pregled*, 4 (Zagreb, 1962).

"Centralističko, decentralističko i policentrično planiranje [Centralized, Decentralized and Polycentric Planning]", *Ekonomist*, 2 (1963); Belgrade and *Naše teme*, 11 (Zagreb, 1963).

"Ekonomski razvoj i planiranje [Economic Development and Planning]", *Ekonomski pregled*, 1 (1963).

"Inflacioni dohodak, administrativne cijene i imperfektna konkurencija [Inflatory Income, Administrative Prices and Imperfect Competition]", *Ekonomist* (Belgrade, 1963) and *Ekonomski pregled*, 3-5 (Zagreb, 1963).

"O monocentraičnom i policentričnom planiranju [On Monocentric and Polycentric Planning]", *Ekonomski pregled*, 1963. (Zagreb, 1963).

"Agrarna prenapučenost [Agrarian Overpopulation]", *Sociologija sela*, 2 (Zagreb, 1964).

"Koje su granice primjeni dohodne cijene [What are the Limits to the Application of 'Dohodni' Prices]", *Ekonomist*, 4 (Belgrade, 1964).

"Medunarodna ekonomska integracija in zunanja trgovina [International Economic Integration in Internal Trade]", *Naše gospodarstvo*, X (Maribor, 1964).

"O planu i sistemu [Plan and System]", *Ekonomska politika*, 624 (Belgrade, 1964).

"Porodica u transformaciji [The Family in Transition]", *Man* (Royal Anthropological Society, London, 1964).

"Pregled razvoja ekonomike i ekonomske politike Jugoslavije 1918-1940 [Survey of the Development of the Economy and of Economic Policy in Yugoslavia 1918-1940]", *Historijski pregled* (1964).

"Problemi planiranja na Istoky i Zapadu [Problems of Planning East and West]", *Ekonomski pregled*, 1-2 (Zagreb, 1964).

"Tri koncepcije ruralnog planiranja [Three Concepts of Rural Planning]", *Sociologija sela*, 5-6 (1964).

"Urbanistički plan Zagreba [Zagreb City Plan]", *Čovjek i prostor*, 133-134 (Zagreb, 1964).

"Nekoliko misli o planiranju i primjedbe na pojedinosti u tezama o planiranju [Some Thoughts about Planning and some Observations on Individual Aspects of the Planning "Theses" of the Institute of Economics SRH]", (Zagreb, 1965).

"O jadranskoj koncepciji ekonomskog razvoja Jugoslavije [The Adriatic Approach to the Economic Development of Yugoslavia]", *Pomorstvo*, 9-10 (1964) and *Izbor*, 3 (1965).

"O odgovornosti planera [The Responsibility of the Planners]", Meeting of the Society of Economists in Maribor, June 1965, and *Ekonomski tehnički pregled*, 4 (Zagreb, 1965).

"Plan i privreda [Plan and the Economy]", *Ekonomist*, 3 (Belgrade, 1965).

"Policentrično planiranje i privredni sistem [Polycentric Planning and the Economic System]", *Ekonomist* (Belgrade, 1965).

"Problem regionalne integracije [Problems of Regional Integration]", *Ekonomski pregled* (Zagreb, 1965).

"Sovjetska planimetrika-ekonomska kibernetika [Soviet Planometrics — Economic Cybernetics]", *Ekonomski pregled*, 9-10 (1965).

"Vasilij Sergejević Nemčinov — In memoriam [In Memoriam — Vasilij Sergejevič Nemčinov]", *Ekonomski pregled*, 1 (Zagreb, 1965).

"Zaokreti u ekonomskom razvoju i agrarna politika [Turning Points in Economic Development and Agricultural Policy]", *Ekonomski pregled*, 11-12 (Zagreb, 1965).

"Privredna reforma, stabilizacija i tehnički napredak [Economic Reform, Stabilization and Technical Advance]", *Ekonomist*, 1-4 (Zagreb, 1966).
"Da li su komputori centralizatori ili liberalizatori [Computers Centralizers or Liberators]", *Automatika* (1967).
"Ekonomske promjene u Hrvatskoj izazvane stvaranje Jugoslavije 1918 [Economic Changes in Croatia caused by the Creation of Yugoslavia in 1918]", *Putovi revolucije* (1967).
"Monocentrična cikličnost ili policentrična stabilnost [Monocentric Cycles and Polycentric Stability]", *Ekonomist*, 1-2 (Zagreb, 1967).
"Odluke o društvenom planiranju [Decision Making and Social Planning]", *Informator*, 26. VIII (Zagreb, 1967).
"Planeri i političari [Planners and Politicians]", *Zbornik Pravnog fakulteta* (Zagreb, 1967).
"Poljoprivreda i stručnjaci za političke nauke [Agriculture and the Experts in Political Sciences]", *Sociologija sela*, 17 (1967).
"Privredna reforma — stabilizacija i tehnički napredak [Economic Reform, Stabilization and Technical Progress]", *Ekonomist* (Belgrade, 1967).
"Radna organizacija i rizika za društvene odluke [Work Organizations and the Risks of Social Decisions]", *Informator*, 2. IX (Zagreb, 1967).
"Reforma, planiranje i samoupravljanje [The Reform, Planning and Self-Management]", *Informator*, 26. VIII (Zagreb, 1967).
"Reforma, planiranje i samoupravljanje [The Reform, Planning and Self-Management]", *Teorija in praksa*, 8-9 (Ljubljana, 1967).
"U sistemu društvenog planiranja bitno je da svaka grupa u raspodjeli prima dohodak prema svom radu [In the System of Social Planning it is Essential that Each Group Take Part in the Income Distribution According to their Work]", *Informator*, 30. VIII (1967).
"Uspješnost planiranja ovisi o kvalitetu predvidanja [The Success of Planning Depends on the Quality of Forecasting]", *Informator*, 23. VIII (1967).
"Proces podruštvljenja i socijalizam [The Process of Socialization and Socialism]", *Praxis* (Zagreb, 1968).
"Statistika i reforma [Statistics and the Reform]", *Statističa revija* (1968), *Ekonomska politika* (1968).

Posthumous

"(Tipologija tržišta u SFRJ) Simpozijum o istraživanju tržišta [Typology of Markets in SFRY]" at Symposium for Market Research (1968).

"Pregledi teorija o agrarnoj prenapučenosti [A Survey of the Theory of Agricultural Overpopulation]", *Sociologija sela*, 23-24 (Zagreb, 1969).

"Problematika jedinstva privrede u Jugoslaviji [Problems of Economic Unity in Yugoslavia]", *Zbornik Pravnog fakulteta* (Zagreb, 1970), spomenica.

b) *Abroad*

"Central European Stability and Yugoslavia", *Journal of Central European Affairs*, 3/1 (Colorado, 1943).

"Excess Agricultural Population", *British Association for Advancement of Science. European Agriculture* (London, 1942) (Also in: *Statement on Agricultural Reconstruction, Bulletin of the Commission to Study the Organisation of Peace*, New York, 1943).

"Effects of War on Rural Yugoslavia", *Geographical Journal*, 1 (London, 1944).

"Cooperation in Yugoslavia", *Yearbook of Agricultural Cooperation*, 1943-1944 (London 1946).

Some Problems of Sectors in the Social Accounting of Different Economic Systems, (=*International Association for Research in Income and Wealth* No. 4, mimeo) (London 1953).

National Income Distribution in Yugoslavia, (*International Association for Research in Income and Wealth*, mimeo) (London 1955).

"La concurrence socialiste en Yugoslavie", *Economie appliquée* (1956).

"Occupational Heterogenity of Peasant Families in the Period of Accelerated Industrialisation", *Transactions of the Third World Congress of Sociologists* (Amsterdam, 1965).

"Bobrowsky, C., *La Yugoslavie socialiste du plan quinquennal de* 1947 *au bilan de* 1955", *Kyklos* (Basel, 1957).

"Economic Growth under Centralized and Decentralized Planning Yugoslavia — a Case Study", *Economic Development and Cultural Change*, 9 (Chicago, 1957).

Interaction of Macro — and Microeconomic Decisions in Yugoslavia, mimeo (Univ. of California, Berkeley, 1957).

"Personal Income Distribution in Peasant Families in Yugoslavia", *IARIW* (De Pietersberg, 1957).

"Lack of Institutional Flexibility in Agriculture", *Proceedings of the International Conference of Agricultural Economists* (Mysore, 1958).

"Economic Growth by Economic Sectors" (*International Association for Research in Income and Wealth*, mimeo) (Portorož, 1959).

The Relevance of Considerations Underlying the Awareness of Need for Industrialisation" (*Mediterranean, Social Science Research Project*, mimeo) (Institute of Social Studies, The Hague. 1959).

"A Dialogue on Planning and Freedom", *Way-Forum*, No. 36 (Brussels, 1960).

"Centralism and Planning: the Hungarian Experience", *Kyklos*, 13 (Basel, 1969).

"Economic Growth, Development and Planning in Socialist Countries", E. Nelson (ed.), *Economic Growth* (Univ. of Texas Press, 1960).

"Economic Growth under Centralized and Decentralized Planning", *Problems of Economic Growth*, M. Hablar, R. Ghish (eds.) (New Delhi, 1960).

"Interaction of Macroeconomic and Microeconomic Decisions in Yugoslavia, 1954-1957", G. Grossman (ed.), *Value and Plan* (Univ. of California Press, 1960).

"Lack of Institutional Flexibility in Agriculture", *Proceedings of the Tenth International Conference of Agricultural Economists* (Oxford, 1960).

"La role du profit dans l'économie socialiste en Yugoslavie", *Economie appliqué* (Paris, 1960).

"Die jugoslawische Agrarpolitik in den Jahren 1953-1959", *Zeitschrift für das gesamte Genossenschaftswesen* (Göttingen, Wandenhoek-Ruprecht, 1961).

Industrialization in Yugoslavia, mimeo (The Hague, Institute of Social Studies, 1961).

"On Comparative Advantages in Agriculture", *Proceedings of the XI International Conference of Agricultural Economists* (Oxford, 1961).

The Role of Socialist Business Enterprise in Yugoslav Economics, mimeo (The Hague, Institute of Social Studies, 1961).

"Produttività del Capitale e lo sviluppo economico", *Mercurio*, 11 (Rome, 1962).

"The Threshold of Economic Growth", *Kyklos*, 15/1 (Basel, 1962).

"A gazdaszagi noveledes kuszobe", *A gazdaszagi fejledes feltetelei* (Budapest, 1963).

"A Grammar for Greek Planning", *Kyklos*, 4 (Basel, 1963).

"Economic Development and Agriculture", *Proceedings of the XI International Conference of Agricultural Economists* (Cuernavaca,

Oxford, 1963).
"La soglia dello sviluppo economico", *Svimez*, 131 (Rome, 1963).
"Review of Michal, Jan M., *Central planning in Czechoslovakia*, 1960", *Kyklos*, Fasc. 3 (Basel, 1963).
On Monocentric and Polycentric Planning, mimeo (Institute of Social Studies, The Hague, 1963).
"Problemas de planification en Oriente y Occidente", *Revista de Economia Latinoamericana* (Caracas, 1963).
"Quelques aspects de la politique des revenus ouvriers en Yugoslavie", *Economie appliquée*, 4 (Paris, 1963).
Research on Turning Points in Economic and Social Development, mimeo (Mediterranean Social Science Research Council, 1963).
"Caire, G. I., *Economie Yugoslav*", *Kyklos*, 4 (Basel, 1964).
"E la concezione Adriatica che deve prevalere nella nostra economia", *La voce del popolo* (Rijeka, 1964).
"Economic Growth under Centralized and Decentralized Planning in Yugoslavia", Marshall I. Goldman (ed.), *Comparative Economic Systems. A Reader* (New York, Random House, 1964).
La planification rurale, mimeo (Institut Agronomique Mediterranéen, Montpellier, 1964).
"Le passage du seuil de dévélopement économique: condition prealables et effets ultérieurs sur le plan social", *Revue Internationale des Sciences Sociales*, 2 (Paris, 1964).
"Review of Nemitchinov, V. B., *Economiko matematskies metodi i modeli*, Moscow, 1962", *Kyklos*, 3 (Basel, 1964).
"Problems of Socialist Agriculture", *Indian Journal of Agricultural Economics*, 2-4 (Bombay, 1964).
"Przemiany spoleczne i progi razwoju ekonomicznego", *Studia Sociologiezne*, 1 (Warszawa, 1964).
"Social Preconditions and Effects of Moving over the Threshold of Economic Development", *International Social Sciences Journal*, 2 (Paris, 1964).
"Some Aspects of Policy of Workers Income in Yugoslavia", E. Stiller (ed.), *Lohnpolitik und Vermögensbildung* (Frankfurt, 1964).
"Three Concepts of Agricultural Over-population", *International Explorations of AER Policy* (Iowa Univ. Press., 1964).
Towards a Typology of Planning, mimeo (Institute of Social Studies, The Hague, 1964).
"'Attitudes to the Zadruga' The Liberation of the Serfs in 1848", *Contrasts in Emerging Societies*, D. Warriner (ed.) (London, 1965).

"La politica dei reditti dei lavori in Jugoslavia", *Mercurio*, 7 (Rome, 1965).

"Le planificateur et le politicien", *Bulletin SEDEIS*, *Futuribles* (Paris, 1965).

"On Comparative Advantages in Agriculture", *Proceedings of the XII. Conference of the International Association of Agricultural Economists* (Oxford, 1965).

The Planner and the Politician, mimeo, *SEDEIS*, *Futuribles* (Paris, 1965).

"Yugoslavia: Agricultural Planning, Organization and Methods", Second FAO Course on Agricultural Development Planning (Rome, 1965).

"Comment ne pas developper un pays", *Le Tiers Monde* (Paris, 1966).

"Economics of Socialism in a Developed Country", *Foreign Affairs* (July, 1966), reprint.

Comparative Economic Systems. Models and Cases, M. Bornstein (ed.) (New York, 1969).

"Turning Points in Economic Development and Agricultural Policy", International Economic Papers, I.E.A. 1966, reprint. Ugo Papi, Charles Nunn (eds.), *Economic Problems of Agriculture in Industrial Societies* (1969).

"Agriculture and the Political Scientist", *International Journal of Agrarian Affairs* (Oxford, University Press, 1967).

"Comment on Farming as a Way of Life: Yugoslav Peasant Attitudes", J. F. Karcz (ed.), *Soviet and East European Agriculture* (Univ. of California Press, 1967).

"Effects of the First World War on the Economics of Yugoslavia. A Lesson in Disintegration and Reintegration", *The Institute of Contemporary History* (London, 1967).

"Gli elaborati di dati nella programmazione policentrica la scuola in azione" (Metanapoli, San Donato, Milanese, Nov. 1967).

"Planer und Politiker", *Der Staat*, 6 Band, Heft 1 (Berlin, 1967).

"Three Models of Planning in Yugoslavia", G. Grossman (ed.), *Essays in Socialism and Planning* in *Festschrift in Honor of Carl Landauer* (Prentice Hall, N.Y. 1970).

"Jugoslawische Stellung in der Weltwirtschaft und das Auslandskapital in Jugoslawien", *Osteuropa Institut* (München 1968).

"The Watershed", *Approaches to the Science of Socio-economic Development*, P. Lengyel (ed.), (1971).

CONTENTS

INTRODUCTION

The main purpose of these essays is to study long-term structural changes in the process of economic development. Instead of centering our interest on starting points of development or on extrapolations of the trends, we have concentrated our research on the turning points.

By turning points in development we mean long-term observable and measurable qualitative and quantitative changes in essential developmental variables which reverse their original direction. Population which grows at a certain point stops growing and begins to decline. Productivity of capital which increases with development, then decreases and increases again. Land which becomes scarce when the frontier is reached, and the area under cultivation declines; yet the volume of production increases.

The importance of such turning points is that they require adequate changes in economic policy, and measures which have in the past produced positive effects become ineffective and even cause damage to development.[1] Because the process of development is complex, it often happens that important changes escape the attention of policy makers at the time. Great errors are made before the lag in political decisions, which trot behind economic changes, is realized and eliminated. Equally damaging is the premature anticipation of such changes by political decision makers, who then take measures which are not appropriate to the real economic situation.

1

The set of turning points we are studying in the first two essays is the change in the capital coefficient. Long considered constant, the capital coefficient can be proved to change in the course of economic development. The capital output ratio after the initial turning point of growth

[1] Structural changes make economic constants which some economists would take for granted suddenly reveal their character as variables in a step function.

becomes considerably greater than that at a later stage of development. This is the period when the infrastructure is being built and the process of creeping over the threshold of growth takes place. Once this process is over and the turning point reached, the capital coefficient becomes lighter, and less capital is required to produce one unit of output. At first the capital mix changes but soon the momentum is provided by technological progress, far more important than the increase in longevity of capital or the mere substitution of labor by capital. Where previously 6 to 8 units of capital were necessary to produce one unit of output, three suffice when the switch from primary industries and transportation to manufacturing industries takes place.

Thus two turning points in the capital coefficient are of great significance for economic policy. At the first turning point, the old school of policy endeavors in vain to go the same slow old way; at the second turning point, the former progressives become conservative and desire to continue their policy of maximizing compulsory saving, concentrating on extractive industries, heavy industries, and rail transport while squeezing the consumer. Others, looking beyond the turning point, lay their hope on innovations due to technological progress.

The cycle is repeated: after a period of building of a threshold based on coal, steam, rail, and steel came a respite, and then another threshold of electricity and oil and internal combustion motors. A relaxing period followed after that. The third industrial revolution, that of electronics, nuclear physics, and chemical industry, is already in full swing, making the capital coefficient heavier again.

The second set of turning points, to be discussed in the third essay, is that of changes in the sharing of the gross domestic product. Again there is no constancy in the shares over the process of development. The shares of labor change in the course of growth. At first they increase at a great pace and then slow down. In the first stages, it is more important for the employees to increase their share of the gross domestic product than the product itself. At a later stage, it is more gainful for them to make the 'cake' bigger, at the same time watching for their fair share.

Similar development takes place with capital formation. At low levels of development, the maximization of the share is considered to be more gainful than the increase of the gross product as a whole. At a later stage of development, the reverse is the case.

This general tendency underwent significant changes in the period 1953-1962. The share of labor grew smaller but their aggregate income increased because of the great overall rate of growth. Capital formation grew from both sources, increasing its relative share and its absolute volume. The bill was paid by the third group, those who neither are employees nor live from capital formation. But this third group consolidated its position in the developed countries while undergoing substantial changes in the developing countries. Some groups preferred to maximize their share, some to maximize growth. The choice was largely motivated by the level of economic development.

The fourth essay in this series of studies deals with changes in the upper structure of economic policy. We have called it an 'Essay in the Pathology of Growth' since these changes show some pathological characteristics in the policy-to-economics relationship.

In this process of developmental policy, we have distinguished four different stages in the black cycle of development: economics of overload, economics of overstrain, economics of underground, and economics of overchange. We have tried to rationalize the process so familiar in the past and present experience of so many countries. At the time of the writing of this essay (in 1963) we did not realize how quickly and in some cases how tragically our points would return in the cycle of Fortune.

2

The second part of this collection of essays deals particularly with changes in agriculture.

The first essay explains the lack of institutional flexibility in agriculture, dealing mainly with the tension between population and institution. We have dealt with extreme cases where fundamental inflexibility causes the exit of some and entry of other institutional units. These inflexibilities are reflected on one hand in the peasant way of life, and on the other hand in the influence of terms of trade between agricultural and industrial products on the institutional inflexibility of agricultural population, which rigidity leads to breakdown.

Our special field of interest is agricultural overpopulation. We have presented in a short essay some results of many years of study of this problem. There are three basic concepts of agricultural overpopulation. One is defined as the point beyond which land cannot support a greater number of agricultural population and the level of consumption begins to decline. The other concept attacks the problem from the perspective of production, and defines agricultural overpopulation as the number of active population in excess of optimal productivity of labor.

There is a third concept of agricultural overpopulation, linked to its mobility. If the forces keeping the population on the spot are stronger than the forces which push or pull them away, agricultural overpopulation is inevitable.

The essay "Agricultural Policy and Turning Points in Economic Development" deals with the three main elements of agriculture — labor, land, and capital — and examines the turning point in their relative and absolute decline. Supporting statistical material shows how widespread these turning points are, at what time periods they occur, and at which levels of development in various countries. On the basis of such development, are presented some ideal types of agricultural policy which correspond to the changes in the turning points in the essential variables of agricultural development. The policy is bound to change when agricultural population falls in absolute terms, when agricultural land and cultivated areas decline, and when capital investments slow down at the same time that production increases.

In the last essay are discussed some problems of agriculture in socialist countries. We have endeavored to find reasons for changes occurring in the agricultural policies of socialist countries, and to discover what turning points in the essential variables could lead to further changes in the agricultural policy of these countries.

PROBLEMS OF ECONOMIC GROWTH

I

AGRICULTURE AND THE POLITICAL SCIENTIST*

The purpose of this paper is to explore how a political scientist should behave in matters of agricultural policy under varying conditions. First an attempt has been made to delimit the political scientist's sphere of action within the framework of the problem. Here four constraints are found: technical, sociological, economic and political, the last being of special significance for the political scientist.

There are so many types of agriculture that the dichotomy developed-underdeveloped simply does not satisfy requirements for an analysis, least of all an analysis from a political point of view. There are peasants, farmers, agricultural labor and scholarly experts, there are sovkhozes, kolhozes and agribusinesses, not to mention feudal, tribal and community forms of agricultural activity. Each of these experience a different process of decision making, all have different objectives in farming and different means to achieve these objectives. For each of them a different type of agricultural policy is optimal.

The problem was how to deal with types of agriculture at various levels of development and under different socio-economic and political systems in order to cover the overall problem of the accelerated changes taking place in world agriculture today. Some rather bold generalizations in choice of types had to be made to meet this situation. These types do not necessarily represent consecutive stages or phases in the process of development. Indeed they can exist simultaneously in one and the same country, and a reverse movement can take place in the change of one type into another. We have distinguished four such ideal types: subsistence agriculture, market (commercial) agriculture, entrepreneurial (industrial) agriculture and contract or planning agriculture (which some

* Paper read at the 13th International Conference of Agricultural Economists, Sydney, August 21-31 1967. Cf. *International Journal of Agrarian Affairs*, Vol. V1, 2 (Oxford, 1967).

people call scientific agriculture). In devising such ideal types we were aware that the old fashioned distinction of money versus natural mechanisms of exchange does not provide the scientist with powerful enough tools for his analysis and that a more refined approach is necessary. The anthropologists speak of the mechanisms in a primitive economy: the gift, redistribution and market mechanisms. To these we need to add two more, those of contract and planning agriculture which are spreading so rapidly with new technological changes.

In order to distinguish between these various types of agriculture we used as general indicator the changes in agricultural population both in absolute numbers and in relative terms to the total population of a country. Thus we divided the whole economy of a country into two sectors only: the agricultural and the non-agricultural. We took the population figures only as a tool in our analytical efforts dealing with the process of change, although not thinking for a moment that such a complex phenomenon as changes in general and agricultural population could be reduced to one single overall cause determining types of agricultural change.

The recently developed analytical tools of cost-benefit analysis or operational research have proved that the market mechanism cannot provide all the answers.[1] Since the cost-benefit analysis has recently spread over many fields and is used to cover varied objectives we feel inclined to proceed to some systematization of these approaches incorporating them into some hitherto considered 'normal' methods of evaluating gains from the economic activities of society. A distinction needs to be made between four methods of the same family: cost-effectiveness, cost-price, cost-benefit and cost-efficiency analysis.

Next came the problem of political action regarding agriculture. All aspects of this vast subject of long standing could not be dealt with in one short paper. So we limited ourselves to marginal cases of political intervention, when political action is motivated by an upset balance of political power. The boundary lines of non-spontaneous return have been called parity lines and the concept set of lower and upper parity lines.

[1] What A. Marshall called external economics, as some sort of fallout from a market economy, are of much more importance than perhaps Marshall and his successors envisaged, and these meta-market concepts should be more fully elaborated. See also the recent book by K. Galbraith, *The New Industrial State* (Boston, Houghton Mifflin Co., 1967), Galbraith acknowledges the importance of meta-market economics for modern development. We disagree with him in that he took the administrative (state) government intervention and planning as one mechanism while we consider them as two distinct socio-economic mechanisms.

In subsistence agriculture these are the hunger line and the waste line. In marketing agriculture the parity lines are those of just price and maximum price. Entrepreneurial agriculture moves between the poverty line and the opulence line, and contract and planning (scientific) agriculture within the technical obsolescence and technical prodigality lines.

The activity of political scientists is to discover these different parity lines in order to find solutions, issue warnings and advise action. Their function has been described according to the intensity of their personal engagement and risk-taking, departing from the indifferent position of expert, adviser, lobbyist or arbiter. Probably the best tool of the political scientist could be forged along the theory of games, using a non-zero game as the most suitable instrument.

Whatever motives are followed or interests served, human action in agricultural policy, as in any other field of social action, is subject to four main constraints: technological, economic, social and political.

(a) *Technological* constraint comes about in answer to the question 'Can it be done at all?' Is a certain action *possible* under conditions of existing knowledge and resources accumulated in the natural sciences? Can the available means achieve the desired ends?

(b) *Economic* constraint poses the question 'Does it pay?' To what extent is one action *preferable* to another in the cost-benefit line.

(c) *Social* constraint puts a brake on action with the question 'Is it acceptable for the survival of the social environment in which the action is taking place?' since no action can in fact take place in a social vacuum.

(d) *Political* constraint deals with the question 'Is the action agreeable to those in control of political power in a society?' i.e. How will it affect the power structure? Will it strengthen or weaken it?

The technological questions must be answered by the natural scientists and technologists, with their ever-expanding field of action. The economic questions are handled by economists who optimize benefits. Social action is covered by all those who pose problems of values: ideological, religious, legal or philosophical, contracting or expanding the field of social action. The political questions fall to the political scientists who explore the power structure and how human relations are affected by it.

The order of these constraints, their magnitude, direction and acuteness may vary, but it is their combined effects that are felt. Natural scientists, economists, sociologists and political scientists may all study the intermixing of influences, the extent they substitute for, conflict with, overlap or complement each other. Their subject matter is the same, but their intentionality in research depends on the laws and principles of their respective disciplines and therefore gives rise to different conclusions. Whose task is it to integrate these conclusions, and provide the best answer? It is our opinion that no solution is scientific enough to justify actions which go beyond the consensus of what is acceptable to those fellow men who work and have to bear the ultimate risk and carry the burden of such actions. In the dilemma between the ideological imposition of a Cause and the democratic consensus of the People, we opt for the latter.

Our particular task in this paper is to explore the special role the political scientist can play and the useful function he can perform in contributing to the improvement of the position of those active in agriculture in the rapidly changing world of today.

1

Political science is comparatively new as an academic discipline. Studies of political behavior go far back into human history. A body of political doctrine, based on generalized experience, was established long ago. But only recently has political science developed as a separate social science, building a consistent system, searching for general laws of political behavior, assessing the scales for weighing rational expectations against probable risks in prediction and attempting to measure complex political activities by quantitative methods.[2] It deals with subjects such as structure and distribution of power over men in societies, the social and economic bases of such power which conditions long-term political action, long

[2] Some recent books dealing with general political theory which we consulted are: R. Bendix and M. S. Lipset (ed.), *Class, Status and Power*; B. de Jouvenel, *The Pure Theory of Politics*; D. Lerner and H. D. Laswell, *The Policy Sciences*; Bert F. Hoselitz (ed.), *A Reader's Guide to the Social Sciences*; R. A. Dahl and Charles E. Lindblom, *Politics, Economics and Welfare* (New York, 1959); Carl Friedrich, *Man and his Government* (New York, McGraw-Hill, 1963).

Soviet sources on political theory are based on the works of Marx, Engels and Lenin and for the former period of Stalin. A short survey can be found in any textbook on political economy, e.g. N. A. Tsagolov, *Kurs politicheskoy ekonomii* (Moscow, 1963).

For a more systematic presentation see L. F. Ilytchev, *Osnovy politicheskyh znanij*, 3rd ed. (Moscow, 1959), Izdatelstvo polytitcheskoj literatury; A. M. Birman, *Nekotory problemy nauki upravleniji narodnim hozjajztvom*, 2nd ed. (Moscow, 1965), Izdavltelstvo ekonomika.

For Yugoslavia see the periodical *Politička misao* (Zagreb, Faculty of Political Sciences, 1964).

and short-term changes in location, the strength and tension of such power. It explores operational ways and means for guiding political decisions and influencing their causes and consequences.[3]

On the one hand we are dealing specially with Agriculture, on the other, in explaining power relations, we are limiting ourselves to *Public* power as a potential for determinative action, or as a determinative action itself exercised by Public Authorities which have an unconditional monopoly of such power.[4] These authorities have the capability of affecting the actions of people engaged in agriculture, using the threat of severe deprivations for non-conformity with the policies intended.[5] Thus the actor *exerting* the influence on agriculturists is the general government, and the actors *subjected* to such influence are the agriculturists. In other terms we are examining what changes in agriculture, occurring at what time, induce the government to act in favor of agriculture, and what changes in society cause the government to take measures which impose certain non-intended behavior upon agricultural producers.

We have developed our explorations along four ideal types of agricultural development, which it seemed to us could be singled out, isolated and explained, from among the great variety of types of agriculture in different countries at various levels of development and under different social and economic systems (see synoptic Table I). We are aware of the shortcomings of these generalizations, but we will be content if, through them, some light is thrown on to the problems of interdisciplinary research in economics, demography, sociology and political science.

We have explored the position of these four types of agriculture along the lines of social interdependence as expressed in agricultural policies seeking life parity, price parity, income parity and technical parity. We found the indicators of such policies first in changes of relative and absolute numbers in agricultural population, taken as independent

[3] "Power consists in the probability of preserving the inner structure of one of the systems in a clash with little or no relevant modification, at the price of bringing about relatively large modifications in the structure of the systems which clash with it. ... Politics ... consist of such production, use, and distribution of power as will prove compatible with social inclusiveness and growth beyond the power field alone. That social group or structure has most strength ... which can undergo the widest range of changes without losing its cohesion in a few essentials, so as to be able to include other patterns and structures within itself without losing its identity or its continued capacity for growth." Karl Deutsch, *Nationalism and Social Communication*, 2nd ed. (Cambridge, M.I.T. Press, 1966), pp. 73, 74.

[4] Laswell Kaplan, *Power and Society* (Yale University Press, 1950).

[5] R. A. Dahl, "The Concept of Power", *The Behavioral Science*, 2 (1957).

variables: when agricultural population increases fast in absolute numbers and declines slowly in relative figures; when there is almost absolute stagnation in absolute population, and great changes in relative population (the population turning-point); when such populations begin to decline absolutely and relatively; and when the decrease is fast in absolute figures and slow in relative.

We have called the four types of agriculture subsistence agriculture, marketing agriculture, entrepreneurial agriculture and contract or planned agriculture. The first maximizes production per hectare, the second production per sale, the third that of the production unit as such and the fourth production per man occupied in agriculture. The corresponding roles of the head of the agricultural production unit are those of family

TABLE I

Types of Agriculture (Synoptic Table)

Type of agriculture	Subsistence agriculture	Marketing agriculture	Entrepreneurial agriculture	Contract and planned agriculture
Agricultural policies	Life parity	Price parity	Income parity	Technical parity
Agricultural population changes	Fast absolute increase Relative decline	Absolute stagnation Fast relative decline	Absolute decline Relative decline	Fast absolute decline Slow relative decline
Maximization of production	Per ha.	Per sale	Per unit	Per man
Main role of agricultural operator	Livelihood provider	Commercial dealer	Capitalist entrepreneur	Technical manager
Main risk	Natural risk	Commercial risk	Financial risk	Innovation risk
Optimalization method	Cost-effectiveness	Cost-price	Cost-benefit	Cost-efficiency
Lower critical policy line	Hunger line	Just price line	Poverty line	Technical obsolescence line
Upper critical policy line	Waste line	Maximum price line	Opulence line	Technical prodigality line
Main instrument of taxation	Poll tax Land tax	Turnover tax, excise, customs duties	Income tax	Corporation tax

livelihood provider; commercial dealer in agricultural produce; agricultural entrepreneur; and technical manager. The first has mainly to fight natural risks, the second the whims of the market, the third the pitfalls of investment and the fourth the intricacies of technical progress.

We shall describe in greater detail the differences accruing from various methods, and how differently gains are assessed in our four types of agriculture. After that government measures will be explored along the corresponding critical upper and lower lines of agricultural policies.[6]

2

In recent years reasonably great advances have been made in attempts to use more exact methods in decision making policy instead of mere 'political intuition', stirred by emotion or 'sound judgment' based on a limited amount of facts or even mature experience of past procedures (see appendix). Advice to policy decision makers is most necessary concerning this new field of policy analysis, since the new methods use procedures which require special technical knowledge of the factors influencing, and elements forming, the connections and interrelations upon which modern decision making rests. This is the particular field of research for a special type of highly qualified political scientist. Agriculture is not debarred from using this opportunity, and the people interested could reap good profit from using quantitative methods to measure gains and losses from agricultural policies.[7] This is of particular importance in countries at a

[6] These types could be defined by partial derivation of the agricultural production function. In a subsistence economy the derivation is arrived at by varying the function with respect to the variable indicating the maximum volume of physical production in the search for an optimum product-mix for family survival. In marketing agriculture the maximizing effect of the price variable on the market was sought by optimizing the sales-mix to give the maximum profit on the market. The entrepreneurial type of agriculture follows the partial derivation for the variable capital, searching for the maximum gain that should be achieved in an optimal production unit called an agricultural enterprise.

In the last, fast emerging type of agriculture by contract planning, partial derivation of the production function with respect to variable technical progress should help to find the optimal innovation-mix for maximum gain.

In general the lower parity line can be observed when the income elasticity of demand of these variables reaches zero in the agricultural sector. When zero elasticity is reached in the non-agricultural sector the upper parity line appears.

[7] Programming systems have as their objective "to sort out all the myriad programs and activities of the defense establishment, and regroup them into meaningful program elements, i.e. integrated combinations of men, equipment and installations whose effectiveness could be related to one ... objective. These are the basic building blocks as well as the decision making levels of the programming process. ... Whenever

lower level of development where the danger of voluntarism and arbitrariness is especially great, because of the limited interdependence of agricultural activities and of lack of political information among decision makers.[8]

Cost-benefit or operations research methods could be applied reasonably well to our four types of agricultural policy.[9] There is quite a family of such methods. We will distinguish four according to the degree of measurability, the directness of the stream of costs encountering benefits and the intentionality of the relationship.[10] These four are cost-effectiveness, cost-price, cost-benefit, cost-efficiency.

We propose to use the cost-effectiveness method when we analyze the life parity policy. Here we have a case where it is least possible to reduce the measurement to a common denominator. The object given is to secure means of subsistence for the family. It is an objective that is so overwhelming that the measurement of cost is not relevant in money terms.

---

possible program elements are measured in physical terms ... as well as in financial terms thus including both 'inputs and outputs', costs and benefits", C. Hitch, *Economics for Defense*, (University of California Press, 1966), p. 32. Forget all about 'defense' and read instead 'agricultural policy', and you will realize that a complex activity such as agricultural policy faces a similar situation. Indeed the Department of Agriculture is among the twenty-two U.S. Federal Government agencies to which the cost-benefit analysis methods will have to be applied.

[8] "In less developed economies the information problem is of capital importance because of the price inadequacy ... the lack of knowledge of resources, of expert surveys, of technical know-how, of the difficulties of assessing economies of scale, and of consumer preferences at higher or variant income distributions, further inhibit the practical use of opportunity costs", M. Kaser, "Analysis of Costs and Benefits in Social Programmes", UN *Problems and Methods of Social Planning*, 1964, p. 52. Under these handicaps action cannot be rationalized, but remains full of political voluntarism ending in dictatorships to correct other people's voluntarism by their own supreme voluntarism — until the mutual checks and counterchecks of each others' voluntarism in the self-interest of survival opens the way towards democracy.

[9] "Government services are not usually sold. Sales and market prices are not good measures of benefits ... The Benefit-Cost analysis provides a systematic way of thinking about allocation problems in government. It makes explicit assumptions which underlie budget figures, determines what activities might be more efficiently performed by private enterprise and what more appropriately carried out by the government. This analysis is most persuasive where the cause-effect relations are clean and the benefit-cost relations measurable. It has the purpose to inform the policy makers of efforts and effects to be considered, thus serves as a tool to aid in policy and budget decisions", Lester, *Manpower Planning in a Free Society* (Princeton University Press, 1966).

[10] For special application of the system in government policy in the U.S.A. consider the PPB (Planning, Programming, Budgeting System) introduced first in the Department of Defense and now spreading gradually to all other U.S. government departments, for which great merit goes to former Assistant-Director of the Bureau of the Budget, Henry S. Rowen. I am indebted to Mr. Rowen for information regarding the general use of these methods and the indication of bibliographical sources.

Performance is stated only in natural effect. The objective is measured by how well subsistence is provided for how many members of the family, and how the family is kept together. — Cost-price analysis belongs to the marketing type of agriculture, which is the classical type of market relation reduced to market prices and costs in money terms. Money is the common denominator and gain is calculated as profit, i.e. difference between cost and price. Nevertheless one must emphasize that the relationship is linear, and profit is calculated by aggregating commodity relationship. Prices and cost are reduced to the *present value* at the market under conditions of imperfect competition. Social costs and social gains are not taken into account. — The method for what we call entrepreneurial agriculture is cost-benefit analysis. It embraces the total stream of tangible and intangible benefits, gains and advantages against the total costs of achieving them, private and social. Both are evalued in money terms expressed explicitly or imputed when natural, non-moneyed elements are concerned. The performance is looked at as a whole with intangible and secondary effects and side-effects added. The choices of alternative uses and mixes of capital are decided taking into account their lifetime operating costs. — The most suitable method for contract agriculture is the cost-efficiency analysis. The efficiency method takes into account natural and money indicators measured in a scientific manner (e.g. money cost per calory unit, fat content of milk, animal proteins in food, capital coefficient of investment, etc.). It implies the maximum use of specified resources at minimum cost, and economies achieved must not affect the implementation of objectives. These increases in efficiency form the main basis for the agriculturists' income.

3

How do changes in the politically exogenous environment of agriculture affect, penetrate or permeate the political sphere of the power structure? We are restricting ourselves to the study of the application of public power or general government as it affects agriculture. In this field we shall study the following three questions: (a) who are the *actors* administering the application of power in agriculture? (b) what are the *means* by which this application takes place? (c) what are the *ends* which make the government intervene so that the levelling mechanism[11] and the

[11] "Levelling mechanisms are ways of forcing the expenditure of accumulated resources or capital into channels that are not necessarily economic or productive. Every society has some form of levelling mechanism, but in primitive and peasant

parity policy are put into action? This parity policy is on the borderline between specific agricultural and 'general social' (non-agricultural) interests.

In the context of this paper agricultural policy implies no other motivation than that of the use of power for making deliberate changes in agriculture in order to preserve an existing social and political system. We are not dealing with other motives of social action affecting the redistribution of agricultural goods and services such as aid, transfers in the form of gifts or religious alms, moral charity, humanitarian equality or national and class solidarity, etc. We are leaving aside also the effects of 'spontaneous' market relations striving towards maximum returns to buyers and sellers of commodities. Nor are we considering such targets as full employment through the firm mechanism conditioned by the observance of technical norms (coefficients).

Our specific concern is the government redistributive system as it affects agricultural goods and services, natural resources and capital income and produce, human labor and technical know-how.

A. *Actors*

Actors in the government redistributive system are politicians and government agency officials on the one hand, and on the other, people engaged in agricultural activities, and those whose wants are being satisfied by agricultural products. (a) These actors are in an asymmetric position, the former using power to influence the actions of the others, the latter accepting the redistribution when it is in their favor, fighting against it when it causes them loss and setting in motion counteracting powers. (b) The specific character of this use of power in agriculture is that the government embodies a concentrated number of actors having a monopoly of power, while on the agricultural side the number of actors is very large and spread over a vast space, therefore their power is diffuse. (c) Power applied in agricultural policy has to pass through several levels of concentration which gives ample chance for deviation and distortions on the cost-benefit line. (d) A government redistributive system presupposes a certain center of action which takes goods and commands services from one social group and gives to another (while keeping the lion's share for itself). In a monocentric system, based on a

economies levelling mechanisms play a crucial role in inhibiting aggrandizement by individuals or by special social groups", Manning Nash, *Primitive and Peasant Economic Systems* (San Francisco, Chandler Publishing Co., 1966), p. 35. For a description of some such mechanisms, cf. pp. 72-80.

monopoly of power this center operates without much control in the form of checking its redistributive effectiveness. Moreover waste can be presented disguised as efficiency if there is monopoly of information in the hands of the monocenter.[12] A polycentric system can be more effective in that it can counterbalance the action of one center by the actions of other centers and integrate auto-regulative and auto-organizing systems to redress the upset equilibrium. In fact, instead of simple mechanical equilibrium we are proposing to strive towards a homeostatic equilibrium. It is our experience that integration by planning is more effective and less wasteful than centralization by command. Centralization does not necessarily equal rationalization.[13] Thus there are limits to the effectiveness of government redistributive systems. In fact, government redistribution is a sign of ineffectiveness in distribution by other mechanisms.[14]

[12] "An actor is subject to a constraint when a state (use of goods or satisfaction) which he effectively desires, is made impossible or prevented from existing", F. Perroux, *Economie et Société. Contrainte-Echange-Don* (Paris, Presses Universitaires de France, 1960), pp. 134ff. Perroux distinguishes the constraints of obstacles, of adversaries and of public authorities who have the monopoly of unconditional constraint. This constraint is limited, as with all monopolies, by potential rivals (in a democracy there are potential rivals who have a chance to replace the ruling group) and checking and mutual counterchecking of more than one centre of decision.

[13] There are two apparently conflicting views as to what the function of the center is. "A redistributive system of exchange is a form of reciprocity with political or economic centricity. Some central agency collects goods or commands services and then distributes them among the social units and persons who have proferred them. ... Redistributive exchange rests on social differentiation along some axis of prestige and power in equality, but operates to minimize that gap, to constrain the use of power differentials in the society and to make status gaps more honorific and ceremonial than economic and political", Manning Nash, *Primitive and Peasant Economic Systems* (1966), pp. 32, 33.

The other view is given by Perroux. "The preferences of the actors can be combined into a social order without the necessity to establish a dictatorship conceived as an order of preferences of a *Centrale*, in opposition to the preferences of a plurality of actors. By these two aspects the total order, the economic order of the global society of all actors, and all variables which characterize their choice, allows theoretically to determine the justified constraints and the requested constraints", F. Perroux, *Economie et Société*, pp. 142-143.

Our views about the role of the centre and polycentricity are expressed in *Problems of Planning: East and West* (*Publications of the Institute of Social Studies*, Series Maior, vol. XV) (The Hague, Mouton, 1967), pp. 82-100. See also "Socialism in a Developed Country", *Foreign Affairs* (New York, July 1966), pp. 647-648.

[14] "In developed societies spontaneous actions and reactions of social groups conveniently managed and transformed into collective habits, spare the Public Authorities an enormous effort of constraint. When the consumers vigorously and intelligently resist unjustified increases in prices, when the producers compete intensely with one another, when workers and employers agree to a certain formula to attach the wages to productivity, the State can intervene discreetly", Perroux, *op. cit.*, p. 140.

B. *The Means*

The method used by the government redistributive system is command instead of demand, and requests to comply instead of supply, i.e. to comply with government orders where supply does not match the claims to satisfy demands as recognized by the government.

This system of redistribution operates under the principle of no equivalence of valuables exchanged, which affects the concept of parity. On the other hand there are no unilateral transfers (in the technical sense) as is often presented, but a reciprocity of interests, often more implicit than explicit. Government action in borderline cases of parities takes the role of equilibrator giving to some what was taken from others. Its gain is in the preservation of the power relationship, and the maintenance of the political structure. The pre-supposition is that the government is the representative of the interests of society. The measurability of effect on both sides is different. On the government side there is a much more easily measurable effect which can be expressed in terms of money. For the other side, since the gain from such action has its effect in physical dimensions, it is much more difficult to ascertain. This means that the burden of the cost and benefit of the gain is blurred.

C. *The Ends*

There are two lines of parity which determine the upper and lower limits of government intervention in agriculture by the redistributive system. The lower line is that where the government intervenes by using state power in order to transfer goods and command services from other sectors in favor of agriculture. Agriculture thus gains goods and services at present values in exchange for the expectations of the government of both survival and gain in the future. The upper line of parity is that where the government orders resources and services to be transferred from agriculturists in order to be distributed to the non-agricultural sectors.

Thus there are two critical lines of parity.[15] We call them critical on the lower level because they require government intervention to redress the upset balance where there is no strength in the agricultural system itself to return back to 'normal', i.e. where the limits of elasticity in the physical sense are approached. This happens in all our four types of agriculture, but in each at a different level, e.g. when hunger threatens the population

[15] For different definitions of standards and levels of living see U.N. *Report on International Definitions and Measurements of Standards and Levels of Living* (March 1954, New York), p. 2.

with physical extermination; or when the price scissors are so unfavorable to agriculture that production needed by the non-agricultural population is seriously hampered below their subsistence level; or when income in agriculture is so unfavorable that the agricultural population (the best part of it) leaves agriculture; or when technical efficiency reaches a stage where work in agriculture is so inefficient and so little productive that it cannot stand comparison in costs with other sectors and countries.

The *upper* line of parity is established on the subsistence level when there is hunger or deficiency among the non-agricultural population, or when prices of agricultural produce increase to such a level that they threaten to reduce the purchasing power of the non-agricultural population, or when non-agricultural incomes fall at the same time that opulence is reached by the reduced number of agricultural producers, sending the bulk of their produce to the monopolistic market. The technical prodigality line demonstrates that agricultural investments have reached a stage where they are stimulated by other than economic motives, such as status symbols, individual or collective, political favouritism or monopoly of power.

It is comparatively easier to establish a lower parity line assessed by objective standards, and to find a common yardstick of measurement. But this cannot be said for fixing the upper parity line. Here political decision-making has a wider field of action, reaching from economic necessity to political party arbitrariness and division of the spoils. Naturally lines of parity change over time corresponding to changed situations and level of development. Changes vary with the change of political power too. Many methods have been devised in order to determine parity lines. The requirements set are that such lines should represent certain values adopted and assured to be the same for all individuals, agricultural as well as non-agricultural, or which differ in a known way within limits of the political system. These values should be able to be commonly accepted,[16] or at least not made unworkable by an upset of the existing power relations. They may be set by political factors, or accepted by them even though set by others (political party, ideology, national ideal, church, class struggle, etc.). Thus they have to be explicitly or implicitly socially recognized.

Parity lines should mobilize sufficient political support ('general social support' as the quoted U.N. Report calls it), to pull the victims of the upset economic balance back to equilibrium on the old or some new level

[16] U.N. *Report on ... Standards and Levels of Living*, pp. 5-8, 45, 47.

through the use of political force.[17] There must be agreed standards of behaviour enabling social adjustment processes of beliefs, customs and accepted values to support such action of power.[18] Finally the degree of tension must be within the breaking-point of elasticity which kept the flexible balance of push-in and push-out, pull-in and pull-out factors in continuous check.[19]

The no return situation in some variables has to be counterbalanced by dynamic equilibrium in the stream of variables of a global balance. In fact we can recognize in the game three systems whose elements have to be put into equilibrium: on one hand is the internal system of power relations, and on the other two external systems, one of them the agricultural equilibrium matching agricultural resources and requirements — the other the non-agricultural system balancing the supply of agricultural resources to their non-agricultural requirements. In the system of redistribution by government action, the government takes the role of the equilibrator of both external systems, transferring agricultural resources to the non-agricultural sector, or goods and services from the latter to agriculture. Such redistribution aims at putting the external system into equilibrium in cases when their own auto-regulative system and other systems of distribution such as the market, the contract or the planning, the village or the tribal mechanisms cease to operate effectively.

The study of such tensions and their discovery and measurement is the object of the research of the political scientist. His role is to locate the field of conflict, to shape the tools of analysis, to find the limits of tolerance of auto-regulation and the breaking-points of resistance to deformations, the connectedness of agricultural interrelations, the effectiveness of the economy and limitations to the use of power.

4

A. *Policy of life-parity*

In this ideal type of agriculture, change is dominated by a considerable increase of agricultural population in absolute numbers, which is of

[17] "When social continuity becomes a conscious goal of most members of a society we may assume the society and culture are under attack from some overwhelmingly threatening other society and culture ... an acculturation situation."

[18] FAO, *Essentials of Rural Welfare*, 1949.

[19] R. Bićanić, *Three Concepts of Agricultural Overpopulation*, R. N. Dixey (ed.), *International Exploration of Agricultural Economics* (Iowa State University Press, 1964), pp. 20-21.

greater rate than its relative decrease in comparison to the total population. The cause may be a demographic explosion, concurrent with lack of outlet in employment in non-agricultural occupations at home or emigration to other areas. There is also shortage of land and capital. This is the well-known and much discussed case of agriculture in most underdeveloped countries.

Agricultural production is carried out within the framework of a subsistence economy due also to a poorly developed infrastructure. It makes the peasant producer little resistant to the pressure of the big landowner whose interests dominate agricultural policy, but these are not considered to be critical any longer from a political power relations point of view. Land is the main factor of production to which labor is subordinated. Yield is so low that the fluctuation in the harvest over years makes a very high percentage of the average harvest. This minimizes efforts to capital intensification and favors extensive cultivation by cheap and dependent labor.

The main worry of the agricultural producer is to provide food and means of subsistence for his family. The greatest threat to this task comes from the blind forces of nature, and his fear of natural risk predominates over all rational considerations. Therefore he values his performance, contrary to all advice and propaganda of agricultural experts, along the lines of cost-effectiveness and not cost-price relationship. He measures his efforts both in terms of natural outlay and monetary expenditure. But he evaluates his gains in terms of his performance expressed in the natural dimension, that of how he manages to keep himself and his family alive. The struggle for survival in physical terms is overwhelming.

The predominant multi-dimensional cost-effectiveness reasoning controls relations with the outside world. The meagre, marginal, market mechanism, with an imperfect price formation, on the brink of natural and moneyed sectors, gives ample opportunity for the greatest exploitation of the peasant. His relationship with the State in terms of taxes and other government services bears a similar character.

This situation determines the power relationship in the field of politics. The basic concern for the survival of the existing power structure is to maintain in existence the social structure based on subsistence economy, and in particular not let it fall below the lower critical point. This breaking-point is reached where the subsistence economy ceases to operate, and the whole social structure based on it blazes up into hunger riots, mob explosions, instinctive and uncontrollable mass movements, peasant revolt. Agricultural policy is dominated by the same factor: the priority goal is to increase food production for the auto-consumption of the agricultural producers themselves. Maximization of such production per hectare is the main policy target.

We propose giving such a policy the name of a *life-parity policy*, because it is based on the idea that the State is obliged to provide a minimum level of subsistence, and not to let anyone starve. If this threatens the agricultural population of an area, the non-agricultural and agricultural population from other areas have to provide means to assure the minimum parity level of subsistence. The measures to keep the agricultural producer above the hunger line are varied. They range from government distribution of free grain and other food to the needy agricultural population to the establishment of emergency village food baskets, regional and national food stock-piling, foreign aid in case of disaster,[20] the U.N. Food Emergency Fund, etc. Homestead laws, exemption from seizure of minimum areas under cultivation for debt or tax and poor laws[21] are all instances of legislation to preserve the peasant above the hunger line. So, too, are the organization of agricultural consumer personal credit, on the basis of government-sponsored mutual aid co-operatives: social, pension and sickness benefits for agricultural population, public insurance against hail, fire, flood and animal diseases. Land tax or poll tax are the forms of taxation considered to be adequate for this situation and level of development.

The policy of expansion of the areas for extensive subsistence agriculture finds its natural or financial limits, and the main emphasis then turns to problems of land redistribution. Removal of the feudal obstacles to individual land inheritance and to commerce in land, and the strengthening of the mobility of landed property by creation of mortgage credit organization are the respective measures of land policy. Above all comes the policy of land reform, both as abolition of rent in labor, cash and kind, and in the form of real distribution of land,[22] which is an outward

[20] E.g. imposition of food rationing in non-hunger stricken areas in order to help the hungry ones suffering from natural disaster (India).

[21] Allocation of land by land reform laws to submarginal smallholders or agricultural labourers.

[22] Many a learned foreign adviser or domestic expert, opposing distribution of large estates, has utterly failed when advocating a policy of cost-benefit optimizing of capital investment where cost-effectiveness of physical survival was at stake at a critical point for the existing power structure. These experts talked a language which was rational, but in another co-ordination system of rationality than the survival of the agricultural population. Their logic was out of place unless other than agricultural sources of income were created for the surplus population.

sign of the changed power structure where big landowners have lost their dominance.

We called the critical upper limit the *waste line*, in opposition to the hunger line. Waste takes place in a subsistence economy when agricultural products are wasted, i.e. used in a less economical way than they would be in the non-agricultural sector, when the latter is threatened with hunger, destitution or food deficiency, and when the market and other mechanisms of supply break down. Government measures taken to meet this situation are those of requisition of agricultural products in case of war, taxation in kind and compulsory deliveries to government agencies — at below real production cost price in some socialist countries, etc. The main concern of those in power is to extract surpluses from the subsistence economy to support the social overhead. The same kind of products are redistributed by the government as are required by the peasants for their subsistence, and stimulation goes to increase the quantity, i.e. surpluses over and above the limits of the needs of the agricultural population. The definition of such 'surpluses' is often very arbitrary. They are extracted either through the intermediary of the market, or the money-lending mechanism, or, when these fail, direct fiscal pressure is used, often acting in collusion with the market.

Maximization of the size of agricultural holdings and land reforms by real distribution are measures to extend the area under cultivation, when there is no more land available. Land above a certain level is considered as wasted surplus — when more than an area necessary for the maintenance of the family is in the hands of the big landowners or rich peasants while the remaining agricultural peasant population cannot exist on their meagre land on the level of subsistence, and where at the same time there is no opportunity for other employment or for emigration.[23]

B. *Policy of price parity*

The situation where a policy of price parity is required is reached when the agricultural population stops increasing in absolute numbers, stagnates and begins to decrease. Therefore we call this stage the turning-point of agricultural population. The agricultural population continues

[23] The land reforms in Yugoslavia show how this upper limit of the critical parity line changes. Consecutive land reforms set the maximum size of agricultural holdings after 1918 at 600-1,200 ha., in 1946 at 25-35 ha. of agricultural land and in 1953 to 10 ha. of cultivated land. Land given to the beneficiaries of the reform amounted after 1918 to 0.5 ha. per member of the household, and in 1948 to 1.5-2 ha. per household.

to decline in relative terms at an accelerated pace. This is the same as saying that an increasing demand is being created for agricultural products by an increase in the percentages of non-agricultural population. The demand is threefold: need for food for the urban population, demand for agricultural raw materials for manufacturing and processing industries and requirements for export in order to meet the demand for import of consumer and capital goods, fuel and raw materials. Subsistence agriculture cannot provide an adequate supply for these purposes either in quantity or in kind. Instead of selling surpluses to producers' own consumption, production specially for the market has to be developed.[24]

Increased demand requires a specific stimulation for production for the market which develops to meet such new requirements. The line of supply and demand now moves along the cost-price axis. The demand is effective in monetary terms of available purchasing power. Supply also has to be effective on the market, which means that the time dimension is reduced to the present value of actual exchange through the market mechanism.[25] Thus the producer's market performance depends on the continuity of his flow returns which secure not only his means of livelihood but also his ability to produce which depends on the inflow of production goods. Thus to the natural risks of production, risks of marketability are added. They provide the lower critical point of operations of the market mechanism.

The agricultural producer's main role becomes that of a commercial dealer in agricultural produce. What his product-mix should be in order to maximize his cost-price differential depends on his personal ability. Maximization of sales for profit becomes uppermost. The price scissors between the product bought and sold by him are the indicators of the producer's performance.[26]

[24] Most of the East European countries experienced a land reform after the First World War, which had to secure, by real division of land, subsistence to millions of peasant families of the region. During the Great Crisis of the Thirties the main problem of the agrarian policy was the problem of the 'price scissors' between agricultural and industrial prices of goods. The same problem seemed to be one of the guiding topics of discussion at the U.N. Conference on Trade and Development in Geneva in 1964.

[25] The production process is conceived of as an isochronic and equivalent process, i.e. the market mechanism is not interested in the time dimension (how long it takes to produce the goods, and how long capital invested will last, etc.); it is equivalent in the sense that all goods at the market are supposed to have the same price whatever the expenses incurred.

[26] The price parity was defined first in 1933 in the U.S., "to re-establish prices to farmers at a level that will give agricultural commodities a purchasing power with respect to articles that farmers buy equivalent to the purchasing power of agricultural commodities in the base period".

The power structure thus depends to a larger extent in agriculture on three areas which communicate through the market mechanism. If the flow of food to concentrations of urban population is upset, serious political problems might arise. Even a reduced flow will manifest itself in an increase of the cost of living, will cause workers' strikes and discontinuity in non-agricultural production, which then brings about unemployment. Exports would seem to be the most adaptable if it were not for the inelastic local demand for imported goods, capital and know-how, which have to be paid for by agricultural exports. Therefore they have a critical influence on the foreign balance of payments. Thus agricultural policy is mainly preoccupied with problems of price parity, with the aim of stimulating agricultural production for the market. It also has to act as a countervailing force in order to keep the flow of domestic agricultural production increasing in spite of any adverse tendency in price relationship on external or internal markets.

This is the lower critical point. The upper one develops when the prices can no longer ensure increase of agricultural production and structural changes become necessary for survival.

C. *Income parity*

When the agricultural population continues to decline in relative terms and also begins to decline in absolute numbers the stage of income parity is reached. The pull-out forces away from agriculture towards other activities become stronger than the pull-in forces, and rural exodus takes proportions which deplete agriculture of labor. Optimalization of production *per unit* (farm, estate) now becomes the main issue in agriculture. Capital investment is the chief factor in the search for greater benefits; and the accelerated process of substitution of labor by capital, and to a larger extent the substitution of capital of lower productivity by that of superior productivity takes place.[27] To the market dimension

It is very interesting to follow the subtleties of the changes in the definitions of the price parity in the U.S.A. from 1933 onwards. Cf. O. V. Wells, "Parity Prices and Parity Income Formulas 1933-1957" (U.S. Congress, *Policy for Commercial Agriculture, its Relation to Economic Growth and Stability*, Joint Economic Committee, November 1957).

[27] There is a marked difference between the income parity and price parity. Poor farmers who sell little to the market would not be protected by the policy of price parity. Therefore suggestions were made to accept an income parity, which was defined in the U.S.A. by the Agricultural Act as "gross income from agriculture which will provide the farm operator and his family with a standard of living equivalent to that afforded persons dependent upon other gainful occupations". And commenting on it,

another important dimension is joined, that of time. The question of the longevity of the capital-mix and the quality of capital (technical progress) plays a predominant role. The main function of the agricultural operator becomes that of a capitalist entrepreneur securing the right capital-mix in order to optimalize his income. Thus to the lessening influence of the natural risk and the extended risk of market relations an ever-increasing financial risk of capital investment is added. The decision-making process involves so many decisions a day among so many variants that only a person living on the spot, used to making decisions and guided by a knowledge of his personal interests, can carry it out.

Capital for investment is available to agriculture in general terms like capital investment in all other sectors.

Capital investment becomes so large that the burden cannot any longer be successfully carried by the producer alone and he increasingly becomes more a technical manager and less an entrepreneur. In a capital intensive agriculture to counteract the long term risk of the market, contract economy and economic planning increasingly come into use.

Specialization and fast technical progress mean that less capital is necessary per product unit, and productivity in agriculture becomes higher and rises faster than in many industrial activities.

The bi-dimensional cost-price relationship is expanded into a multi-dimensional cost-benefit relationship, where the differences between a stream of cost and a complex concept of benefit are optimalized.

Power relations are affected by this in many ways. On the one hand the number of agricultural voters is declining fast. The ever-increasing need for capital investment per man puts a brake on the entrance into agriculture of all those who are short of capital. This would lead to further social differentiation of agriculture into capitalist agriculture and proletarians if the 'pull' forces outside agriculture were not to attract the latter at a faster rate than they were proletarianized. Thus the agricultural proletariat is reduced just at the time when entry into agriculture has become difficult.

Agriculture is no longer a sector, outside the business sector, run according to exceptional economic considerations. It has become part of the general entrepreneurial economic system. In this situation an income-

---

O. V. Wells said: "The determination of equivalent standards of living involves much more than equivalent dollar incomes. A family's well-being depends not only on income but also on other factors such as the accumulation of assets and consumer goods over the years, the availability of adequate health and educational facilities, and such intangible factors as are involved in evaluating country versus city life." (U.S. Congress, *Policy for Commercial Agriculture*, p. 520.)

parity policy becomes the main preoccupation of government policy[28] with triple purpose: to paralyze the influence of rural exodus, to assure an adequate rate of general interest for the capital invested in agriculture and to offset the effects of monopolistic and monopsonistic power over agricultural producers in an integration process.

A parity policy finds its lower critical point at the income level of the *poverty line*.[29] This line can be described in absolute terms as income per family of agricultural producers of a certain level (say $3,000 p.a.).[30] Or it can be more adequately expressed as the income which still keeps the agricultural farmer on land together with the members of his family. The line can be differentiated according to the income differentials in various countries, and regions within the country. As there is no question of earning a rate of profit for invested capital but of survival on land as owner of a distinct production unit, it is necessary to introduce into the parity comparison also all items measurable in money and in kind as well as non-measurable elements of the standard of living, such as cost of health and educational services, opportunity costs for employment, leisure time, recreation, etc., and other elements which in a comparison of town and country life might act in favor of the peasant leaving the land in search of a better level of living.

Thus instead of a relatively simple cost-price line or cost-profit relation an overall cost-benefit is required to define the poverty line.

Therefore other elements are added to mere agricultural economic policy of production, marketing and of subsidies and tax exemptions, such as educational and health facilities for farmers' children, special agricultural or overall national health service including the agriculturists, youth clubs, community development centers, etc.

The top critical line of income points is that of *opulence*, by which is

[28] The dominant trend in agricultural policy in European socialist countries in the 1960s became ever more the problem of income parity. The policy manifests itself in measures to increase the incomes of the kolkhozniks, and to secure them by regular payments, social insurance and pensions, e.g. in the U.S.S.R. in 1966. Cf. R. Bićanić, "Problems of Socialist Agriculture", *Indian Journal of Agricultural Economics* (Bombay, July-December 1964).

[29] In the U.S.A. the povery income line was defined as income of all those families which is below $3,000 a year. The Social Security Administration defined a poverty income standard taking into account family size, composition and place of residence. Of all farm households 30 per cent were classified as being under the poverty line (*Economic Report of the President*, 1966, p. 113).

[30] The problem of poverty is widely treated in the U.S.A. in Reports of the President. "Poverty is the inability to satisfy minimum needs. The poor are those whose resources — their income from all resources, together with their asset holdings — are inadequate", *Report*, 1964, p. 62.

meant an income level which, when overstepped, puts in motion redistributive action by the government for reasons of adequate sharing of the burden of the social overhead, or social equity, or political pressure against unearned incomes. The main instrument of such redistribution today is the progressive income tax and progressive inheritance tax (death duties). In socialist countries it is the capital tax, profit sharing between socialist agricultural estates and the government, etc. Some measures of legislation in favor of agricultural labor can be put into the same category in redistributing parts of the opulence income to those who labored for it. Nationalization of landed estates is the most radical measure to end the opulence of a limited number of people.

D. *Technical parity policy*

This type of agriculture develops when the decline in agricultural population slows down in relative terms, i.e. when the division of labor has reached stagnating level, but the absolute number of agricultural population declines rapidly.

Replacement of labor by capital is no longer a matter of profitableness but an absolute necessity since there is siuply no labor available for agricultural work at any price. Abundance of capital in the country makes heavy capital investment possible in agriculture, and spectacular technical progress reduces the capital-output ratio in agriculture as elsewhere. Therefore less capital per unit of product is required.

Personal abilities are less demanded of the farm operator and his risks reduced by contracts in marketing, by technical services and various forms of insurance. His main risk is the risk taken for capital investment in innovations. Personal abilities are greatly supplemented by extension services, education and government production research (farming by recipe!). Integration relieves the farmer of threefold heavy risks, natural, commercial and financial, but he has to pay for this by a considerable reduction of his independence.[31] This is so because combinations of production factors are no longer so dependent on farmers' personal skill and experience as before, but more on research, and development of formulae for production factors. Capital remains the main factor of

[31] In America the idea of the freedom of the farmer is linked to the minimum of government intervention. Arguments put forward in favour of this are: that freedom to decide the use of one's resources is a basic value essential to the fullest development of the individual; farm income and efficiency will be greater if farmers are free to work out their own decisions; government intervention involves cost to taxpayers and is an inconvenience to farmers. U.S. Congress, *Policy for Commercial Agriculture*, p. 505.

production and a common denominator of success. Therefore economies of scale can operate optimally and concentration of farms into bigger units dominate. Rewards for resources used are similar in all farms in function of capital invested, thus depending on accumulation and indivisibility of capital. Prices are also similar in all agricultural enterprises and consequently the differential pay-off depends on the managerial skill of the farm operator; technical management becomes his main function.[32] Cost-efficiency becomes the leading criterion of performance.

In such a type of agriculture the bottom line of parity is the technical *obsolescence* line. Competition subordinated to the predominance of technical progress simply cannot let the farmer operate below a certain technical level. Neither can this be in the interest of the national economy as a whole. The gap between technical possibilities and actual performance reaches the lower critical point in receptive capabilities of agriculturists, in comparison to non-agricultural occupations. The discrepancy between hard labor in the fields and ever softer labor in factories and in town further creates pressure for technical progress. Vocational and managerial training, general education up to college level, government agricultural extension services, expansion of research and development facilities, are the measures of government policy. Technical aid is the outward recognition of such endeavors both in national and international fields in order to bring about technical parity and spread minimum technical knowledge in international comparisons.

Some more coercive redistributive measures have been taken in connexion with technical parities. Such are laws (e.g. in the U.K. and Yugoslavia) ordering private owners to work their lands according to some minimum technological standards under threat that land might be taken from them and rented to more able managers; obligation to work one's own land, etc. Use of technical norms prescribed by law in socialist agriculture is another example of such minimum technical lines.

The upper critical line of technological parity is what we call the

[32] D. R. Kaldor (Iowa State College) set the following requirements of economists for efficient farm industry: 1. The output of each farm product would be produced at minimum cost. This would mean that all producers would be using the best practices and the lowest cost combinations of land, labour and capital. 2. The composition of farm output — the relative amount of each product — would be geared to the pattern of demand for agricultural commodities. This would imply that the rewards for resources would be similar in all farm enterprises. 3. The total output of farm products would be adjusted to the total demand to give a level of prices that would be similar in all farm enterprises.

D. R. Kaldor, "Farm Policy Objectives: A Setting for the Parity Question", U.S. Congress, *Policy for Commercial Agriculture* (November 1957), p. 505.

technical *prodigality line*. This is the level of technical work above which the government redistributive mechanism is set into operation, because of application of technical progress beyond economic reasoning (e.g. what is technically possible but economically does not pay or cannot be permitted in terms of the social values accepted by the society).

This is the case of over-capitalization in agriculture, which some government measures try to reduce, and of conspicuous production (e.g. use of some means of production as a status symbol). Government measures restricting production and paying premiums for not using available capital can be put into the same category of technical prodigality, like the production restrictions in the U.S.A. (soil bank, subsidies, etc.). Government prescribed standards of production can also be classified in a similar category.

5

Having established the existence of constraints to social action, and examined the types of agriculture from the point of view of their social recognition by government action in *parity* relation to other interests in society, we ask ourselves what role the political scientist can play in making and implementing agricultural policy. We emphasize that we are not talking about politicians, men of action, but about political scientists, men of science. Our purpose is not to determine the field of action and poles of attraction of politocrats, who make choices of final decisions and pass value judgements. We are opposed to the idea that such choices should be made by bureaucrats, people who run government affairs from offices by rules and regulations, or by technocrats, who think they know all the answers and therefore have the divine function to run human affairs.

We believe that politics, including agricultural politics, is too serious a business to be left either to the technicians or the economists alone, nor should it be left unconditionally to the politicians. Each of these has a specific role and acts under specific constraints in the complex game of policy-making.

We agree that politics and economics have a common basic ground, and that "politics is the concentration of economics" (Lenin). When an economic situation becomes so 'thick' that it requires government action, then it becomes a political question. On the other hand, we recognize the danger (expressed by Max Weber) of giving advice without bearing the responsibility. In this mixture of various roles it is not only useful and advisable, but imperative that all those engaged in formulating agricultural policies or implementing political measures in agriculture be trained in essential matters of political science. Reliance on experience and common sense in politics, justified as it is neither in agricultural technology nor agricultural economics, is no longer enough in view of the increasing complexity and improvements in scientific knowledge.[33]

What then is the specific role of the political scientist in agricultural policy? In our opinion his main task is to rationalize the process of decision-making and implementation. It is for him to prepare the logistics of decision-making and to find functional relationships in the political game. The political scientist can perform his role in different capacities such as:

(a) He can act as an *expert*, a research scholar, engaged in finding facts and exploring their relationships; (b) he can act as an *adviser* giving his opinion on alternatives presented and exposing the consequences of alternative decisions to be taken; (c) he can be employed as an *apologetic lobbyist* presenting, advocating or defending those agricultural interests which hired him; (d) he can also act as an *arbiter* weighing arguments and counter arguments in a conflict of interests and finding whose ends are best served by what means.

There are various approaches to political conflicts which the political scientists have to explore. Among many theories we believe that special attention should be given to the Dahl-Harsanyi theory of political games. Dahl[34] found the following elements of power relations: (a) the *base* of power, that is the resources that the actor can use in order to influence other people's behavior, such as facts about the number of voters and their class structure, the weight of economic interests, the existing legal situation and institutional framework, etc.; (b) the *means* of power, i.e. the tools of action by which resources can be applied to influence the opposite opinions; such as public meetings, publicity, speeches in parliament; (c) the *scope* of power, which represents a set of actions undertaken as a whole, covering the purported ends; (d) the *amount* of

[33] Here is the advice given by a prominent American scholar to the famous Mexican National School of Agriculture at Champingo: "We need to know more about institutions of law and government and to find how they can be better employed in agricultural development. ... Political sciences and law have never directly been considered part of the rural social sciences in the U.S., probably because so many of our agricultural colleges are part of universities that emphasize law and government in other faculties. Yet these subjects may well be part of an adequate social sciences program under your conditions", Bryant E. Kearl, *Agricultural Development Council Papers* (New York, May 1966), p. 5.

[34] R. A. Dahl, "The Concept of Power", *Behavioral Science*, 2 (1957), pp. 201-215.

power set in motion compared to the tasks to be performed, that is the probability of actually performing the desired action; (e) the set of individuals over whom power is exercised by the actor.

To these, in our opinion, another important element should be added, that is the number of actors taking an active part in the action and forming the power structure of a society.

Harsanyi[35] has added two important dimensions to Dahl's elements of power. His main contribution is the effort to measure the gain from the political game. His elements are: (a) the costs to the actor of attempting to influence the opponent's behavior; (b) the strength the actor has to apply in order to make his opponent yield to his influence in the game.

By these methods experts in political game theory can quantify to a considerable degree of probability some gains and losses from political action which may be useful for all concerned to know.

APPENDIX

There is considerable difference of opinion[36] as to the definition, methods and objectives of the cost-benefit analysis, which is the most popular name for a family of concepts and overlapping methods dealing with the choice of alternative uses of means for intended ends.[37] Some authors talk of cost-benefit, others of cost-utility and still others of cost-effectiveness, of operational research, and of system analysis, etc. A stage has been reached when some efforts at systemization would be useful.

All authors dealing with these methods have in common the extension of the computation over and above micro-economic costs by bookkeeping methods, to total social or external costs and gains, in order to maximize the ratio of achievements to costs. To quote a few examples of

[35] John Harsanyi, "Measurement of Social Power, Opportunity Costs, and the Theory of Two Person Bargaining Games", *Behavioral Science*, 1 (1962), pp. 67-80. "In more precise words the costs of A's power over B will be defined as the expected value of the costs of his attempt to influence B. It will be a weighted average of the net total costs that A would incur if his attempts were successful and of the net total costs that A would incur if his attempts were unsuccessful."

[36] Robert Dorfman (ed.), *Measuring Benefits of Government Investments* (Washington, The Brookings Institution, 1966), Introduction, esp. p. 7.

[37] The most systematic presentation, including an ample bibliography of the cost-benefit method is given by R. A. Prest, Survey in the *Economic Journal* (London, December 1965), which is reprinted in the *Surveys of Economic Theory*, vol. III, issued by the American Economic Association and the Royal Economic Society (London, Macmillan, 1965). See also an excellent report to the Canadian Conference of the *Resources for Tomorrow* by W. R. D. Sewell, *et al.*, *Guide to Benefit-Cost Analysis* (Ottawa, Roger Duhamel, Queen's Printer, 1965).

differences of approach: Alan Dean[38] defines cost-*benefit* analysis as an effort to measure tangible and intangible benefits against the costs of achieving those benefits. Cost-*effectiveness* for him is "selection of alternative approaches to the achievement of a benefit already determined to be worth achieving". Cost-*utility* analysis is defined by him as "a specialized technique of operations research utilizing advanced mathematical techniques, particularly model building, as an aid to decision making". G. Steiner[39] defines the various methods differently. Cost-*benefit* analysis is a method to "measure the benefits, gains or advantages for achieving the objectives by each alternative means chosen for examination ... requiring calculation of all major costs and benefits that make comparisons relevant ... alternatives from measurement of a common denominator, usually money". And he defines cost-*utility* as the "most objective evaluation possible of the cost of alternative programs in relation to their values ... measuring the advantages of achieving an objective by the use of dollar expenditure in one way versus another".

Of special interest to us is the distinction between cost-effectiveness and cost-efficiency methods, both of which we used in our paper. Both are of the same linguistic origin (*ex facere*=work out).[40] Effectiveness can be taken as actual production of an effect; a result as the function of working out an intentional accomplishment. Efficiency means action resulting from the exercise of energy or still; action adequate to intended result. While the term effectiveness is correlated to the cause and effect relationship, efficiency is the antonym of wastefulness. The former could be described as a result produced irrespective of magnitude of effort, while the latter is connected with the idea of producing results adequate in relation to the energy, action or power used. Most authors warn against the arbitrary use of either term. Some, nevertheless, e.g. Arthur Smithies, make a clear distinction between effectiveness and efficiency.[41] Effectiveness in a program relates the program to the achievement of its objectives, while efficiency is concerned with the action which is carried out. The distinction depends on the possibility of measurement which is smaller when dealing with effectiveness. Efficiency implies measures taken to

[38] As quoted in David Novick (ed.), *Program Budgeting* (Harvard University Press, 1965), p. 311.

[39] G. Steiner, "Problems in Implementing Program Budgeting" Novick, *op. cot.*, pp. 310ff.

[40] Based on definition given in the *Shorter Oxford English Dictionary* and *Webster's Dictionary of Synonyms.*

[41] Arthur Smithies, "Conceptual Framework for the Program Budget", D. Novick, *op. cit.*, pp. 48-51.

achieve economies which will not affect the attainment of the objectives of the program. McKean reserves the method of cost-effectiveness to tests of a maximum effect for a *given* budget, or to a specified effectiveness at *minimum* cost. For this latter we would prefer to use the term efficiency.

Cost-benefit and similar methods first found widespread and ample use in water resources projects (including agricultural use), in defence, in preservation and use of natural resources,[42] in road and railway building, in project evaluation, in educational and health research, and also in estimating effects of government services, especially the PPB (Planning, Programming, Budgeting Method). Its use in agricultural policies provides ample opportunities for further development.

[42] Advocating the creation of an Office of Secretary of Resources in the U.S.A., R. McKean and M. Anshen propose a comprehensive programme. This hypothetical natural resources programme would include a package of measures including agriculture, water supply and use, forests, outdoor recreation facilities and grazing.

II

THE THRESHOLD OF ECONOMIC GROWTH[1]

1

The problems of economic growth are not adequately demonstrated when they are represented as changes in real income per head of population over a considerable time period. The prime need for economic growth is more capital, and since the limiting factor of growth is capital, the increase of real capital per head of population provides a more realistic picture of economic growth.

But change in the quantity of capital or of national wealth does not give a clear enough indication of problems of economic growth, nor does it measure this growth process adequately.

What matters most in the process of economic growth is, to our mind, not only the magnitude of the income or the quantity of capital; the crucial factor is the change in the quality of capital, i.e. in its productivity. This change can be measured by the change in the aggregate capital coefficient which brings to the fore the most difficult problems of economic growth.[2]

Expressed in symbols the formula of economic growth thus changes from:

$$m = \frac{P}{L}$$

[1] The author of this article shares the views of those who consider economic growth as a multidimensional process. In this article one dimension only, that of capital coefficient, is analyzed. For penetrating criticism of concepts of economic growth see F. Pérroux, *La théorie générale du progrès économique* (*Cahiers de l'Institut de Science Economique Appliquée*, 47, 59, 60, Paris, 1956-1957).

[2] It is not the purpose of this article to deal with the difficulties of measuring capital or product. With regard to these problems we refer to J. Robinson, *Accumulation of Capital* (1956), p. 118, and also "The Production Function and the Theory of Capital", *Review of Economic Studies*, Vol. XXI, 2.

where m is the measure of growth over time, and P is product net or gross, and L represents total population, into:

$$m = \frac{K}{aL} \qquad P = \frac{K}{a} \qquad a = \frac{K}{P}$$

where a is the aggregate average capital coefficient, and K stands for capital. This capital coefficient[3] can be looked at not only as a capital-to-income proportion, but also as a simplified production function with only one sector.

The use of the capital coefficient in economic growth analysis, after some initial enthusiasm, became less popular when more data were collected. The capital coefficient for very developed countries, such as the U.S.A., the U.K., Germany and France was found to be roughly the same (2-2.5) as in India, Ceylon or Burma and some Latin American countries.[4] This caused confusion and the realization that the dynamics of the capital coefficient had not been fully realized. In recent years still more data have been obtained and these allow some general conclusions to be drawn which make the use of the capital coefficient more meaningful.

In general there are three approaches to changes in the capital coefficient. One is the theory of the constancy of the capital coefficient. Its origin is linked to the beginning of the application of this concept in economic analysis, starting with G. Cassel.[5] According to this theory, capital coefficient shows a constant relation between capital and product, and does not change in the process of economic growth (in the observed period). A constant capital coefficient is also used in the Harrod-Domar model of economic growth. W. Leontief himself used partial, constant capital coefficients in his input-output tables. R. Solow and P. Samuelson, dealing with short-term periods, also assume constancy of the capital coefficient in a more refined way.[6] Solow's assumption that the change in the productivity of capital is compensated for by the changes in technical progress accepts as the end result an approximately constant capital coefficient.

[3] R. G. D. Allen, *Mathematical Economics*, pp. 332, 362. The problem of a one-sector model and its relationship to a multisectorial analysis is dealt with in L. Johansen, *A Multisectorial Study of Economic Growth* (1961).

[4] K. Martin, "Capital Output Rates in Economic Development", *Economic Development and Cultural Change*, 1 (1957), pp. 24-31.

[5] G. Cassel, *Theoretische Sozialökonomie* (1952), pp. 23-35, especially p. 33.

[6] R. Solow, "Technical Change and the Aggregate Production Function", *Review of Economics and Statistics* (1957), p. 312. Compare also Dernburg-Macdougall, *Macroeconomics* (1961), pp. 191-193, and Johansen, *op. cit.*, pp. 24-37.

The second approach is the theory of a constantly diminishing capital coefficient, i.e. a steady increase in the productivity of capital. One of the first to observe this tendency in the capital coefficient was R. Goldsmith, who calculated the capital coefficient for the U.S.A. in 1897-1950 as decreasing from 3.5 to 2.5.[7] More recently collected data regarding the capital coefficient of 18 countries[8] also show a general tendency toward downward movement of the capital coefficient. This tendency is observable for the following countries:

TABLE I

Long Term Changes in Capital Coefficient

Country	Years	Fall in capital coefficient
Belgium	1846-1950	from 9.3 to 5.4
West Germany	1913-1955	5.4 3.6
Norway	1900-1955	4.1 3.4
U.S.A.	1897-1949	5.9 4.3
Australia	1903-1956	6.4 4.0
South Africa	1917-1955	7.0 3.5
Colombia	1925-1954	4.4 2.9
Argentina	1917-1955	5.8 3.4

Source: Th. van der Weide, "Statistics of National Wealth for 18 Countries", *Income and Wealth Series*, VIII (1959), pp. 30-32.

An overall fall in the capital coefficient is also observed in the U.S.S.R., where the capital coefficient fell from 98 in 1928 to 79 in 1956 (taking 1913 as 100).

The first interpretation of this tendency was given by H. Leibenstein.[9] Dealing with the full complexity of the problem, he comes to the final conclusion that the general decrease in the capital coefficient has two causes. One is the actual decrease of the capital coefficients for particular

[7] Goldsmith, aware of the further implications of this change in the capital coefficient, asked for more research in this matter. R. Goldsmith, "The Growth and Reproducible Wealth of the U.S.A. from 1805-1950", *Income and Wealth Series*, II, pp. 296-300.

[8] Th. van der Weide, "Statistics of National Wealth for 18 Countries", *Income and Wealth Series*, VIII, pp. 30-32.

[9] H. Leibenstein, *Economic Backwardness and Economic Growth* (1957), pp. 176-184, 246ff.

products, and the other the change in the structure of production in the sense that more goods which require less capital per product unit are produced.

TABLE II

Fixed Capital and National Income in the U.S.S.R.

Year	Fixed capital		National income	Fixed capital per national income unit
	total	productive	aggregate	
1	2	3	4	5
1913	100	100	100	100
1928	120	136	138	98
1940	375	603	611	98
1950	462	806	1003	81
1956	775	1480	1904	79

Source: *Dostizheniye Sovyet-vlasti za 40 let*, pp. *15*, *SSSR v cifrah v 1957*, p. 22.

The third school found changes in the capital coefficient, i.e. starting from a first phase of a low coefficient to a second phase showing a rise followed by a third phase showing a decrease. This tendency has been observed by a number of economists, including S. Kuznets, Colin Clark, J. Spengler, G. Bombach.

Studying the long-term changes in economic growth, S. Kuznets[10] observed that the capital coefficient for some developed countries started first at a low level, then increased, and after some time began to decrease again. This means that the productivity of capital was greater in an earlier stage, then became smaller, and in the subsequent phase increased again. In the U.S.A. the capital-income ratio around 1880 was 2.5 and showed an upward trend until 1919, when it reached 3.5. After that it fell below 3 till 1938. In Great Britain the capital coefficient in 1865 was around 4.5 and then reached 6.5 in 1895 and kept at that level until 1913. In France the capital coefficient was at 4 in the middle of the nineteenth century and reached 6 in 1913. The fact that these two countries were capital exporting countries has to be taken into account as this greatly influenced the change of their capital coefficients.

The moving average of the capital coefficient in the U.S.A., counting

[10] S. Kuznets, "Population, Income and Capital", Round Table Conference on Economic Progress, Santa Margherita, 1953; *Economic Development and Cultural Change* (April 1959), pp. 63-70.

fixed capital only (land value excluded) increased from 5.5 level in the 1879-1889 to 6.17 in the 1909-1919 period, and from this period onwards decreased until 1934 to 5.5 again, and in 1949 reached 4.68 (total capital: net national product).[11]

Colin Clark[12] attributed changes in capital coefficients, besides those owing to the change in the structure of investment and to technical progress, as being due to the unused capacity of invested capital in the first period of economic development, and its fuller use in the subsequent period. To J. Spengler the change in capital coefficient is due to the increase in the volume of capital by 20 to 30 per cent, and to improvement in technique and organizational skill by 25 to 50 per cent. G. Bombach[13] has linked the changes in the capital coefficient to economic growth, as we shall see later. A capital coefficient dependent on the structure of the national economy corresponds to each stage of growth.

In the U.S.S.R. when the rigid system of priorities was softened up two trends emerged regarding capital coefficient. One used the capital coefficient (giving it different names) for measuring the effectiveness of investments, while the other tried to find some other specific criteria for socialist economics.[14] Strumilin[15] has shown that capital coefficient in Soviet industries changed from 1.65 in the first Five-Year Plan down to 0.88 in the period immediately before the Second World War, increasing again in 1956 to 2.08. M. Z. Bor also noticed a change in the capital coefficient which (taking 1928 as 100) has fallen from 100 to 79.[16]

The Polish economist O. Lange[17] took the view that the concept productivity of capital belongs to the mystical nimbus of capitalist economics, as the effectiveness of investments depends on a purely technical constant coefficient in a planned economy. M. Kalecki[18] also,

[11] The data for different countries are not comparable as the methodology of computing them varies from country to country. This refers also to other tables in this article.

[12] Colin Clark, *Conditions of Economic Progress* (1957), pp. 503, 569ff.

[13] G. Bombach, "Quantitative und monetäre Aspekte des Wirtschaftswachstums" (=*Schriften des Vereins für Sozialpolitik*, Neue Folge, 1959) (Bd. 15: Bombach, Giersch, Senf, *Wachstum und Konjunktur*, 1960, p. 23).

[14] Cf. Recommendations of a Symposium on Investment Policy published in *Voprosy ekonomiki*, No. 9 (1958). See also *Cahiers de l'Institut de Science Economique Appliquée*, G. 6, 83 (Paris, 1959).

[15] S. G. Strumilin, *Ocherky socialistitcheskoy ekonomiki SSSR* (Moscow, 1959), pp. 234-242.

[16] See note 34.

[17] O. Lange, "Produkcyjno-tehniczne podstawy efektiwnosci investycji", *Ekonomista*, 6 (Warszawa, 1959).

[18] M. Kalecki, "Czynniki kreslajace tempo wzrostu dochodu narodowego w gospodarce socjalistycznej", *Gospodarka planowa*, 8 (1958), pp. 1-5.

examining the efficiency of investments, takes into account the steady decrease of the capital coefficient because of technical progress. Another Polish economist M. Rakowski[19] proposes to introduce the concept of rate of maximum growth which depends on the optimal productivity of labor and optimal capital coefficient.

2

The capital coefficient is a complex aggregate which can be separated into its component parts. There are three main elements in the change of the aggregate:

(a) change in the longevity of capital goods;
(b) change in the capital mix;
(c) change in technical progress.

(a) According to R. Goldsmith's[20] inventory of the American economy in the last decade, about 60 per cent of all goods produced were of short duration. Around 15 per cent of goods were of an average duration of 2 years, and only 10 to 15 per cent of the total production were durable consumer goods and capital goods which had an average life of 10 years or more. On an average the 'age' of American products was 7 years, which at a static level of production represents a capital coefficient of 3.5.[21] If the rate of increase were 3 to 4 per cent the corresponding capital coefficient would improve to 3.0. If the U.S.A. has such a small percentage of durable goods, one can imagine how lesser developed countries fare in this respect. In India, for example, dwellings represent only 13 per cent of the national wealth while in the U.S.A. the percentage is 27. If goods of longer durability are produced, the capital coefficient naturally increases. This can be overdone, as is the case in many underdeveloped

[19] M. Rakowski, "Efektivnost procesa akumuliranja u narodnoj privredi", *Poljski ekonomisti o problemima socijalističke privrede* (Beograd, 1960), p. 175-199.

[20] R. Goldsmith, "The Growth of Reproducible Wealth of the U.S.A. from 1805-1950", *Income and Wealth Series*, II, p. 298.

[21] In 1952 the U.S.A. had 54 per cent of all machine tools younger than 10 years and 79 per cent younger than 20 years. West Germany had in 1952 30 per cent of all machine tools younger than 10, and 69 per cent younger than 20 years. In the U.S.S.R. about 55 per cent of all machine tools in the metal industry were older than 20 years. In Hungary the average age of machine tools was 17 years, and by reducing it to 13 or 14 years an increase in product of 50 per cent per factory space unit was expected. *U.N.-E.C.E. Economic Survey of Europe in 1959*, p. 111, 4. A. I. Mitrofanov, "Modernizaciya kak faktor vosproizvodstva osnovnih fondov", *Problemy politicheskoy ekonomii socializma* (1959).

countries.[22] There are many complaints that too much money is being spent on too expensive and massive buildings and too little on equipment in factories, agricultural estates, administrative buildings, etc.[23]

(b) The change in the capital mix is one of the most important causes in the change of the aggregate capital coefficient. Partial capital coefficients vary extensively among various branches of the economy. These partial coefficients vary also within particular industries for different firms.[24]

In the U.S.A. the capital coefficient (investment to returns ratio) in railways was 3.3, in agriculture 2.7 and in sources of energy 2.2, in metal and mechanical industries 1.2, in metallurgy 1.0, in the automobile industry 0.5 and in the garment and leather industries 0.3.[25]

In England[26] the capital to income ratio varied from 8.0 in coke, 9.2 in oil refineries and 5.1 in sugar refineries down to 1.1 in shipbuilding, 1.4 in ceramics and 1.6 in food processing. The average capital coefficient in 1954 was 2.8.

In the U.S.S.R. Notkin[27] estimated partial capital coefficients in Soviet industry (fixed funds: gross output) in 1938 at 0.66, and in 1956 at 0.55. Electric power stations showed a coefficient of 3.0 in 1938 and of 2.76 in 1956, production of fuel 2.0 and 3.9 for the same years, and ferrous metallurgy 1.5 and 1.2, while the non-ferrous metals dropped from 1.5 to 1.4 in the same period.[28]

For India the following capital coefficients were given in the Second

[22] For influence of durability on economic growth cf. W. A. Lewis, *The Theory of Economic Growth*, p. 313; R. C. Blitz, "Capital Longevity and Economic Development", *A.E.R.* (1958), p. 313; Leibenstein, *Economic Backwardness and Economic Growth*.

[23] In the U.S.A. investments in buildings in 1922 amounted to 69.7 per cent and in equipment to 30.3 per cent of total investments in fixed capital. In 1952 the corresponding proportions were 55.7 per cent for buildings and 44.3 for equipment. In the first Five-Year Plan in the U.S.S.R. investments in buildings reached 80 per cent, in equipment 18 per cent and in the rest 2 per cent. In the years 1956/57 the investment in buildings covered only 63 per cent, that in equipment increased to 32 per cent and the rest 5 per cent. In Yugoslavia in 1948 the share of buildings in total fixed capital investments was 65 per cent, of equipment 30 per cent and the rest 5 per cent. In 1957 the proportions changed to 44.5, 41.0 and 14.5 per cent.

[24] Nber, "Problems of Capital Formation", *Studies in Income and Wealth*, XIX, pp. 287-471.

[25] W. Leontief, *The Structure of American Economy*.

[26] T. Barna, "The Replacement Cost of Fixed Assets in British Manufacturing Industries in 1955", *Journal of the Royal Statistical Society*, 1 (1957).

[27] Notkin, "Technitcheskiy progres i preimushtchestvenniy rast proizvodstva sredstv' proizvodstva", *Xoprosi ekonomiki*, 12 (1955), p. 35.

[28] For capital coefficients in Eastern European countries see *U.N.-E.C.E. Economic Survey of Europe in 1959*, 111, pp. 13-27.

Five-Year Plan (non-monetary investments excluded): agriculture 1.0, cottage and decentralized industry somewhat below 1.0, centralized modern industry for new factories 3 to 4.0, and for the manufacturing industry as a whole 2.2.

In Latin America[29] the aggregate capital coefficient for the 5 largest countries in 1950 was 2.5 while the partial coefficients for particular industries were: agriculture 2.5, industry 1.47, manufacturing, transportation, electric power and communications 5.0 and services 2.9.

We have computed for Yugoslavia[30] the following coefficients (based on fixed capital: total sales minus turnover tax): for the total socialist sector 0.75. The railways show a coefficient of 8.95 and transportation as a whole 5.66, sea transport 4.0, manufacturing industries 1.01, agriculture (large estates in the socialist sector) 3.32, public electric power stations 5.35, coal mining 1.97, oil drilling 1.14, chemical industry 1.12, metal industry 0.74, textiles 0.6, timber 0.75, and leather industry 0.41.

The particular groups of industries in the U.S.A. show, for 1956, a dispersion from 0.55 to 0.05, with an average of 0.31.[31] The Soviet industrial groups stretch over a span of 3.2 to 0.13, averaging 0.49 in 1957. The Yugoslav partial group coefficients spread from 8.95 to 0.31, the average being 1.01.

This great dispersion of partial capital coefficients clearly shows the importance of changes in the capital mix for the aggregate capital coefficient. Even if the influence of the formation of groups is taken into

TABLE III

Investment in the U.S.A.

Years	Capital coefficient	Industry	Agriculture	Communications	Others
1880-1890	4.04	13.3	7.2	22.9	55.6
1890-1900	3.72	19.1	9.2	19.9	49.1
1900-1912	3.80	21.5	9.6	15.2	51.8
1924-1929	3.53	25.0	8.6	10.5	45.9
1952	2.55	33.8	15.0	7.7	45.5

Source: A. Bergson (ed.), *Soviet Economic Growth*, p. 34; J. F. Dewhurst, *America's Needs and Resources, A New Survey*, p. 476.

[29] A. Ganz, "Problems and uses of national wealth estimates in Latin America", *Income and Wealth Series VIII*, p. 230.

[30] Computed from Index No. 4 (1960).

[31] D. Creamer, "Postwar Trends in the Relation of Capital to Output in Manufactures", *A.E.R.*, 2 (1958), p. 251.

account, the span of 1:12 in the U.S.A. or of 1:25 in the U.S.S.R. or of 1:17 in Yugoslavia is too large to be neglected.

Therefore changes in the capital mix, by making some heavier capital coefficients instead of the lighter ones, can greatly increase the aggregate capital coefficient (Tables III, IV, V). Thus a change in the structure of capital investments one way or the other changes the overall capital coefficient.

TABLE IV

Investment and Capital Coefficient in the U.S.S.R. 1918-1957

	Years	Index of the capital coefficient	Percentage of investment*			
			Industry	Transport	Agri-culture	Housing
	1918-1928		38.4	23.8	6.1	22.1
1. Five-Year Plan	1929-1932	100	42.6	18.6	13.9	11.8
2. Five-Year Plan	1933-1937		41.8	21.5	8.1	10.2
3. 3½ years	1938-1941	71	40.9	20.4	5.3	12.7
1/7/1941-1/1/1946			54.0	18.1	2.1	7.8
4. Five-Year Plan	1946-1950	52	48.9	14.2	7.3	12.7
5. Five-Year Plan	1951-1955	47	51.1	10.1	9.6	15.5
	1956-1957		47.6	9.0	11.3	17.1

Source: *SSSR v cifrah*, pp. 260-263. *Narodnoe hozhyaystvo SSSR v 1958*, p. 58.
* Other investment groups left out.

TABLE V

Indian Investment Plans

	Plan I	Plan II	Plan III
Agriculture and communal services	15.1	11.8	14.5
Irrigation and electric power	28.1	19.0	15.9
Industry and mining (including decentralized industries)	7.6	18.0	28.8
Transport and communications	23.6	28.9	16.2
Social services	22.6	19.7	16.9
Housing	2.1	2.5	} 7.8
Others	3.0	2.1	

Source: Government of India *Second Five Years Plan*, 1956, pp. 21/22, *The Third Five Years Plan* (a draft outline), p. 26.

(c) The third factor influencing changes in capital coefficients is technical progress.

Not going into an intricate definition of technical progress, we have to register the importance which technical progress has on economic growth and in particular on changes of the capital coefficient. R. Solow[32] measured the effect of the productivity of labor in the U.S.A. and came to the conclusion that the increase of production amounted to 65 per cent from 1909 to 1949. Of this, 8 per cent was due to the substitution of labor by capital, and 57 per cent to technical progress. S. Fabricant[33] refers to the period 1895-1955 in which the increase of the gross national product was 87.5 per cent due to technical progress and only 12.5 per cent due to the substitution of labor by capital. G. Bombach[34] gave for West Germany the following figures for the period 1950-1956. The productivity of labor increased by 40 per cent, of which the substitution effect was responsible for 4 per cent and technical progress for 36 per cent. In the manufacturing industries in the U.S.S.R. Strumilin[35] calculated the marginal investment effect (investment in new technical capital goods) during the First Five-Year Plan at 51 per cent of the total increase in production; in the Second Plan the effect of technical progress amounted to 79 per cent, in the Third Plan it fell to 69 and in the last planning period (1951-1955) to 68 per cent. M. Bor also estimated that the capital coefficient fell from 100 (in 1928) to 79 in 1956 due to the technical progress in manufacturing industries in the U.S.S.R., thus showing an improvement of more than 20 per cent.[36]

For Yugoslavia we found the change in the capital coefficient 1950-1953 to 1957-1959 moving from 3.92 to 3.19. At the same time that the productivity of labor increased from 100 to 151 and the productivity of capital from 100 to 123, technical progress improved from 100 to 113.[37]

[32] R. Solow, *op. cit.*, p. 312ff.

[33] S. Fabricant, "Basic Facts on Productivity Changes", *N.B.E.R.*, occasional paper No. 63 (1958).

[34] G. Bombach, *op. cit.*

[35] S. G. Strumilin, *Ocherky socialisticheskoj ekonomiki S.S.S.R.*, p. 237.

[36] M. Bor, "K voprosu o vzaymosvyazi ekonomiceskih faktorov socialisticeskogo vosproizvodstva i ego dinamiki", *Problemi politicheskoy ekonomi socializma* (1959), pp. 43ff.

[37] The measurement of technical progress, however imperfect it may still be, shows indisputably that this factor is much more important than was sometimes thought when the development of underdeveloped countries was discussed. The burden of the increased capital coefficient is such that the building of infrastructure would be possible only under conditions of a considerable lowering of the level of living if it were not counterbalanced by technical progress. On the other hand technical progress (diminishing the capital coefficient and through it also the burden of investment) can make the process of growth less painful. Discussions on projects of economic growth simply by intensification of local labor must take into account the above.

3

Sufficient data have been collected to enable us to present a theory of economic growth with regard to the changes in the capital coefficient.

In the second stage the capital coefficient increases; i.e. capital is small capital coefficient. This is low because the product is small. The main burden of production is carried by physical labor. The aggregate capital is small, labor is abundant, cheap and not very productive, therefore the productivity of capital is comparatively high, as the total product has a larger labor input than it will have later. The capital coefficient moves between 2 and 2.5.

In the second stage the capital coefficient increases; i.e. capital is becoming less productive although more abundant, but much more capital is required to produce a unit of product. The change in the capital coefficient is due primarily to the change in the capital mix as the bulk of investments goes to capital intensive goods such as building of railways and ports, opening of mines and canals, regulation of rivers and laying the foundations of the extractive industries.[38] Land reclamation and irrigation add to heavy capital investments (i.e. great capital coefficient). Most of these investments represent technologically indivisible and large sums of capital investment which push still further towards an increase of capital coefficients. To this must be added expenditure for defense purposes as well as prestige or political investments for conspicuous production.[39]

In other words, where previously 2 units of capital were necessary to produce one unit of income, now six units are needed. (See diagram.)

The rate of saving which initially sufficed to keep the established level of production must now be considerably increased in order to provide investment for further stages of economic growth. 4 per cent of the national income saved and invested could increase the national income by 2 per cent when the capital coefficient equalled 2. But when the capital coefficient reaches 6 the rate of savings has to be 12 per cent in order to achieve an increase of the national income by 2 per cent. The increased

[38] Transport took the lion's share of foreign capital "Two thirds of all English capital invested abroad before 1914 went to railways". A. K. Cairncross, "The Contribution of Foreign and Indigenous Capital to Economic Development", *International Journal of Agrarian Affairs* (April 1961), pp. 78, 79, 80.

[39] We are not discussing here the influence of human factors such as: inefficient labor, inexperienced management, overoptimistic planners and irresponsible politicians. Considerations of monetary policy and the inflationary price push caused by excessive investment expenditure are left out. The partial overcapitalization in underdeveloped countries is also not taken into consideration in this long-term analysis.

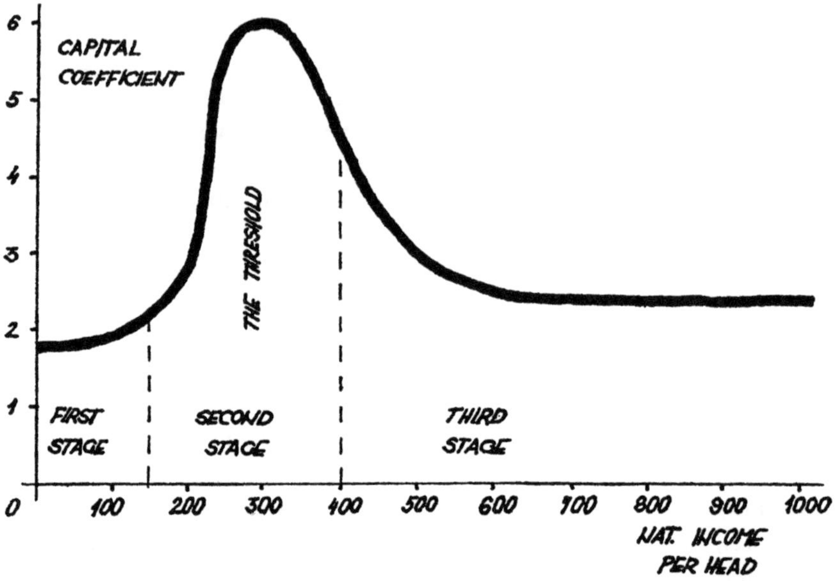

burden of investment puts an exceptionally high demand on the level of consumption, as it takes a larger share of the national income than in the first, the traditional stagnant stage.

This second stage can therefore be described more realistically as a painful process of creeping over the threshold of economic growth, rather than an elegant 'take off', which does not adequately convey the difficulty and intensity of the problems of this stage of economic growth. In one word the infrastructure of the national economy and the opening up of the country is taking place. This shows an increase in the capital coefficient from 2 or 2.5 up to 4 or even 6.

Capital and consumer goods of more durable quality are being produced. The primitive hand-to-mouth life is replaced by a larger reach in satisfying human wants, which means an increase in the longevity of national wealth. All this requires a more than proportional increase in capital investment, for life would be rendered impossible and the level of living considerably lowered if technical progress did not affect the changes in productivity of capital in the opposite direction. At this stage production of capital goods has normally a greater rate of increase than production of consumer goods.

The third stage is marked by a decrease in the capital coefficient. It moves from the previous 4 to 6 back to 3 or even less. This happens when the basic infrastructure of the national economy has been built, the proportion of durable producers' and consumers' goods to non-durables improved, and technical progress more firmly introduced.

This means that capital has become more productive, and one unit of income is produced by only 3 units of capital instead of almost double that amount at the peak of the second stage. It also means that the same income effect will be achieved with a much smaller rate of investment. If the capital coefficient has fallen from 6 to 3 the same rate of saving of, say, 12 per cent will increase the national income by 4 per cent instead of the increase which in the previous stage was only 2 per cent. Another consequence is that more attention is paid to production of consumer goods instead of capital goods. During the second stage production of capital goods increased faster than the production of consumer goods, as more capital was required for production of one income unit. In the third stage less capital is necessary than before for the same amount of income. Thus the production of consumer goods can increase faster than production of capital goods, a very controversial problem in socialist economics.

It was for a long time considered as a law in socialist economies that production of capital goods ought to be increased at a higher rate than production of consumer goods if economic growth was to be achieved. In our opinion this law is valid only in a period of rising capital coefficient. In the period of its decrease the opposite is true, and the rate of growth of consumer goods can be greater than that of capital goods. If there is a constant trend of decrease in the capital coefficient, a steady increase of consumer goods is possible. It is possible because of constant technical progress.

Building of large, centralized enterprises where great indivisibility of capital is necessary can now be given less priority, and a greater number of smaller enterprises built round the larger ones; thus the external economies are felt to a larger extent. Also the multipliers begin to show their effect as the economy becomes more closely knit and the markets operate more effectively. The process of urbanization and industrialization introduces a way of life in which the population increase becomes less, and technical education improves the skill of the labor force.

This third stage usually brings a sudden improvement in economy which sometimes surprises even the optimistic planners and politicians. It also brings new problems of economic policy and requires new and more complex methods and more subtle instruments of economic policy of which policy makers are not always fully aware.

The economic policy of a country also plays a significant role. If the process of growth is spontaneous, then the changes in the up and down swing of the capital coefficient are slow and protracted, with a small amplitude. If a country practices a deliberate development policy, then the upward swing of the capital coefficient may show a steeper line with all consequences involved. If a policy of planning is carried out, the upward swing may be quite steep, almost vertical. On the contrary the downward swing is not so regular, as many factors of economic policy may cause a lag in the switch from the second to the third stage.

The stages of upward and downward trends of capital coefficients are sometimes blurred by a geographical difference in phases of economic growth. This is particularly true of large countries in which the building of the infrastructure is gradually spread from one geographical area to another, so that, whereas in one area the second stage is passing, and the capital coefficient is beginning to decrease, in another the second stage is advancing, and therefore the capital coefficient is increasing. The end result is a cancelling out of changes which prevents us from seeing clearly what is going on. Table VI shows this process in the U.S.A. where the gradual shifting of economic growth at different stages is demonstrated.

TABLE VI

Years of the Relatively Greatest Contribution of the Various Regions of the U.S.A. 1870-1950

Region	Population	Income per head	Labor force agriculture	Labor force extractive industries	Value of industrial production
New England	1870	1880	1870	1870	1870
Middle Atlantic	1870	1880	1870	1880	1870
Great Lakes	1870	1880	1920	1890	1930
Southeast	1870	1950	1910	1950	1950
Great Plains	1890	1900	1950	1900	1890
Southwest	1950	1950	1930	1950	1930
Mountain	1950	1910	1950	1880	1900
Far West	1950	1950	1950	1940	1950

Source: Perloff, Dunn, etc. (ed.), *Regions, Resources and Economic Growth* (Baltimore, J. Hopkins Press, 1960), pp. 12, 13, 134, 238, 153, 252.

4

Some empirical data in support of the above theory are shown in Table VII.

The capital coefficient in the United Kingdom, during the period for which data are available, shows an increase from the beginning of the nineteenth century up to the middle of that century, moving from 5 or 6 up to an average of 7.5 in the fifties, which corresponds to the central and last phase of the second stage, the climb over the threshold. From that period onward the capital coefficient decreases, capital becomes more productive and its coefficient moves gradually down to 2.6 and remains almost unchanged from the thirties into the fifties of the twentieth century. The U.K. reached the third stage at the end of the nineteenth century.

Belgium was already in the second stage in the middle of the nineteenth century; moving over the threshold she reached the third stage toward the end of the same century.

In the long-term range of coefficients for the U.S.A. we can distinguish the first, second and third stages. Data are available reaching into the first stage. Starting from a low level of less than 1.0 in the beginning of the nineteenth century the change of the capital coefficient shows an upward trend until the end of that century when a coefficient of 3.3 is reached. From this time a downward trend is observable, which (when cyclical movements are excluded) shows a 2.5 coefficient. Kuznets has shown a similar trend. His capital coefficient for the U.S.A. moves from the eighteen-eighties at 2.5 up to 3.5 in 1919, then turns in a downward movement to less than 3.

TABLE VII

Economic Growth and Capital Coefficients

Country	Year	Net national product per head (international units)	Capital coefficient
Australia	1890	505	4.02
	1903	355	4.11
	1915	373	4.33
	1929	465	4.01
	1942	—	4.37
	1949	640	3.67
Japan	1905	159	5.09
	1913	146	4.90
	1924	159	7.76
	1930	189	5.31
Netherlands	1893	329	6.21
	1915	356	3.75
	1927	410	3.65
	1939	480	3.31

Country	Year	Net national product per head (international units)	Capital coefficient
Great Britain	1801	164	6.0
	1811	182	4.9
	1841	173	8.9
	1889		
	1858–	236	7.5
	1865	—	3.1
	1875	344	3.51
	1885	390	4.04
	1895	495	3.72
	1906	492	3.84
	1909	496	3.8
	1914	514	3.4
	1928	535	3.53
	1938	624	2.68
	1953	604	2.65
U.S.A.	1805	—	0.77
	1850	362	1.59
	1880	337	2.54
	1890	368	3.35
	1900	467	3.32
	1912	508	2.84
	1922	563	3.21
	1929	725	3.02
	1939	712	3.38
	1948	1021	2.54
Norway	1900	180	3.98
	1916	250	3.68
	1925	295	4.03
	1930	327	3.46
	1939	399	3.4
	1946	389	2.96
	1947	—	2.72
	1951	496	2.95
	1956	—	3.31

Sources: Colin Clark, *Conditions of Economic Progress*, third edition, p. 572. Data for Norway: Odd Aukrust, "Investeringenes Effekt po Nasjonalproduktet", *Statistisk Sentralbyra*, Artikler 1 (Oslo, 1957).

The U.S.A., Norway and West Germany moved over the threshold and entered the third phase toward the end of the nineteenth century. Some non-European countries now in the process of development and for which data are available give a similar picture.

Japan moved over the threshold from the beginning of the first decade of this century until the twenties. The case of Argentina is typical, and there is long-range data available. We witness an almost constant coefficient, characteristic for the first stage, then its upward trend from 4 to almost 6 between 1900 and the nineteen-twenties, and after that a downward trend changing this coefficient to 3.4 in the fifties. India and Mexico also show characteristic coefficients for the first and second stage, while Yugoslavia reached the peak of the threshold in 1953. These data correspond closely to the economic development as described by economic, historical and other research.

5

Overall changes in the capital coefficient show long-term stages in economic growth. Moreover whenever there is a change in the structure of capital investment which causes heavy investment in infrastructure, an increase in capital coefficient occurs. In the course of time, when this is finished, the benefit of such investments is reaped, and the capital coefficient decreases. This means at the same time an increase in the level of living because of a faster increase in the production of consumer goods, etc. Thus a country has time to gain and recover from the efforts made in the period when an increase of the capital coefficient was made.

So far there have been three such periods of heavy capital investment — we might identify them with the three industrial revolutions. The first industrial revolution based on steam, coal and steel, railways and steamers, started toward the end of the eighteenth century and was carried out until the middle of the nineteenth. This stage of development happened in what we described as the second stage of economic growth, demonstrating an increase in the capital coefficient.

Most of the developed western European countries experienced the change we described; it is a very well known process. The second wave of increase of capital investment, based on internal combustion engines, electric power, oil, metalled roads and the electric grid represented the main investment in infrastructure. This took place in most advanced countries at the beginning of the twentieth century.

The third industrial revolution is now taking place, based on automation, nuclear energy, the chemical industry and rockets.[40]

[40] These waves can best be shown in Germany. From some of the latest data on capital-to-income relations we computed the capital coefficients. In 1860 it was at 3.3, but fell until 1880 to 3.1. From that period a second industrial revolution took place demanding more heavy capital investments, and in 1900 the capital coefficient was at 3.7. It continued to grow so that in 1920 the top 4.6 mark was reached. From that period the capital coefficient began to decrease, in the beginning at a slower rate

The investment per worker in the first period amounted to some 500-1000 dollars, in the second around 3000-5000 dollars were necessary, and in the present period the investment per head has risen to several tens of thousands of dollars.

Now the characteristic feature in the development of developed countries was that they had, after each period of increase of the capital coefficient, a period of halt, or recuperation and respite, where they reaped the fruits of increase of the productivity of capital, and gathered strength to carry on a new wave on a higher level of economic development.

The position of the economically undeveloped countries of the present day is such that they have to achieve all three industrial revolutions compressed in one time period: to build railways and electric power-stations, metalled roads and the electric grid, nuclear power generators and automatic factories. The competition on the world market, effective or potential, makes it imperative to move in all three fields. This compression makes economic growth today such a burden that such countries are not able to carry it out by their own strength. Therefore foreign aid becomes not only friendly help but is an economic necessity. As soon as the stage of building the infrastructure is over, these countries might show an almost unexpected and more than proportional increase in economic growth, due to the greatly increased capital productivity, and all that goes with it in skilled labor, increased consumer demand, multiplier effect, external economies, etc.

6

Until recently not much data was available from which general, macroeconomic conclusions could be drawn. Evidence in support of our thesis can however be found in the latest data of Kuznets' analysis of economic growth of as many as eleven nations at different levels of economic development. This is to be found in his data relating to the ratio between the percentage of growth of capital formation and the percentage of growth of national product. In other words, the ratio shows how many per cents of growth of the capital formation are required to produce one

standing still in 1935 at 4.4, but keeping at 3.9 in 1940. After the Second World War the coefficient in 1950 remained at the 3.6 level, and then, in the period of prosperity fell to 3.1 in 1955. After that year another increase took place and the coefficient rose again — a sign of the impact of the third industrial revolution, and in 1960 the increase marked 3.3. Computed from W. Waffenschmiedt's article in: "Die Konzentration in der Wirtschaft", 11, *Schriften des Vereins für Socialpolitik* (Berlin, 1960), p. 804.

per cent of growth of the national product. This is a kind of relative marginal capital coefficient.

From Table VIII we can see that the U.K. reached the first peak in the eighteenth century. Germany had her first peak in the decade beginning in the eighteen-seventies. Italy achieved it at the same time, but with much greater efforts (much higher capital coefficient). Norway and Sweden also crept over the threshold at about the same period, and Denmark was also on the downward move in the eighteen-seventies. The U.S.A. had its main peak a little later, in the eighteen-eighties, and Japan about 30 years later, just before the First World War. Argentina shows a climb to the peak in the same period as Japan.

The second peak was attained by the U.K. in the decade of the eighteen-nineties. Germany already caught up, and had her second peak in the same decade as the U.K. The U.S.A. also speeded up and had her second peak before the First World War. Sweden and Norway also showed a similar movement of the capital coefficient, while Denmark was a little slower and Japan had her second peak in the thirties.

Looking at the time which elapsed between the two peaks we see that the U.K. took almost a century to pass from one to the other, but always stayed abreast of the others. The span between the two peaks was much closer in Germany, hardly 20 years. The U.S.A. moved very fast from the first to the second peak, and the move did not show great amplitude in the rather high capital coefficient. Italy's movements of the marginal capital coefficient show a much slower pace, but always under the pressure of a comparatively high coefficient (i.e. low productivity of capital). Norway and Sweden were faster with a lesser amplitude of the wave. Japan had also a short distance, although much later than Germany.

The case of Australia is significant: the two peaks came almost at the same time. Argentina's movements are such that the two peaks are not clearly visible. The same applies to South Africa.[41]

Almost all countries show an increase in the capital coefficient in the nineteen-fifties. But the period is too short to draw any far-reaching conclusions. It is likely that the third peak will appear more clearly when data for the second half of the nineteen-fifties is available.

[41] Our concept of phases in economic growth differs from that of the Kondratieff or Schumpeter kind; the main difference is their idea of cyclical periodicity, while we think in terms of cumulative changes marking the thresholds of economic growth.

TABLE VIII

Marginal Capital Coefficients

Decade beginning with year	United Kingdom	Germany	Italy	Denmark	Norway	Sweden	U.S.A.	Australia	Japan	Argentina	South Africa
1740-1770	6.1										
1770-1880	4.3										
1801-1811 1821-1830	2.9										
1851-1861		3.6									
1861-1870 1871-1880	4.2[1]	4.6	9.8			2.8		1.3			
1871-1880 1881-1890	4.1	5.9	17.2	3.0[6]	9.3[9]	5.1	3.2[10]	2.2			
1881-1890 1891-1900	4.0	4.7	11.7	2.2	4.6	3.3	6.7	2.3	1.3[12]		
1891-1900 1901-1910	8.0	6.0	5.8	3.7	4.1	3.5	5.3	2.1	0.8		
1901-1910 1911-1920			7.3[3]	3.4[7]	4.0	4.3	7.4	3.9	1.4	6.3[14]	
1911-1920 1921-1930					5.5	6.6	6.4	3.7	2.6	1.2	
1921-1930 1931-1940	3.8		7.2[4]	5.4	4.3	6.4	42.8	7.6	1.6	4.9	3.5[15]
1931-1940 1941-1950						4.6	4.7		2.8[13]	0.9	2.8[16]
1941-1950 1951-1958			2.7[5]	4.8[8]			4.8			3.7	4.3[17]
1952-1958	6.6	2.9[2]	3.4	6.7	9.2	6.1		6.8[11]	3.7	2.8	5.3

Source: S. Kuznets, "Quantitative Aspects of the Economic Growth of Nations", VI, *Economic Development and Cultural Change* (July 1961), Part II.

Notes: GNCF = Gross national capital formation; NNCF = Net national capital formation; NNP = Net national product; GNP = Gross national product; GDP = Gross domestic product; NDP = Net domestic product:

UK: GNCF/GNP (p. 60), current prices; [1] Decades start with 1860-1869, etc., until 1921. *Germany:* NNCF/NNP (pp. 64, 68), constant prices; [2] West Germany only for 1952-1958. *Italy:* GNCF/GNP (p. 69), current prices; [3] 1896-1905 to 1915; [4] 1921-1939; [5] 1946-1956. *Denmark:* GNCF/GDP (p. 76), current prices; [6] Decades beginning with 1870-1879, etc.; [7] 1900-1909/1914; [8] 1948-1952. *Norway:* GNCF/GNP (p. 82), current prices; [9] Decades beginning with 1870-1879, etc. *Sweden:* GNCF/GDP (p. 88), current prices. *United States:* GNCF/GNP (p. 95), current prices; [10] Decades beginning with 1869-1878, etc. *Australia:* NNCF/NNP (p. 107), constant prices; [11] 1952/53-1958/59. *Japan:* NNCF/NNP (p. 115), constant prices excluding military investments; [12] 5 year periods starting with 1885-1889/1895-1899; [13] 1930-1934/1941. *Argentina:* NNCF/NDP (p. 118), constant prices; [14] Decades beginning with 1900-1909, etc. *South Africa:* GNCF/GNP (p. 122), current prices; [15] 1919-1928/1929-1938; [16] 1929-1938/1939-1948; [17] 1939-1948/1949-1958.

3

SOCIAL PRE-CONDITIONS AND EFFECTS OF MOVING OVER THE THRESHOLD OF ECONOMIC DEVELOPMENT

The increase of the capital coefficient in the course of economic development and its subsequent decrease is called 'moving over the threshold'. During the climb to and the descent from the threshold of development, turning points are usually reached in economic policy depending on trends of economic development.

1

By 'threshold of economic development' we mean the increase of the capital to output ratio or capital coefficient in the process of economic development.[1] In a stagnating or slowly growing economy there is a 2:1 ratio of capital used per unit of output, since capital is scarce but labor abundant. Labor has to carry the main burden of production; only a small amount of capital can be used per unit of product. During the initial stage of the development process the aggregate capital coefficient moves up to 6:1 or more. There is a subsequent stage when the infrastructure has been built and the capital coefficient begins to decrease, down to say 3:1, thus easing the process of development. This means that in the initial stage a much greater burden is put on saving as a source of investment. In the stagnating stage, 4 per cent of the national income saved was sufficient to increase the national income by 2 per cent, but in the second stage 12 per cent is required for the same additional increase. For this reason the process of economic development places such a heavy burden on the whole economy that we have found it more appropriate to describe it as 'creeping over the threshold' rather than to use another, more fashionable label.

[1] This very simple single-factor production function gives only a first approximation to the problem of development, as capital also represents changes in labor that activate it and all other factors of production.

There is not just one single threshold in the course of economic development. Already three distinguishable thresholds have occurred which coincide with different industrial revolutions. The first industrial revolution was based on coal, steam, steel and railways and took place in Europe towards the end of the eighteenth and up to the middle of the nineteenth century. The second was based on the internal combustion engine, oil and electricity, and in most advanced countries began to take place in the seventies of the last century. The third industrial revolution is now taking place, in mid-twentieth century, based on automation, electronics, nuclear energy and the chemical industry.

In its initial stage each of these industrial revolutions implied an upward movement of the capital coefficient, making investments a heavier burden on the national economy. It also meant that expenditure on producer goods increased faster than consumption of consumer goods. In the subsequent stage of development, when the infrastructure has been built, the reverse tendency arises: a faster increase in the production of consumer goods than in that of producer goods. The fruits of the 'hard' period are thereby reaped. This is prolonged into a third stage, that of a comparatively stable capital coefficient.

Various countries, and even various regions within one country, move over the thresholds at different times. Therefore, the speed of changes has different effects. Although the changes are very uneven and complex there is a general tendency for the period between the peaks of the various revolutions to become shorter and shorter. The late-comers are stimulated to faster growth by competition on the world market, by national defence requirements, by the demonstration effect and the spread of technical knowledge. The later they come, the higher the thresholds, until finally two of the three revolutions may be compressed into one, making the periods of respite shorter.

There is sufficient empirical data from different sources to support this theory. Let us take the United Kingdom as the most significant example. Its capital coefficient rose from the beginning of the nineteenth century and reached 7.5 in the middle of it, then declined to the third stage of development by the end, and in the middle of the twentieth century was at 2.6. Belgium reached the second stage by the middle of the nineteenth century, and toward the end of it moved over the threshold. The United States of America, Germany and Norway also moved over the threshold in the second half of the nineteenth century, Japan in the first and second decades of the twentieth century. India and Mexico reached it deep in the twentieth century, Argentina crept over the threshold in the thirties and during the Second World War, and Yugoslavia reached the peak round 1953. Great Britain had almost a century to pass from the capital coefficient peak of the first revolution to the capital coefficient peak of the second. In the meantime, when the capital coefficient decreased she had a period of almost sixty years to relax from the strain of the initial climb. The span was much shorter for Germany where it lasted some twenty years (1880-1900); thus there was little time to enjoy the period of relaxation. The U.S.A. moved quickly from the first to the second peak (1890-1910).[2] Italy (1880-1920) shows a much slower pace, approximately twice that of Germany, since it was continuously under the pressure of the low productivity of capital (gradual construction of the infrastructure). Sweden and Norway were faster and had some twenty years between the two peaks. All these changes took place around the turn of the twentieth century. Japan also experienced rather fast movement (twenty years) from peak to peak. Australia developed in such a way that the two peaks fell close together (1930). In Argentina (1920-1950) and South Africa (1930-1950) the peaks are so blurred that they cannot be clearly distinguished.

It seems that the climb over the threshold of a third industrial revolution is now taking place. Heavy capital spending and the increase in the capital coefficient in the most advanced countries are signs of this. The particular difficulty being faced by underdeveloped countries is that they have to compress all three revolutions over one time period, hurried by world economic and political competition.

2

Until recently predominant opinion held that the capital coefficient was constant, but further research has shown that this is not so.

Changes in the capital coefficient are due to three main causes. One is the change in the durability of the goods produced. Even the national wealth of developed countries is very short-lived. In the U.S.A., for example, 60 per cent of the national income has a very short life span; only 10 to 15 per cent of consumers' durables and producers' equipment lasts over ten years, and buildings last fifty years, the overall average being not more than seven years (a capital coefficient corresponding to 3.5). This is much shorter in the less developed countries where life 'from

[2] The peaks do not show great amplitude here because of the geographical differences in economic development. When the East was already comfortably over the first threshold the Western States were still climbing uphill.

hand to mouth' is frequently the general rule.[3] An increase in the durability of national wealth is the first cause of an increase in the capital coefficient.

The second factor causing changes in the capital coefficient — and the most important in the short run — is the change in the capital mix. Different industries have very varied partial capital-to-product ratios.[4] Some do not require more than one unit of capital per unit of product. These are mainly the light industries such as textiles and apparel, leather and rubber, food-processing and tobacco, but also mechanical and transport vehicle industries, shipbuilding, etc. The industries with a heavy capital coefficient are mining and fuel, particularly sea, river and rail transport (railways up to 20), iron and steel, but also the paper industry, agriculture (especially land reclamation, irrigation, forest clearance) and, above all, housing. Emphasis must be laid here, too, on the building of roads and railways, the electric grid, harbors, canals and airports. The switch to these activities means at the same time a sudden increase in the capital coefficient, which is out of proportion to the propensity to save or the investment quota of the national income. On the contrary the move from such heavy partial coefficients makes the aggregate capital coefficient lighter.

The third source of changes in the capital coefficient is technical progress. It has a long-term effect, although not a very long one. This is likely to be so particularly in countries where the imitative technique prevails over the creative, and technical progress can be imported. Some recent studies by American (F. S. Fabricant, R. Solow), German (G. Bombach) and Soviet (G. Strumilin) economists[5] have shown that, in

[3] Cf. R. Goldsmith, "The Growth of Reproducible Wealth of the USA from 1805-1950", *Income and Wealth Series*, II, p. 298; *UN/ECE, Economic Survey of Europe for 1959*, III, p. 4; A. I. Mitrofanov, "Modernizaciya kak faktor vosproizvodstva osnovnih fondov", *Problemy politicheskoy ekonomii sociyalizma* (Moscow, 1959); W. A. Lewis, *The Theory of Economic Growth*, p. 312; R. C. Blitz, "Capital Longevity and Economic Development", *AER* (1958), p. 313; H. Leibenstein, *Economic Backwardness and Economic Growth*.

[4] NBER, "Problems of Capital Formation", *Studies in Income and Wealth*, 19, pp. 287-471; W. Leontief, *The Structure of the American Economy, 1919-1939*; T. Barna, "The Replacement Cost of Fixed Capital Assets in British Manufacturing Industries in 1955", *Journal of the Royal Statistical Society*, 1 (1957); A. Notkin, "Tehnicheskiy progress i preimushtchestvenniy rast proizvodstva sredstv'proizvodstva", *Voprosy ekonomiki*, 12 (1955), p. 35; UN/ECE, *Economic Survey of Europe for 1959*, III, pp. 13-27; A. Ganz, "Problems and Uses of National Wealth Estimates in Latin America", *Income and Wealth Series*, VIII, p. 230; D. Creamer, "Postwar trends in Relation of Capital-to-output in Manufactures", *AER*, 2 (1958), p. 251.

[5] R. Solow, "Technical Change and the Aggregate Production Function", *Review of Economics and Statistics* (1957), p. 312; S. Fabricant, "Basic Facts on Productivity Changes", NBER, Occasional paper, 63 (1958); G. Bombach, "Quantitative und

the long run, technical progress is responsible for some two-thirds to more than nine-tenths of the increase in productivity, and this change has a growing effect on the process of development (e.g., in the first Soviet plan it amounted to 51 per cent, and in the last one to 66 per cent). Thus technological progress, which means also an increase in the quality of capital or a decrease of the capital coefficient, is in the long run the most important factor in economic growth.

The time dimension is very important. The change in the capital mix occurs much faster and has a more direct effect than the change caused by technological progress. Therefore, though in the long run the capital coefficient becomes lighter, it increases in weight in the short run of the process of development. *It takes time for the change in the capital mix to be partly compensated for by technological progress.*[6] This lag has many important implications in the social, political and cultural spheres. The qualitative improvement of capital is the main factor in the easing of the process of economic development.[7]

3

Since we are dealing here with the specific effect of social pre-conditions on changes in the capital coefficient during the process of economic development, there are several important points to stress.

A. *Three kinds of change in a stagnating economy which trigger a movement toward the threshold of development*

(a) An increase of population, not as such alone, but in relation to the use of natural resources available at customary and established levels of consumption, and exploited with traditional techniques. The condition is one where labor exists in abundance, which means rural overpopulation. For a large proportion (usually one-third) of those occupied in agriculture the marginal productivity of labor is zero, and they can be taken out of the production process without lowering its level. Since the

---

monetäre Aspekte des Wirtschaftswachstums", *Schriften des Vereins für Sozialpolitik*, 15 (1951); S. G. Strumilin, *Ocherky socialistitcheskoy ekonomiki SSSR*, p. 237.

[6] So even if the assumption were valid that increase in the capital coefficient is compensated for by technical progress over time, the span required would be several decades or generations.

[7] It makes matters more optimistic, but does not justify the theory of a constant capital coefficient.

average income of the agricultural population is lower than that of any other group, a rural exodus takes place as soon as opportunity offers. Obviously we are dealing here not exactly with the agricultural, technological or occupational problem but with the problem of a complex peasant sector where primary, secondary and tertiary activities are all carried out within one and the same institutional framework. Upsetting of the balance, be it on the demographic side, on the resources side, or on the production side can open up a movement, or create pre-conditions for a movement towards a developmental threshold.

The impulses may come from a sudden change (consecutive bad harvests, famine, flood, war, etc.) or from some more long-term causes such as exhaustion of natural resources, deforestation, repeated floods, soil erosion, fertile land shortage, confiscated products, uneven increase of population, changed consumption habits and levels, induced changes in technique of production.

(b) The inability of the established local governing classes to control society by old methods in the stagnating economy. This may manifest itself in the necessity for new techniques: for modern armaments to keep law and order (communications and transport systems), and maintain established consumption on the previous prestige level. New techniques may require fresh personnel with new skills who compete with the old ones (e.g. new military leaders). The competition makes itself felt in commerce, in administrative power, at the consumption level (conspicuous consumption) as well as on the production side (conspicuous production).

(c) A threat from abroad to exploit resources with improved techniques (penetration of foreign capital, military aggression, some national and international integration movements, export of revolutions).

It is important to stress that all these factors are brought to bear within an established institutional framework, thus creating tensions which the usual macroeconomic analysis does not show.

B. *The increased investment quota*

Changes in the capital coefficient mean in the first stage of development an increase in the investment quota of the national income. What social machinery is necessary so that (a) the investment quota can be increased, (b) capital can be concentrated, and (c) capital can be diverted from traditional to novel purposes?

(a) To increase voluntary savings in population groups which can afford it means at the same time establishing an efficient modern banking or co-operative credit system which will be able to compete with and divert funds from the traditional local moneylenders, dealing mainly in consumer credits, and to direct the flow of credit to productive purposes. Compulsory saving by taxation implies the existence of an effective administrative system for tax collection with as little administrative waste, arbitrariness, and corruption as possible. A third source of investment funds consists of tapping available natural resources, exploiting them with local labor and traditional techniques and making the accumulated proceeds available for further productive investment. Export of capital controlled by the ruling élite, so frequent in politically and economically unstable countries despite patriotic professions, is another source that can be exploited. This, and the decrease of luxurious or conspicuous consumption and transfer of acquired savings to the production sector is another source of investment, which also implies the existence of an administration governing against the interests of the established élite.

Avoiding waste of what is already being produced is a source of investment funds often overlooked. To exploit this source it is necessary to have an efficient administrative machinery from top to bottom, as centralized administration is not always the most efficient mobilizer of funds for national investment purposes.

Proper use of foreign aid is not only linked with an efficient administration in the recipient state, but depends also on the donor having adequate technical services at the top and efficient operative organization on the local level.

(b) In order for them to be used for climbing over the threshold, it is not enough for investment funds to attain a certain magnitude; they must also be concentrated so as to correspond to the indivisibility, both technical and economic, of the necessary means of production in major developmental projects. This concentration can be achieved through banking machinery for private savings, or through a taxation system which in a way performs a transfer service by moving capital from the taxpayers' small pockets to the treasury. Bulk exports of divisible but homogeneous agricultural products and raw materials, exchanged for indivisible and specific imports of productive equipment, is another mode of transformation. Foreign aid and credits are normally already available in adequately concentrated magnitudes.

(c) The available concentrated funds must be diverted from their traditional use. Development implies restriction of traditional capital use and expansion of novel capital uses for the initial building of the infrastructure. A new investment policy pattern must therefore be created, in which those responsible, the targets, the instruments and the milieu are modified.

Change also implies much greater risk-taking with centrally allocated funds than with small doses of capital application. Centralization of decisions is linked to centralization of risks, where the law of great numbers ceases to operate. As the responsibility of the central administration for its decisions increases, there is a tendency for central bureaucracy (including top managers and *apparatchiks*) to avoid social control or prevent it from being effective in this period. The infallibility of government by the expert, technocrat or politocrat is used as an excuse for such a policy.

The diversion of funds also opens up the problem of the interrelationship between investments in physical and in financial terms. In other words, an increase of investments at the expense of consumption posits channels through which consumer goods can be used to increase the stock of producer goods. For this purpose the transfer of labor, fed and kept by peasants (voluntarily or compulsorily) and used in productive sectors other than agriculture, is often resorted to. Exports of consumer goods to pay for imports of producer goods is another instrument of this policy, and so also are inter-regional shifts from agricultural to industrial areas, or from villages to towns and from provinces and colonies to the metropolitan centers.

C. *The capital coefficient proper*

A greater (heavier) capital coefficient means that more capital is required for the production of less income, macroeconomically speaking. The main reason for this is the change in the capital mix, which moves faster than technological progress. This lag is often also followed by a fall in the average rate of profit, and means that developmental activities cannot be carried out by existing machinery on the basis of 'business as usual'. In the past, special privileges, concessions or guarantees were given to the promoters of the first industrial revolution in foreign countries, by the receiving or by the donor countries and their financial establishments. It is particularly to be stressed that most European countries had their infrastructures built at government expense, particularly railways, harbors, water supply and roads. The foreign capital exported before the First World War was allocated mainly to railway building (e.g., two-thirds of British capital abroad before the First World War was invested in railways).

Today, most capital investment by the World Bank is allocated to finance the building of the infrastructure for the first and second industrial revolutions (metalled roads, railways, electric power stations, national electric grid, etc.). Private capital investment now plays a role of subsidiary investment in developing countries, waiting for the average capital coefficient to fall. Therefore government machinery, or rather, to broaden the issue, public developmental activity, is a necessary requirement for development at least during the period of moving over the threshold. It is another question, when this stage is over, why those who have not carried the burden in difficult times should enjoy, at the expense of the consumers, the benefits of the subsequent period of a lighter average capital coefficient and of increased rates of profit.

D. *Technological progress*

Technological progress is an independent developmental variable which reduces the capital coefficient. It requires, without delay, complex imports of imitative technology from more advanced countries. Nevertheless there are examples (Italy) where creative techniques based on local traditions have managed to compete successfully with countries of a higher level of development. Technological progress demands increased facilities at all educational levels as a most vital 'economic' investment. The training of skilled labor of the lowest educational standard takes two to five years, that of technicians and professional people twelve to sixteen years, and that of highly qualified experts for the creative technology of the future some twenty-four years (bearing in mind that a highly qualified expert cannot be trained in less than eight years of university attendance). But the crux of the matter, as Mahalanobis rightly pointed out, is that one must start at once if one wants to have adequate experts in twenty-years' time.

Here there lies the danger of the old élite frustrating the education or aspirations of the new, and trying to repair its leadership, based on traditional techniques. Less evident is the tendency of the new élite, more or less overtly, to appropriate a privileged position by using educational attainments for the control of society in their own interest, allegedly in the name of technical progress, while in fact preventing it by their monopoly. '*La trahison des clercs*' is not a phenomenon reserved to developed countries only, and the damage done by the sergeant mentality of the half-educated is matched only by the intolerant arrogance of economic staff officers.

The technical progress during the first industrial revolution favored the concentration of population, of capital and of enterprises in large urban agglomerations. The second industrial revolution acts in reverse, enabling the population, the capital and the products to disperse. The effect of the two revolutions occurring simultaneously depends very much on whether a clear economic policy exists, taking both counteracting and compensatory effects into account.

E. *Social changes during movement over the threshold*

During this period there is a faster movement away from agriculture than from other occupations. This means that increases in income levels work to the advantage of those outside agriculture. Even the poorly paid industrial worker in this first period of industrialization has a higher income than most of the peasants. Therefore there is a steady rural exodus, encouraged by economic policy. In this respect one must distinguish two periods: the construction period when the infrastructure is being set up, and the operational period when this structure is mainly established and the industries begin to operate. In the first period the bulk of the labor force is unskilled, employed in building, on roads, railways and similar work. In the second period, unskilled labor becomes redundant and skilled factory labor is in ever-increasing demand. As many of the unskilled cannot acquire the necessary skills, and have broken their links with the village, the problem arises of an urban sub-proletariat, suspended in an economic no-man's-land, following the rule: last into town, last out of town. They resist being pushed back to villages by a new economic policy. The exodus from agricultural occupations has as its effect changes in the internal structure of the peasant family. The burden of productive labor falls more and more on the shoulders of the women just at a time when intensification of agricultural production is required because of increased demand for agricultural products.

New social relationships are created in the family; there is a shifting of responsibility and the establishment of new rights of the family members. A large joint family can more easily afford to dispense with some labor, but the problem of income distribution plays a more disruptive role within a family embracing several earners. On the other hand, off-farm activities occasion the rise of a tendency towards separating the productive from the consumption functions in the family, thus making it less of a productive unit, under the father's authority, and more of a consumptive unit, with the mother as the main organizer of the family consumption. This switch from one authority to the other is followed by complaints about 'demoralization' of youth, which finds fresh opportunities for work in newly created industries.

These changes in the trends of development demand another set of measures in economic policy, since those which produced good results in the first stage of development seem to be ineffective in the second stage. Such turning points in economic development as the change in the capital coefficient must therefore be watched very carefully by all policy makers.

IV

SHARES OF LABOR AND CAPITAL IN THE GROSS DOMESTIC PRODUCT OF 40 COUNTRIES IN THE DECADE 1953-1962

The purpose of this empirical research is to explore some changes that took place in the structure of the world economy during the process of general economic growth in the decade 1953-1962. In particular our interest is concentrated on two specific problems:

What changes occurred during the process of growth in the share of the gross domestic product (GDP) going to labor and the share going to gross domestic capital formation?[1]

[1] Long-term changes in the distribution of income have been studied by many authors. There is the pioneering work of E. H. Phelps Brown in the U.K., *Economic Journal*, VI (1952) and the subsequent study of G. Feinstein for the same country, "National Income and Expenditure, 1870-1963", the London and Cambridge Bulletin of the *Times Review of Industry*, June 1964. There are several studies related to long-term trends in the U.S., such as F. S. Kuznets, "Long Term Changes in the National Income of the USA since 1870", *International Association for Research in Income and Wealth*, 1952, p. 85; Gale H. Johnson's "The Functional Distribution of Income in the U.S., 1850-1952", *Rev. Ec. Stat.* (May 1954); I. G. Kravis, "Relative Income Shares in Fact and in Theory", *AER* (Dec. 1959); E. C. Budd, "Factor Shares, 1850-1910", *Trends in the American Economy in the XXth Century* (=*Studies in Income and Wealth*, No. 24, NBER, 1960); M. Kalecki, *Theory of Economic Dynamics* (London, 1954), pp. 28-41.

P. J. Bjerve did an excellent study of the long-term national income distribution in Norway, *Income and Wealth Series*, and there is also an official publication, *Nasjonalregnskap 1930-1939 od 1946-1951* (Oslo, 1952), following that of Lindahl regarding Sweden, one of the first historical analysis of income distribution, *Wages, Cost of Living, and National Income in Sweden 1860-1930* (London, 1933).

S. Goldberg did a very useful study of Canada, "Long-Run Changes in the Distribution of Income by Factor Shares in Canada", *The Behaviour of Income Shares* (= *Studies in Income and Wealth*, Vol. 27 NBER [Princeton, UP 1964]); W. Woytinski published for some countries an historical series regarding national income shares for Great Britain, Germany, France, and the U.S. (*World Population and Production*, pp. 374, 376, 383). The international comparison started with Livio Livi's *Primo Computo del Reddito distributto al fattori della produzione* (Roma, 1958); Jean Marchal and J. Lecaillon gave an extensive treatment, both theoretical and analytical, to the problem of shares in the income distribution on a comparative basis: *La repartition du revenu national*, I: *Les participants*, 1 (Les salaries, Paris, 1958). S. Kuznets, in his "Quantitative Aspects of the Economic Growth of Nations", *Economic Development*

An analysis has been made here presenting GDP distribution in the process of economic growth assuming that only three sectors exist: labor, the gross domestic capital formation, and a residual 'Third Group'.

The second question asked is whether there is any empirical rule by which we can establish a relationship between the economic development of different countries and the distribution of the gross domestic product among these three sectors. In a way we are turning space into time, geography into history, assuming that the GDP per capita of different countries provides the conventional basis for a quantitative measurement of development.

1. SOME CONCEPTUAL REMARKS

We have tried to find a functional relationship between figures representing national economic growth — arranged according to gross domestic product per capita in U.S. dollars — and figures showing the percentages in the GDP that go to the employees and to the gross domestic capital formation. The residuum is what remains after the sum of these two percentages has been subtracted from the total share of the Third Group.

For our research we have used a country-wide, cross-section analysis,[2] and our 'world' is confined to the 40 countries for which the *U.N. Yearbook of National Accounts Statistics* supplies relevant data.[3]

---

and Cultural Change (Chicago, particularly the issues of April, 1959, July, 1960, and July, 1961), gave the most comprehensive review and analysis of the available data.

[2] Some economists object to the cross-section analysis method for research into long-term economic growth; others are using it to an ever greater extent. Of course, we must bear in mind the imperfections of the method and the broad set of assumptions by which the functional relationship is determined. On the other hand, if we divide the countries into groups by levels of income per capita, we also have to make similar assumptions in order to obtain the income distribution by groups.

No socialist countries are included in this analysis — either of the Yugoslav, Soviet, or Chinese type — because data is not comparable among them, nor between them and the nonsocialist world. So, with regret, we have to leave the socialist countries aside, but we believe that the results in product sharing in socialist countries would not show a general tendency other than we found in this analysis. This belief is based on some partial research of product distribution in the USSR and Yugoslavia.

[3] In the first *Yearbook of National Accounts Statistics*, 1957 (*YNAS*, 1957), there were 70 countries, and in the 1963 *Yearbook* there were 74. The turnover was considerable. Fourteen new countries reported their national accounts, but 10 disappeared from the later *Yearbook*, in which only 40 had comparable data for 1953 and 1962. We have tried to explore to what extent the method of cross-section analysis provides meaningful information. If the experiment gives positive results, the great wealth of facts accumulated in the national accounts of many countries could be used for quantitative research in global and regional changes in the world economy. At present

How representative are our 40 countries of the world economy? (See Table I).
They are distributed by geographical areas as follows:

Europe	16	Asia	7
North America	2	Africa	3
Latin America	10	Oceania	2

If we divide them into four groups of ten countries each, according to the gross product per capita, the division runs like this:

Group	Number of countries in sample (UN National Accounts)	Number of countries for which GP per capita is given by UN statistics	Percentage of coverage
I	10	10	100
II	10	13	77
III	10	14	72
IV	10	58	17

It is not possible for us to compare our sample with the world as a whole; all we can say is that it is quite representative for the first three groups. In the *National Accounts Statistics Yearbook*, gross product per capita is given for 95 countries, with our 40 countries representing 42 percent of the total; the first group is 100 per cent covered, the second 77, the third 72, and the lowest 17. But 40 countries constitute a substantial element. Moreover, as the sample is identical for the years 1953 and 1962, it provides quite a satisfactory basis for comparison if we bear in mind the skewness of the sample when drawing our conclusions.

Unfortunately the fourth group of countries, with a GDP of less than 250 dollars per capita, is rather poorly represented.[4] The very making

we must be satisfied with modest results, although considerable progress can be made by improving the system of national accounts and by extending the comparisons to a greater number of countries and data.

[4] The smallest gross domestic product per capita of 95 countries recorded in the *YNAS*, 1963, was that of independent mountainous Afghanistan and of colonial tropical Mozambique, neither having more than 25 dollars per capita in 1953. Upper Volta followed with 34, Ethiopia with 38, Burma with 42, and Cameroun with 50 dollars gross product per capita. Whatever the imperfections of the computation methods may be, and however questionable the reliability of data, the desperate lowness of the figures is really striking. Can we conclude either that life at a gross product of 7 cents a day is so poor, or that provision of goods and services is so cheap that human beings can maintain their existence under such conditions? Is this realistic at

of national accounts demands a substantial set of recorded numbers which only a country of a certain statistical culture can supply.[5] We have to bear in mind this shortcoming of our research.

The 1962 *National Accounts Statistics* improved the international comparison considerably by providing corrected conversion rates of national currencies into dollars.[6]

The *U.N. National Accounts Statistics* present data of the gross domestic product,[7] both aggregate and per capita. The other two figures

---

all? Or had we better adapt our statistical methods to their conditions of life and existence? Nevertheless, thirteen African, five Asian, and one Central American country had a gross product of less than 100 dollars per capita, accepted by UN statistics. Perhaps still more important is the relative level of GDP per capita between the less developed countries and the highly developed countries. The former have a GDP per capita which is more than seventeen times smaller than the GDP p.c. of the most developed countries. In twenty of the forty countries the GDP per capita is more than ten times larger than the per capita figure of the country with the smallest income The two extremes, the U.S. and Uganda, show a difference in the ratio of GDP per capita as follows: GDP per inhabitant is forty-five times greater in the former than in the latter; that of France is twenty-four times, and of Belgium twenty-one times greater than of the Congo. This gives enough background for developing the complex attitudes of *developmental nationalism*. Two further remarks have to be made in connection with the use of per capita incomes. One is that such a measurement excludes the influence of the *size* of the country. This problem of scale is very important, especially in an age of international economic integration. The other effect of the per capita approach is that it includes the overall population increase, but does not take into account other qualitative and quantitative changes of population which also have a great bearing on the process of economic growth. This throws a special light on the use of per capita GDP in view of the fact that usually the population increase is much greater in countries at a lower income level.

[5] In most cases (55 out of 95), figures for compensation of employees were not available, and as these figures are essential for our analysis, the employees had to be left out.

[6] The value of gross domestic product per head is expressed in U.S. dollars in the *UN Yearbook of National Accounts Statistics*, 1963, pp. 318-331. There are two tables, 3A and 3B. We took figures preferably from Table 3B, in which calculated parity rates of exchange were used. Conversion of national currencies into dollars (see note, p. 390) was estimated by adjusting the official or free market exchange rates in 1938 for each country by the relative change in the level of prices from 1938 to the years 1953 and 1962, between the U.S. and the country concerned.

The relative change in prices was measured by means of implicit price indices of the gross domestic product wherever data were available. Estimates were made in current and constant national prices of the gross domestic product for 1938, 1953, and 1962. Where such data were not in existence, index numbers of consumer prices were used or producers' price indices applied.

For a few countries where such corrected parity rates were not available, we used the gross product per capita data from Table 3A in which the prevailing dollar exchange rates were applied.

[7] The gross domestic product is used here at factor cost on the expenditure side. The figure stands for the value of the total production in a country in a year. This gross

for each country indicate the percentages of the gross domestic product represented by employee compensation and gross domestic capital formation. These percentages we computed from data given in national currency.

By the term 'labor', or workers in a wider sense, we refer here to all employees, whether white or blue collar workers, wage or salary earners, actively providing goods and services in business and in general government, as defined in the *U.N.National Accounts.*[8]

Gross domestic capital formation includes the formation of capital in enterprises proper, in households, private non-profit institutions, and general government agencies.[9]

The third portion of the GDP, that not classified as employee compensation or gross capital formation, consists of the final consumption of all non-employees (e.g., peasants, capitalists, and those practicing handicrafts or liberal professions), and of general government as well.

The *U.N. Yearbooks of N.A.S.* for 1960 and 1963 give figures for 1953 and 1962, completing the decade. By using annual figures available for the first and the last year only we have not been able to exclude the influence of all short-term movements. Nevertheless, the span of one decade represents a time period in which changes occur which have more than short-term meaning.

---

domestic product at factor cost is defined as "the value at factor cost of the product taken at market prices before deduction of provision for the consumption of fixed capital, attributable to factor services rendered to resident producers of a given country, excluding the excess of indirect taxes over subsidies. In this way the value of the gross domestic product is equal to the value of production for final consumption and for gross capital formation." (*YNAS*, 1963, p. XI.)

[8] Compensation of employees includes all wages and salaries in cash and in kind, payable to normal residents employed by private and public enterprises, households, private non-profit institutions, and general government, as well as labor income payable by the rest of the world to normal residents. Armed forces stationed at home and abroad, the overseas diplomatic and consular staff, employees on ships and aircraft or domestic carriers operating abroad are also included (*YNAS*, 1963, p. XIV). Employers' payments to social security agencies on behalf of employees is part of this compensation. See also footnote 22.

[9] This gross domestic capital formation consists of sums spent on construction of dwellings and non-residential buildings, other construction or work, machinery and equipment including transport equipment. It also comprises increase in stock in the country, excludes investment from abroad and includes replacement of fixed capital. (*YNAS*, 1963, p. XIV.) The use of the *gross* domestic product required that for capital formation the corresponding *gross* domestic capital formation figures also be used. See also footnote 27.

TABLE I

Gross domestic product distribution of 40 countries, 1953-1962.
(Ranking by GDP p.c. in 1962)

No.	Symbols used in Chart 1	Country	(1) Year	(2) Gross Domestic Product Per Head (X)	(3) Compensation of Employees AS % Observ. (Y_L)	(4) Of GDP Comput. (Y_L^*)	(5) Deviation (Col. 3 — Col. 4)	(6) Percentage of Deviation	(7) Gross Domestic Capital Formation as Percentages Observ. (Y_K)	(8) Of GDP Comput. (Y_K^*)	(9) Deviation (Col. 7 — Col. 8)	(10) Percentage of Deviation	(11) Residual percentage of the Third Group
1.	U.S.A.	United States	1962	2691	58.77	54.90	3.87	7.05	17.18	26.33	−9.15	−34.74	24.05
			1953	2080	57.37	55.61	1.76	3.16	17.21	22.37	−5.16	−23.07	24.42
2.	Swi.	Switzerland	1962	1951	51.85	52.78	−0.93	−1.75	30.06	25.03	5.01	20.01	18.09
			1953	1173	53.35	51.02	2.33	4.57	21.34	20.70	0.64	3.08	25.31
3.	Ca.	Canada	1962	1887	51.01	52.56	−1.55	−2.95	22.45	24.92	−2.47	−9.91	26.54
			1953	1475	47.72	52.81	−5.09	−9.64	24.48	21.35	−3.13	14.64	27.80
4.	N.Z.	New Zealand	1962	1860	50.27	52.47	−2.19	−4.19	22.86	24.86	−2.00	−8.06	26.87
			1953	1324	46.86	51.96	−5.10	−9.81	19.05	21.04	−1.99	−9.48	34.09
5.	Al.	Australia	1962	1843	50.77	52.41	−1.63	−3.13	26.18	24.83	1.35	5.45	23.05
			1953	1127	49.35	50.71	−1.36	−2.69	26.33	20.59	5.74	27.88	24.32
6.	Sw.	Sweden	1962	1833	62.71	52.37	10.34	19.74	23.30	24.81	−1.51	−6.07	13.99
			1953	1177	58.57	51.05	7.52	14.74	19.07	20.71	−1.64	−7.92	22.42
7.	No.	Norway	1962	1608	51.04	51.54	0.50	−0.97	29.58	24.31	5.27	21.68	19.38
			1953	1066	47.36	50.29	−2.93	−5.83	29.39	20.44	8.96	43.82	23.25
8.	Lx.	Luxemburg	1961	1543	46.48	51.28	−4.80	−9.36	25.78	24.15	1.63	6.73	27.74
			1953	1060	46.13	50.25	−4.12	−8.20	24.20	20.42	3.78	18.51	29.67
9.	De.	Denmark	1962	1492	47.98	51.07	−3.09	−6.04	19.44	24.03	−4.59	−23.60	32.58
			1953	965	45.95	49.54	−3.59	−7.25	18.78	20.16	−1.38	−7.32	35.27
10.	U.K.	United Kingdom	1962	1454	61.29	50.91	10.39	20.40	16.85	23.93	−7.08	−29.59	21.86
			1953	1028	57.31	50.02	7.29	14.58	14.45	20.34	−5.89	−28.94	28.24
11.	Ge.	Germany F.R.	1962	1439	48.87	50.84	−1.97	−3.88	26.69	23.89	2.80	11.70	24.44
			1953	751	45.22	47.71	−2.49	−5.21	21.58	19.49	2.09	10.73	33.20
12.	Fr.	France	1962	1437	46.32	50.83	−4.51	−8.88	31.19	23.89	7.30	30.56	22.49
			1953	861	42.45	48.70	−6.25	−12.83	16.60	19.85	−3.25	−16.38	40.95
13.	Ne.	The Netherlands	1962	1250	50.42	49.97	0.45	0.90	25.84	23.38	2.46	10.53	20.74
			1953	780	43.20	47.98	−4.78	9.96	20.33	19.59	0.74	3.79	36.47
14.	Be.	Belgium	1962	1239	47.46	49.92	−2.46	−4.92	19.46	23.35	−3.89	−16.65	33.08
			1953	831	41.62	48.44	−6.82	−14.08	15.38	19.76	−4.38	−22.16	43.00
15.	Is.	Israel	1962	1232	48.01	49.88	−1.87	−3.75	31.31	23.33	7.98	34.22	20.68
			1953	558	45.03	45.62	−0.59	−1.30	27.61	18.72	8.89	47.49	27.36

18.	Fl.	Finland	1962	771	51.60	47.09	4.51	9.57	16.92	21.69	−4.77	22.00	31.48
			1953	442	50.59	44.05	6.54	14.85	24.43	18.14	6.29	34.69	24.98
19.	Ir.	Ireland	1962	755	47.89	46.97	0.92	1.96	17.63	21.62	−4.00	−18.47	34.48
			1953	513	44.33	45.05	−0.72	−1.59	17.20	18.51	−1.31	−7.07	38.47
20.	Tr.	Trinidad	1962	650	36.91	46.12	−9.21	−19.96	28.06	21.13	6.93	32.81	35.03
			1953	305	41.54	41.66	−0.12	−0.28	20.47	17.25	3.22	18.67	37.99
21.	Jp.	Japan	1962	551	42.81	45.19	−2.38	−5.27	38.24	20.59	17.65	85.69	18.95
			1953	217	38.59	39.57	−1.00	−2.49	27.87	16.47	11.40	69.20	33.54
22.	Ar.	Argentina	1962	462	42.76	44.22	−1.50	−3.31	22.22	20.04	2.19	10.88	35.02
			1953	390	50.04	43.23	6.81	15.76	16.05	17.83	−1.79	−10.00	33.91
23.	Cy.	Cyprus	1960	432	23.47	43.86	−20.39	−46.49	24.48	19.83	4.65	23.43	52.05
			1953	332	25.97	42.19	−16.22	−38.45	13.63	17.45	−3.82	−21.88	60.40
24.	Pa.	Panama	1961	429	58.58	43.82	14.76	33.68	18.59	19.81	−1.22	−6.16	22.83
			1954	287	56.69	41.28	15.41	37.34	10.81	17.11	−6.30	−36.81	32.50
25.	Ja.	Jamaica	1961	418	50.41	43.68	6.73	15.40	21.23	19.73	1.50	7.59	28.36
			1953	235	49.96	40.05	9.91	24.74	13.16	16.65	−3.50	−20.96	36.88
26.	Gr.	Greece	1962	374	35.09	43.09	−8.00	−18.57	23.68	19.39	4.29	22.10	41.23
			1953	210	27.51	39.38	−11.87	−30.14	15.42	16.40	−0.98	−5.97	57.07
27.	Sp.	Spain	1962	372	42.08	43.06	−1.00	−2.28	19.30	19.38	−0.08	−0.41	38.62
			1955	242	46.21	40.23	6.00	14.86	17.81	16.72	1.20	6.54	35.98
28.	Ml.	Malta	1962	371	49.29	43.05	6.24	14.50	22.02	19.37	2.65	13.68	28.69
			1954	260	45.04	40.67	4.37	10.75	14.20	16.88	−2.68	−15.88	40.74
29.	Co.	Colombia	1964	285	29.92	41.68	−11.86	−28.21	17.81	18.60	−0.79	−4.22	52.27
			1953	204	31.03	39.21	−8.18	−20.86	15.08	16.33	−1.25	−7.68	53.89
30.	Cr.	Costa Rica	1962	260	53.75	41.21	12.54	30.43	15.95	18.33	−2.38	−13.00	30.30
			1953	227	50.31	39.84	10.47	26.27	21.21	16.57	4.69	27.98	28.48
31.	Ma.	Mauritius	1962	210	49.69	40.14	9.55	23.78	16.96	17.74	−0.78	−4.38	33.35
			1953	181	50.66	38.51	12.15	31.55	15.99	16.07	−0.69	−4.24	33.35
32.	Ho.	Honduras	1962	194	56.70	39.75	16.95	42.62	14.08	17.52	−3.44	−19.64	29.22
			1954	160	42.95	37.80	5.15	13.62	13.55	15.81	−2.26	−14.27	43.50
33.	Ec.	Ecuador	1962	188	42.05	39.60	2.45	6.18	16.03	17.44	−1.41	−8.06	41.92
			1953	139	38.73	37.01	1.72	4.65	13.50	15.51	−2.01	−12.94	47.77
34.	Rh.	Rhodesia & Nyassa	1962	178	49.96	39.34	9.62	24.46	20.41	17.29	3.12	18.06	29.63
			1954	158	36.75	37.73	−0.98	−2.59	24.43	15.78	8.65	54.83	38.82
35.	Pe.	Peru	1962	173	35.80	39.20	−3.40	−8.67	20.94	17.21	3.73	21.66	43.26
			1953	153	28.87	37.55	−8.68	−23.11	24.49	15.71	8.78	55.89	46.64
36.	Ce.	Ceylon	1962	137	43.27	38.09	5.18	13.59	14.20	16.60	−2.40	−14.47	42.53
			1953	108	43.20	35.63	7.57	21.25	10.64	14.99	−4.35	−29.00	46.16
37.	Ph.	Philippines	1962	125	35.18	37.67	−2.49	−6.60	12.91	16.37	−3.46	−21.12	52.63
			1953	90	36.50	34.66	1.84	5.30	8.12	14.62	−6.50	−44.46	55.38
38.	Ta.	Taiwan	1962	121	40.00	37.52	2.49	6.62	20.96	16.29	4.68	28.70	39.04
			1953	78	38.15	33.93	4.23	12.45	16.59	14.34	2.25	15.69	45.26
39.	Ko.	Korea	1962	110	34.89	37.08	2.20	−5.91	15.68	16.05	−0.37	−2.29	49.43
			1953	65	26.82	33.01	−6.19	−18.74	11.95	13.99	−2.04	−14.58	61.23
40.	Ug.	Uganda	1962	60	24.90	34.42	−9.52	−27.66	9.93	14.61	−4.68	−32.03	60.49
			1953	66	23.10	33.08	−9.98	−30.18	21.00	14.02	6.99	49.80	62.88

2. GENERAL TENDENCY IN PRODUCT DISTRIBUTION

The prevailing general tendency in the decade 1953-1962 was a considerable increase in gross domestic product all over the world.[10] It is also significant for the forty countries of our sample.

TABLE II

Population and gross domestic product of 40 countries (by groups of 10 countries) 1953-1962

		Ranked by GDP Groups				
		I	II	III	IV	Total
Population						
— in millions	1953	257	130	158	87	632
	1962	294	143	175	111	723
	±	37	13	17	24	91
— in percentages	1953	40.6	20.6	25.0	13.8	100%
	1962	40.6	19.8	24.2	15.4	100%
		+ .0	−0.8	−0.8	+1.6	0
Gross Domestic Product						
— in million dollars	1953	442	97	38	8.7	586
	1962	675	188	83	14.9	961
	±	233	91	45	6.2	375
— in percentages	1953	75.4	16.6	6.5	1.5	100%
	1962	70.3	19.6	8.6	1.5	100%
	±	−5.1	+3.0	+2.1	0	0
Gross Domestic Product						
per Head	1953	1724	748	241	99	817
	1962	2298	1318	471	134	1328
1962 Increase (1953 = 100)						
Population		118	110	111	127	114
Gross domestic product		152	194	218	172	165
Gross domestic product p.c.		133	176	195	135	162

This general tendency can be demonstrated by using aggregate figures for the gross domestic product in the four groups of countries of the sample.

The total sum of the gross product of all forty countries increased from 586 to 960 milliard dollars; in 1962 it reached the index 165 (taking 1953 as 100), averaging a 6.2 per cent increase per year.

The greatest change occurred in the third — the developing — group,

[10] Of all 95 countries whose income figures were published in the *YNAS*, 1963, for the decade 1953-1963, only 5 countries in Africa and 1 in Asia showed a decline in the production per capita, and 3 in Africa and 2 in Asia demonstrated a stagnation.

including countries from Japan and Argentina to Colombia and Costa Rica, in which the aggregate GDP increased to index 218; the average annual rate of economic growth was 9.5 percent while its population grew at the rather low rate of 1.1 percent. The next largest change took place in the second group, consisting of developed countries from Germany and France to Finland and Ireland, which showed an index of 194 of GDP aggregate increase and an annual economic development rate of 7.6 percent over the decade but also had the lowest increase of population (1.2 percent p.a.).

In the fourth or least developed group, countries from Mauritius and Honduras to Korea and Uganda, the GDP rose from 100 to index 172, but the rate of economic growth p.c. was only 3.5 per cent because of the large population increase (2.7 per cent p.a.).

The smallest relative change was in the first group of most developed countries, ranging from the U.S.A. and Switzerland to Denmark and the United Kingdom. The aggregate GDP rose from 100 to 152 (5.2 per cent p.c.) at a low growth rate of 3.3 per cent p.a., but the population also increased considerably (1.4 per cent p.a.).

Another significant impression is obtained when ABSOLUTE figures are compared. The first 10 countries in the highest GDP per capita group increased their income from 442 to 675 milliard dollars. Their share in the 1953 total aggregate gross product of all forty countries was 75.5 per cent but fell to 70.2 per cent in 1962. Nevertheless these 10 most developed countries contributed 62.2 per cent of the total increment of the gross domestic product of the forty countries.

The second group, that of developed countries with 650 to 1450 dollars GDP per capita, showed a decennial increase of 91 milliard dollars. Their relative importance increased from 16.5 per cent to 19.5 per cent, and they contributed almost one quarter (24.2 per cent) to the total increase of the GDP.

The third group, that of the developing countries with 250 to 650 dollars per capita product, witnessed the greatest relative increment of 45 milliard dollars. Their share in 1953 was 6.5 per cent of the total and in 1962 rose to 8.6 per cent. Their contribution to total increment of the GDP amounted to 12 per cent.

The group of 10 countries with the smallest product per capita of 60-250 dollars showed a total gain of 6 milliard dollars. Their relative share remained almost the same, i.e., 1.5 per cent, and they contributed only 1.6 to the increase of the total gross domestic product of the forty countries.

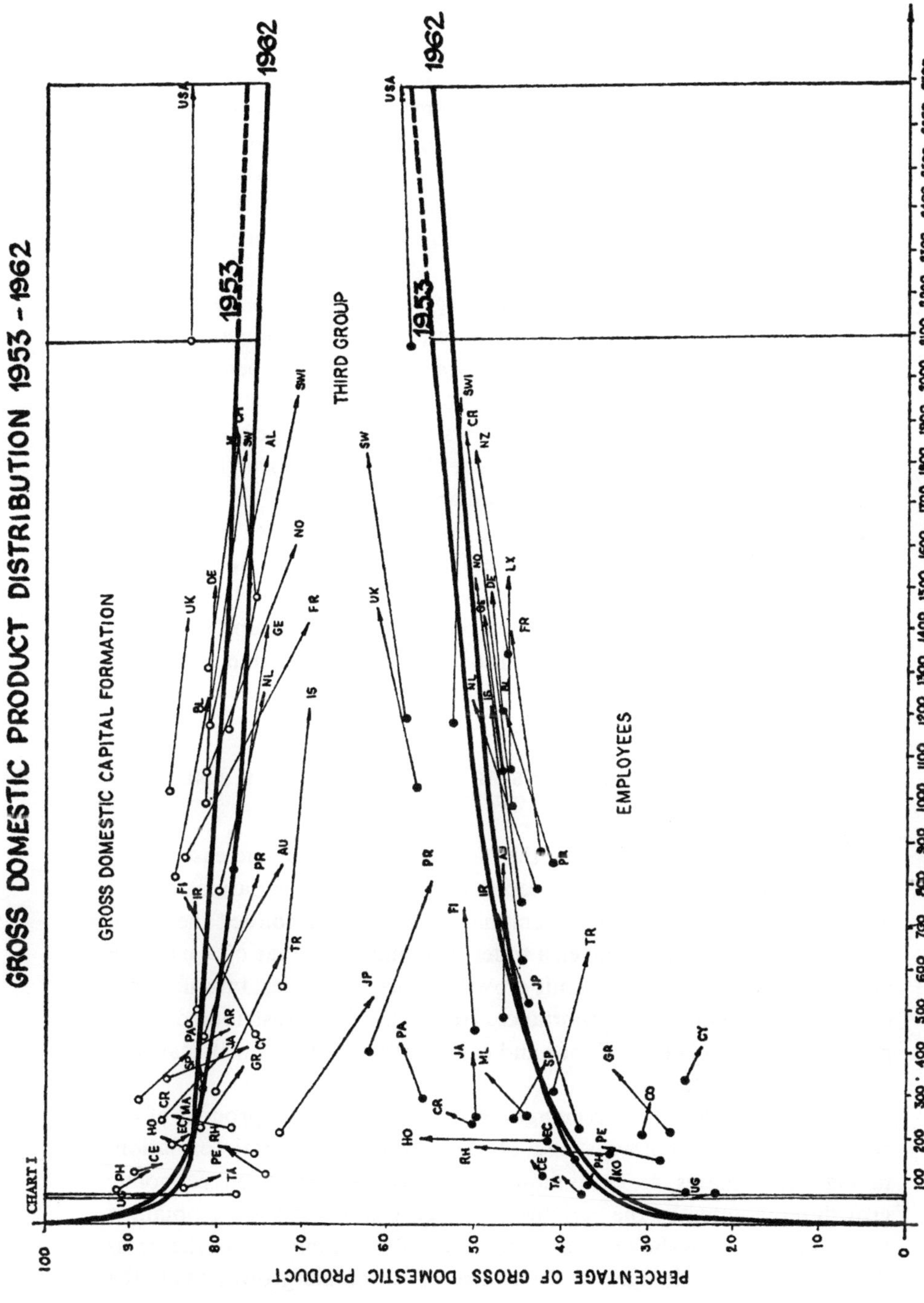
CHART I
GROSS DOMESTIC PRODUCT DISTRIBUTION 1953 - 1962
GROSS DOMESTIC CAPITAL FORMATION
THIRD GROUP
EMPLOYEES
1953
1962
PERCENTAGE OF GROSS DOMESTIC PRODUCT
GROSS DOMESTIC PRODUCT PER CAPITAL IN DOLLARS
100
90
80
70
60
50
40
30
20
10
0
100
200
300
400
500
600
700
800
900
1000
1100
1200
1300
1400
1500
1600
1700
1800
1900
2000
2100
2200
2300
2400
2500
2600
2700

On the whole, our world sample moved one step further in the direction of relative equality. The most developed of the 40 countries incurred a relative loss (5.2 per cent) of total gross product. This loss was gained by the second and third groups, which increased their shares by 3.1 and 2.1 per cent. But the least developed group, with less than 250 dollars GDP, remained in 1962 (with a slight increase in their share) as they were in 1953, i.e., at 1.5 per cent with no betterment of their relative position. Thus the greatest relative gain from development went to the second and third groups.

This general upward tendency of the gross product has had a great effect on the growth variable (X). The average value (arithmetical mean, $\bar{X}$) rose over the decade from 554 dollars to 852 dollars per capita (54 per cent). True, the range of the sample was extended a little at the bottom level, from 66 down to 60 dollars per head (9.3 per cent down), but this was amply compensated for since the top level moved from 2,080 to 2,691 (nearly 29 per cent higher) dollars per capita.

The employees' average share in the GDP (Y_L) also rose, from 44 per cent in 1953 to 46.29 in 1962. The average gross domestic capital formation ($\bar{Y}_K$) moved from 18.26 to 21.38 per cent in the same decade. This double increase lowered the average share of the third group from 37.74 per cent in 1953 to 32.33 per cent in 1962. Its relative importance declined in the decade 1953-1962 by 5.41 per cent of the GDP.

3. FUNCTIONAL RELATIONSHIP BETWEEN GROWTH AND SHARES OF THE GDP

We defined economic growth in the conventional way as increase of the real gross domestic product per capita and plotted the variations of this figure on the axis S. We wish to emphasize that in this context the figure of the GDP per capita is given a wider meaning., i.e., that of a measure of the overall process of economic growth of forty countries. International comparison magnified its importance. How is the GDP distributed in the process of growth between labor and capital? We shall deal with statistics first and policy afterwards.

On axis Y we put the percentages in the gross domestic product of the compensation of employees and of gross domestic capital formation, taking these shares as continuous functions dependent on economic growth represented by the variable X. By regression analysis we obtained two equations: one showing how the share of the employees in the gross domestic product changes in the course of economic growth (Y_L); the second giving the same functional relationship for gross domestic capital formation (Y_K).

The space between these two lines is residual and represents the share of the Third Group in the gross product. We carried out the same procedure for both 1953 and 1962 (Table I and Chart I).[11]

The curves do not express a 'law' of economic growth. They say only that the forty countries have maintained certain relationships in growth in the years 1953 and 1962. Thus these empirical curves show a general tendency of behavior derived from the data of our sample countries. Only by implication can we develop some further speculations regarding the changes over time, and other characteristics of gross product distribution.[12] We shall analyze first the general tendency expressed in both curves, then compare the 1953 and the 1962 curves, and after that make some comparisons of the changes by countries over the decade.

In our analysis of the effects of growth on product distribution, we shall deal first with the part pertaining to the employees, and second with that accruing to capital formation. Finally, we shall analyze the role of the Third Group. For that purpose we have computed the regression equations from Table I searching for the functional relationship between the shares of economic growth and of the employees and of the capital formation. (Chart I, Table I).[13]

[11] In order to make the chart more presentable we drafted the capital formation function in the form of $100 - y = ax^b$.

[12] See Appendix. Gain from growth and gain from distribution.

[13] Our model is built on the following equations:

$$X_i = \frac{Y_i}{P_i};\ Y_{Li} = \frac{Y_{Li}}{Y_i} \cdot 100;\ Y_{Ki} = \frac{Y_{Ki}}{Y_i} \cdot 100;$$

$$Y_L = a\,X^b$$

$$Y_K = c\,X^d$$

$$Y_L + Y_K + Y_{III} = 100$$

In this model Y stands for aggregate gross domestic product, Y_L for the percentage of the gross domestic product distributed to wage and salary earners, Y_K for the percentage of the gross domestic capital formation as percentage of the GDP, P for total population, and Y_{III} for the share of the total product accruing to final consumption of independent producers, government, and the leisure classes; *a*, *b*, *c*, and *d* are constants. The symbol *i* stands for countries.

The regression equations were computed on the following assumptions: a) no product — no shares, i.e., both curves were forced to pass through the point of origin; b) the data for the GDP per capita of different countries represent a continuous function of economic growth; c) the population increase was taken into account by the computation of the product per capita. The change in number of the wage and salary earners was not directly taken into account.

The regression lines obtained by the method of least squares runs as follows:

Regression Equations	Standard Deviation (log.)
$Y_{L\,62} = 20.82 \times {}^{0.123}$	0.18
$Y_{K\,62} = 7.75 \times {}^{0.155}$	0.25
$Y_{L\,53} = 17.61 \times {}^{0.151}$	0.19
$Y_{K\,53} = 7.95 \times {}^{0.135}$	0.26

The lines show a quite good fit, better for 1962 than for 1953 for both equations.

4. THE SHARE OF THE EMPLOYEES (Y_L)

A. *Statistics*

a *Aggregate change, 1953-1962*

As we can see from Table I the compensation of employees in 1962 in countries with a low level of development varies around the median of 40 per cent of the GDP; in developing countries around 43 per cent; in

Thus there are several underlying assumptions which a more detailed analysis over time would have to take into account. The gross domestic product is taken in the aggregate in both years and, consequently, does not show the inter-industry shifts, the declining role of agriculture and forestry, the changed degree of monopoly, nor the change in scale. It assumes an unchanged product mix and no changes in the quality of products, etc. All data are given in current prices, which also have changed.

When discussing the share of income accruing to employees over the decade, we assumed the homogeneity of the employment structure (government to business sectors; the white and blue collars; no changes in productivity). No account was taken of the rate of domestic unemployed and foreign labor employed, etc.

Similar assumptions were made also in the field of capital formation — no changes in structure nor in productivity of capital. It was assumed that the capital coefficient had not changed over the decade, that there had been no technical progress, etc.

In other terms, most of the assumptions usually made in macroeconomic analysis are retained in this paper, as such analysis is conventional in such types of *prima facie* international comparisons where research spreads over a great range and variety of countries. Therefore, one should not expect too much precision, particularly when individual countries are compared. Nonetheless, the general tendency of changes seems to be quite satisfactorily established with regard (a) to the shape of a functional relationship which is not directly proportionate to development and (b) to the changeability in the exponent of the curves of the shares of both capital and labor. How and why these exponents change we expect to be able to investigate when more internationally comparable data are collected.

developed countries 48 per cent; and in the most developed countries it moves around 51 per cent. The highest percentage reached so far was in Sweden (62.71%), the second highest in Great Britain where the share of the employees was 61.29 per cent, and the third in the United States (58.7%). The lowest share appeared in Uganda (24.90%) and Colombia (29.94%) (Table III). Thus we can say that the share of the GDP representing wages and salaries of employees increased with economic development. This process takes place mainly at the expense of the "Third Group" of independent producers.[14]

TABLE III

Countries ranked by labor share in GDP in 1962

Sweden	62.71	Canada	51.01	Denmark	47.98	Ecuador	42.05
U.K.	61.29	Australia	50.77	Belgium	47.46	Taiwan	40.00
U.S.	58.77	Netherlands	50.42	Ireland	47.89	Trinidad	36.91
Panama	58.58	Jamaica	50.41	Austria	46.93	Peru	35.86
Honduras	56.70	New Zealand	50.27	Luxemburg	46.48	Philippines	35.18
Puerto Rico	54.69	Rhodesia N.	49.96	France	46.32	Greece	35.09
Costa Rica	53.75	Mauritius	49.69	Ceylon	43.27	Korea	34.89
Switzerland	57.85	Malta	49.29	Japan	42.81	Colombia	29.42
Finland	51.60	F.R. Germany	48.87	Argentina	42.76	Uganda	24.90
Norway	51.04	Israel	48.01	Spain	42.08	Cyprus	23.47

In 1962 the share of employees in the GDP was 36.7 per cent in countries at the 100 dollars p.c. development level, and it increased steadily until at the 2500 dollars growth level it reached 54.4 per cent of the GDP (Table IV). It is significant that this increase in the share of labor is not linear. On the contrary, it shows a regression in the growth of the share.

[14] We were not in a position to analyze how the employees' income is distributed between the share of the wage earners and the share of the salaried. The distinction between the two groups is rather blurred and has changed throughout history, but there is an undoubted tendency for the share of the salaried to increase faster than that of the blue collar workers. To give one example:

From 1870 to 1950 the share of the employees in the national income of Great Britain increased from 55 to 65 per cent. In this sum the share of the wage earners showed a small increase from 39 to 42 per cent while the percentage accuing to the salaried rose from 16 to 23. In the same period the number of wage earners fell from 84 to 66 per cent of the total of employees while that of the salaried went up from 16 to 34 per cent. Cf. E. H. Phelps Brown and P. E. Hart, "The Size of Wages in National Income", *Economic Journal*, No. 246 (1952), pp. 276-277.

The conclusion that we draw from these studies termed as 'inexplicable' or 'miraculous constancy': the constancy of the labor share in the GDP is a result of methodological niceties of occupational statistics and has little to do with either social relations or the technological process.

TABLE IV

Computed shares of labor, capital and third group in the GDP
(Percentages)

GDP p.c. (in dollars)	Labor Shares 1953	Labor Shares 1962	Labor Shares diff.	Capital Shares 1953	Capital Shares 1962	Capital Shares diff.	Residual Third Group 1953	Residual Third Group 1962	Residual Third Group diff.
1	17.61	20.82	3.21	7.95	7.75	0.20	74.44	71.43	−3.01
50	31.84	33.68	1.84	13.51	14.21	0.70	54.65	52.12	−2.52
100	35.22	36.65	1.43	14.83	15.81	0.98	49.95	47.54	−2.41
200	39.19	39.95	0.76	16.26	17.62	1.36	44.55	42.43	−2.12
500	44.87	44.65	−0.22	18.44	20.29	1.84	36.68	35.06	−1.62
600	46.27	45.74	−0.53	18.85	20.89	2.04	34.88	33.37	−1.51
1000	49.81	48.62	−1.19	20.26	22.59	2.33	29.93	28.80	−1.14
1100	50.70	49.27	−1.43	20.46	22.95	2.49	28.84	27.78	−1.06
1500	52.94	51.10	−1.84	21.40	24.05	2.65	25.65	24.85	−0.80
1600	53.65	51.50	−2.15	21.53	24.32	2.79	24.82	24.18	−0.64
2000	55.29	52.94	−2.35	22.25	25.14	2.89	22.46	21.92	−0.54
2100	55.90	53.35	−2.55	22.33	25.36	3.03	21.77	21.29	−0.48
2500	57.18	54.41	−2.77	22.94	26.03	3.09	19.89	19.57	−0.32
3000	58.99	55.74	−3.25	23.43	26.81	3.38	17.58	17.45	−0.12
3100	59.29	55.96	−3.33	23.53	26.94	3.41	17.18	17.10	−0.08
Increment									
1- 100	17.61	15.83		6.88	8.06		−34.49	−23.89	
100- 200	3.97	3.30		1.43	1.81		− 5.40	− 5.11	
500- 600	1.40	1.09		0.41	0.60		− 1.80	− 1.69	
1000-1100	0.89	0.65		0.20	0.36		− 1.09	− 1.02	
2000-2100	0.61	0.41		0.08	0.22		− 0.69	− 0.63	
3000-3100	0.30	0.22		0.01	0.13		− 0.23	− 0.35	

This general tendency can be demonstrated by measuring how an increase in the GDP of 100 dollars corresponds to a rise of the share of labor. The increment of 100 dollars is functionally related to an increase of the share of employees in the GDP of 3.3 per cent at a low 100-dollar level of development. The same amount of dollars added at the 500-dollar development level increases the labor share by only 1.1 per cent. At a 1000-1100-dollar level the increase amounts to only 0.65 per cent and at a 2000 to 2100 level it is not much more than 0.4 per cent of the GDP.

Thus, if the workers wish to achieve 100 dollars' increase in the GDP at the lower level of development, they must increase their share in the GDP by more than 3 per cent while at the 3000-dollar level it is enough to increase their share by 0.2 per cent only.

The considerable economic growth in the decade 1953-1962 had a favorable effect on the income of the employees. The average per cent (arithmetic mean) of the gross product of the sample, distributed to the employees increased, as said before, from 44.04 to 46.29 per cent or 2.25 per cent of the total gross domestic product. It corresponds to an average annual percentage increase of 0.23 per cent of the GDP for the forty countries. This relative increase is not a spectacular change, as the gross domestic product per capita increased in the same period by 29 per cent or 2.9 per cent per year. The increase in the volume of the product earned by the employees was obtained more from economic growth than from changes in the product distribution. Their gain was derived (a) from the increase of the aggregate gross domestic product which over the decade added 29 dollars to each 100 dollars of total increase, (b) from the increase of their share from the average 44.0 to 46.3 per cent of the GDP. This relative increase when put in absolute terms meant an increment from 44 to 60 units, or when expressed by the index 1953 = 100, reached 136 in 1962. The employees absorbed 45 per cent of the total increase of the GDP while the remaining 55 per cent went to capital formation and the Third Group.[15]

Year	Increase of the Global GDP	Per cent of the GDP accruing to employees	Comparable increase $(1 \times 2) - 100$	Index
	(1)	(2)	(3)	(4)
1953	100	44.0	44	100
1962	129	46.3	60	136
Percentage of the increase	100	45	55	—

The coefficients of the regression equations represented in 1953 a value for Y of 17.6 per cent and in 1962, 20.8 per cent when x = 1 (a theoretical case outside the range of empirical data, used for measurement only). This means that in present times even the least developed countries allocate to the wage and salary earners one sixth to one fifth of the value of their GDP. The rise indicates the increasing role the share of the employees plays in gross domestic product distribution. Of course, most of this increase at the lower level of development is due to the increase in the number of people employed, and only secondarily to the increase of their income per head. Moreover, this *prima facie* analysis does not give any indication of the income differentiation within the social

[15] See also Appendix

group of employees, nor does it give information on the income differentials between the government employees, and the salaried and wage earners in the business sector. This could be a subject for further analysis.[16]

b. *Change and development by groups of countries*

The increase in the labor share was unequally distributed among countries at different levels of development. This is clearly visible from Chart I. Both curves, representing the labor share for 1953 and 1962, move steeply up at the beginning, near the origin, for the less developed countries. As development proceeds and more developed countries are involved the curve gets flatter. Nevertheless, it does not become parallel to the axis S, i.e., the employees' share is neither constant nor proportionate to the development, but increases in the course of development although the increment rate is steadily diminishing.

To get an idea of the role that general government expenditure plays in economic development, we are giving here a few figures relating the total general government expenditure to the net national income. This sector comprised in some European countries in the mid-fifties (1950-1956) up to 45.6 per cent of the equivalent of the national income in Germany, in France 40 per cent, in Luxembourg, the Netherlands, and Austria 30, and in the United Kingdom 33.3 per cent. In the U.S.A. it redistributed the equivalent of 29.2 per cent of the national income, and in Canada, New Zealand, Sweden, and significantly, Panama, 31 per cent. The percentage amounted to between 20 and 25 in Greece, Japan, Costa Rica, and Ecuador, Taiwan, and Rhodesia-Nyassa. In some countries there was no larger general government sector than around 15 per cent, e.g., in Spain, Colombia, Honduras, the Philippines, Mauritius, and Jamaica.

Both curves (Y_L for 1953 and 1962) moved up sharply to the range of 100 dollars, the developmental level of most of the African countries, where the share of employees attained 34.5 per cent in 1953 and 36.5 in 1962, an increase of 2 per cent of the GDP (Table IV). The change from 100 to 500 dollars of GDP per capita involved an increment of Y_L of

[16] Growth of government functions and tertiary services more than industrialization are the probable causes of this tendency, which turns 'independent' producers into wage and salary earners in the least developed countries of Africa, Asia, and Latin America. This pressure for an increased percentage of the GDP explains the tendency of the local bureaucracy towards dictatorial regimes, be it in the name of social progress, military efficiency, or political stability.

10.6 per cent in 1953 but only 8 per cent in 1962. In the upper group of countries, those between 500 and 1000 dollars GDP per capita (the level of Austria and Japan), Y_L changed by 1 per cent; but in the range of 2000 to 2500 dollars GDP p.c., its structural change amounted to little more than 2 per cent (2.14). The maximal computed share of the employees at the top level of growth achieved 54.72 per cent of the GDP.

B. *The Policy*

Economic growth cannot be separated from changes in the product distribution because they are in a functional relationship. Economic growth brings with it a structural change in the GDP distribution which benefits the employees. The empirical evidence leads to the conclusion that the workers as a social class (i.e., all wage earners and all salaried, together called employees) at the lower level of economic growth increase their income faster by increasing their share of the GDP than through the general economic growth of the country. But this situation changes at a higher level of economic development, where the workers' income is increased faster when the GDP per capita is increased than when only their share is augmented.

This objective situation when transferred to the field of economic policy lends itself to two different approaches, each of which can have two different policy interpretations. The first is concerned with the meaning of the workers' share of the GDP for working class policy. The second is related to the meaning of the curve for the national income policy.

a. *What comes first: the workers' share in the GDP or the economic growth of the country?*

On the basis of the first stage of the above empirically established situation, a workers' policy can be envisaged in which the primary consideration is the maximation of the labor share. This is seen in the classical trade union policy limited to wages only, where the class struggle is narrowly conceived and workers' interests considered to be isolated from other economic problems of the country. This policy is limited over time, not looking to further perspectives, but firmly dealing with current wage problems.

In the second situation, where the workers get more income from economic growth than they do from increase of their share, the prevailing tendency is to focus and increase the influence of the workers and the working movement on the overall national economic policy dealing with economic growth (the development of production forces). This necessitates a complex economic policy for the workers' movement: policy of economic growth, national economic planning, general investment and credit policy, etc. It does not mean that their interest in the share of the income must be weakened. Awareness that their income depends on at least two factors leads to a search for an optimal solution of both.[17]

In other words, in the first lower-level growth, there is a desire to get a bigger share whatever size the cake is. At the second higher level, the dominant tendency is to make the workers' income bigger by making the cake bigger. Usually this difference is attributed to different levels of general education; to various degrees of maturity and responsibility of the workers' movement and their leaders; to the experience and the class-consciousness of the working class, etc. But the underlying material factor is of primary importance; behind these psychological attitudes stand the level of economic growth and the structural changes connected with it.

In the first case, the workers feel too weak to influence the growth of the whole cake by their political pressure, or they have not confidence enough in themselves and their organizational ability to undertake it. So they limit their objectives to immediately attainable short-term objectives.

In the second case, they feel stronger and better organized, their views are wider and their experience stretches over a longer period of time, so that they can visualize a policy to make the cake bigger according to their ideas and feel strong enough to secure an appropriate share of it for themselves.

The actual situation is complex and the tendency of development described cannot be taken as an 'economic law', valid for all and sundry. Lagging in policy objectives behind the actually achieved level of growth and anticipations of future development are often only too evident. But

[17] It is not difficult to find elements of these two approaches in the history and in the present-day politics of working-class movements; the struggle between the labor politicians and the syndicalist leaders; the tension between the industrial and the political wing of the labor party in Great Britain, etc.; the conflict between the Second and the Third International in the 1920's; the present day Stalinist and the post-Stalinist policies; the Soviet and the Chinese conflict, etc., can partly (but not wholly) be explained by the difference in policy approach determined by the existing level of economic growth.

These tendencies may appear also within one country according to the level of economic growth at which different workers' groups work in different regions of the country or different branches of industries (e.g., Yugoslavia).

on the other side stands the fact that the coefficient of variation of our regression curve shows a pretty good fit. Then the big question arises whether this coefficient of shares is constant over time.[18] So far we think we have proved that it changed even over the short time of a decade.

b. *Does growth limit the workers' income, or the income limit growth?* The second approach is centered on the macroeconomic interpretation of the general tendency in national policy of GDP distribution. Here again two different policies may be evolved from the same situation, each depending on the class position of the policy makers. Both policies are connected with the interchange of independent and dependent variables. The commonly accepted view is that the difference between the political and the analytical approach can be explained by the change of the independent and the dependent variables in the functional relationship. The result of the analysis becomes the objective of the policy.

In the first instance the question is asked: What should be the workers' share at a certain level of development? In the second instance the question is reversed: What share of the GDP should the workers get in order to be stimulated to increase the national product per capita to a desired level? Of course there are certain limits to this, as economic growth does not depend only on the workers' stimulation but also on their adequate provision with other factors, among which capital investment and technical progress are the most important. We shall deal with these at a later stage of this analysis. But few people would deny the existence of a functional relationship between the workers' income and their performance.

The first policy is presented as follows: A certain definite share of the GDP accruing to the workers corresponds to each level of economic growth; therefore there exists an objective limit to the workers' demands at each level of economic development. This is a passive and also an

[18] The interpretation by P. Douglas of the constancy of the shares was: the greater the wages bill, the greater the product — the effect of steady proportions. Here the imperfect competition was treated as perfect; the monopolist was supposed to share with the workers the surplus at the expense of the consumer. Equilibrium was sought in expanded demand which led to reduced competition and to sub-production, while reduced demand led to hyperproduction and increased competition.

M. Kalecki accepted the empirical results of the developed countries but gave them a different interpretation. He found the reason for constancy of the shares to be in the degree of monopoly, particularly in price leadership — increased overhead costs, advertising expenses, the industrial composition, the ratio of material bill to the wage bill; and on the labor side, the increased overall pressure of the organized labor. (M. Kalecki, *Theory of Economic Dynamics*, London, 1954, pp. 28-41, particularly p. 31.)

analytical technocratic approach to the problem, taking the share of the employees as a dependent variable which automatically depends on the level of development. Economic development is taken to be an independent variable, i.e., independent of the efforts and activities of workers and salaried labor.

The other attitude, also taking the functional relationship as the starting point, is based on the opposite reasoning: As there is a functional relationship between the workers' share of the GDP and the level of economic growth, the workers' share in the GDP should be increased if a greater level of growth is required. This interpretation is an active one, a policy approach which gives workers and salaried labor an active role and treats their share as an independent variable on which the development variable depends. As a result of it the greater the share attributed to the workers and salaried, the greater their contribution to economic growth can be, and therefore the faster the economic growth of the country. This is also a humanistic and a dynamic approach, where domestic growth is considered to be primarily a function of labor and its productivity.

The first approach is practiced in many capitalist entrepreneurial circles, in conservative public administration, and in the state bureaucracy in some socialist countries with the mentality of a lower level of economic development. The second attitude is visible in the provisions for profit sharing in workers' co-partnership in decision making, in certain advanced policies of some trade unions, and in its most developed form in the principle of workers' management (e.g., in Yugoslavia).

c. *The statistical evidence*

How have these different policies manifested themselves in the statistics of the general tendency of the GDP distribution during the decade 1953-1962? On Chart I the line for 1953 starts from a lower level and moves up more steeply than the second line, that of 1962, which means that the share of the employees in relation to the economic growth rate increased faster in 1953 than in 1962. The curve for 1962 started at a higher level than in 1953 but moved up at a slower pace. The discrepancy between the two lines increased in the course of economic growth (Chart I, Table IV). This increased pace was positively correlated only in the first group of least developed countries (+2 per cent) while in the course of development, the gap between the curves opened ever wider. This widening gap is a sign of a decreasing rate of growth of the share of employees in the decennial course of development. In other words the period 1953-

1962 was a period of negative changes in gross domestic product distribution to the employees and of slowing down of the rate of increase of the employees' share.

The regression line showed a flattening of the curve after around 200 dollars value of GDP p.c., and after that demonstrated an ever decreasing structural change, as Chart I shows. In the higher levels of growth, the curve flattens. But it never became parallel to the growth axis S. The share of the employees in the GDP does not change much, but the absolute amount varies in direct proportion to the change in the GDP p.c.

The employees' share expressed by the variable Y_L increased in 1953 with the power of 0.151 over X, and this small exponent is responsible for the curvature of the line. At the end of the decade, in 1962, the curve became flatter, demonstrated by the decline in the exponent to 0.123. This again is a sign of the decreasing influence of the structural share changes component in the GDP distribution in this decade.

The less developed countries, at the bottom of the scale, follow a general tendency: THE LESS DEVELOPED A COUNTRY, THE MORE STRUCTURAL CHANGES IN THE PRODUCT DISTRIBUTION ARE TO BE EXPECTED IN THE PROCESS OF GROWTH. In fact, the process of fast growth is a process of great structural change in GDP distribution. But there is a point where the distribution becomes less important than growth, as the coefficients of the curve show. We have seen that the one for 1962 as compared to 1953 rose from 17.61 to 20.82, meaning that the 1962 curve comes closer to the axis Y than that of 1953. So, to a certain extent the range of countries where great structural changes take place has narrowed.

In the flattening of the curve in the decade one can read that the process of growth as expressed by the increase of the variable X prevails over the process of GDP product distribution, whatever the impression based upon outward appearances may be. The structure of the product distribution has stiffened; the shares did not change much; growth was steady and continuous, without spectacular changes. In the nineteen-fifties the employees gained more by the process of growth than by the increase in shares of the GDP. Or to be more explicit, the increase of the share achieved great improvement in the lesser developed countries, and had less impact in the more developed countries. This is more true the more developed a country is. The way in which the changes were distributed over the forty countries at different levels of growth is demonstrated in Chart I and Table IV where we have compared the course of both curves. We have also added the course of changes of different countries in the decade for both the employees' share and the capital formation.

C. *Change in the Labor Share by Countries*

To make the tendencies for the forty countries clearer, we have also drawn in Chart I lines connecting the points of the initial and the final years in the decade.

The length of the line along the axis X shows the change in absolute figures, i.e., change in dollars of the GDP per capita, and its vertical distance demonstrates the change in the share. Thus the slope of the line gives the functional relationship of the magnitude of the absolute to the magnitude of the relative change, i.e., its developmental elasticity, which we shall analyze later. (Table XI).

Only Uganda had a negative change in the global sum of its GDP. The decennial line for each of the countries in the sample moved from left to right.[19]

Another situation is demonstrated when the relative figures are analyzed. Here some countries, such as Spain, Argentina, Trinidad, Cyprus, Philippines, Colombia, Puerto Rico, Mauritius and also Switzerland, Austria, and Denmark, belong to the group of the declining share of the workers and therefore have a negative developmental elasticity of the share. Most of the developed European countries such as the Netherlands, Sweden, Belgium, the United Kingdom, and Ireland have a marked increase of the employees' share. An almost vertical climb in the share is shown by some less developed countries like Honduras, Costa Rica, Peru, and Korea, meaning that the increase of the employees' share took place only by changes in the distribution and with practically no change in the absolute figure of the GDP p.c. The developmental coefficient of elasticity of the labor share was greater than 1.

Most of the other developed countries moved along the general trend with a small change in the share but a considerable gain from the development of the country (U.S.A., Canada, France, West Germany, Norway, Ireland, but also Greece, Panama, and Japan, etc.).[20]

The impression one gets at first glance is that the employees' variable showing the share of the GDP for 1953 was higher than that for 1962.

[19] See Chart I. Points for the year 1953 are marked by a black point and those for 1962 by an arrow.

[20] It is not the purpose of this research to explore further conclusions as to political and other implications which might be drawn from these figures. This is left to the experts in these matters. But one cannot miss the obvious correlation between the distribution of the gross domestic product and the political position of the workers. Another significant factor is that this period coincides with the last stages of colonial regime or of the liberation struggle.

It is true that the general tendency of the employees' share AT THE SAME LEVEL OF GROWTH over the decade shows a smaller percentage of the product in their hands. Although the curve for 1962 started from a higher percentage (at X = 1.0), 20.8 as compared to 17.6 in 1953, its smaller power over X (0.123 as compared to 0.155 in 1953) does not let it climb faster than the 1953 curve. Therefore, a difference during the decade progressed with economic growth. At 100 dollars per head, the increase for the decade in the share of the employees was +1.95 per cent of the GDP. But at a higher level of development, it decreased to −2.22 per cent for the 1000 dollars product p.c. level, and to −4.09 per cent for the 2000 level. In other words IN THIS DECADE THE EMPLOYEES IN LESS DEVELOPED COUNTRIES IMPROVED THEIR SHARE WHILE THOSE IN MORE DEVELOPED ONES HAD IT REDUCED, AT THE SAME GDP PER CAPITA LEVEL.

This static disadvantage was greatly compensated for by the dynamics of growth in the decade. Two conclusions can be drawn from this situation. One is that if it were not for the change in growth the position of the wage earners and the salaried would be worse in 1962 than it was in 1953.[21] Such development was convenient or less detrimental to the interests of the employees in those countries in which growth was considerable. It was less favorable where such gains from growth were lacking.

The second lesson drawn from the experience of the decade is that if countries at a certain level of growth (say 1000 dollars p.c.) are considered in a static analysis, the position of the employees in product sharing for the same growth level as such has deteriorated. In other words, growth did not have the same effect for countries at the same level of growth at the end of the decade as it had at the beginning.

Therefore, one should not expect that increased GDP per capita will lead automatically to an increase in the percentage of the product accruing to the employees. From this we can conclude that if it were not for the prosperity of growth, employees would have to struggle more intensely for a share of the final product increase in order to increase or maintain their income level. One ought also to expect that after 1962 the

[21] The result of a more detailed analysis can be demonstrated by the change in the composition of the developmental group of 500-1000 dollars product per capita. This very mobile group, which in 1953 consisted of 7 countries and in 1962 of 6 countries, from the beginning to the end of the decade lost 6 countries to a higher GDP bracket group, that over 1000 dollars (Denmark, Germany, France, Netherlands, Belgium, Israel) and gained five new countries (Austria, Puerto Rico, Finland, Trinidad, Japan). Only Ireland remained in this group, in which the average percentage of the employees' share fell by 2.22 per cent.

TABLE V

Deviation of labor shares in GDP in 1962

Country	Negative	Country	Positive
Cyprus	−46.49	Honduras	42.62
Colombia	−28.21	Panama	33.68
Uganda	−27.66	Costa Rica	30.43
Trinidad	−19.96	Mauritius	23.70
Greece	−18.57	Rhodesia-Nyassa	24.46
Luxemburg	−9.26	U.K.	20.40
France	−8.88	Sweden	19.76
Peru	−8.67	Puerto Rico	15.17
Philippines	−6.60	Jamaica	15.40
Korea	−5.91	Malta	14.50
Denmark	−6.09	Ceylon	13.59
Japan	−5.27	Finland	9.57
Germany	−3.88	U.S.	7.05
Belgium	−4.92	Taiwan	6.02
New Zealand	−4.19	Ecuador	6.18
Israel	−3.75	Ireland	1.96
Argentina	−3.31	Netherlands	0.90
Australia	−3.13		
Canada	−2.95		
Spain	−2.28		
Switzerland	−1.75		
Austria	−1.53		
Norway	−0.97		

struggle for the increase in the share should be intensified in both political and industrial fields as soon as the rate of economic growth slows down.

Deviation of Labor shares in particular Countries from the General Tendency. — The general tendency expressed in the regression equation described above represents the 'rule' of how gross domestic product (at factory cost) was distributed at the beginning and end of the decade 1953-1962 between labor and capital or, to be more precise, between income of the employees and the expenditure on gross domestic capital formation. Some countries showed quite a significant deviation from the general line in both the positive and the negative senses. Others followed more closely the general tendency.

In Table V we grouped the forty countries according to percentage of deviation from the general tendency. Some countries were marked by a very great deficiency in the share of labor in product distribution. The greater negative deviations in 1962 were those of Cyprus, Colombia, and Uganda, and of developed countries such as Luxembourg, France, and Germany. The closest to the general tendency, but still on the negative side, were countries such as Canada, Austria, and Norway which showed smaller shares than the general line would allow.

On the positive side, having a greater share than the general tendency would allocate were, besides some Latin American countries like Honduras and Panama, some African countries, the United Kingdom, Sweden, and the United States. They deviated from the general line up to 7 per cent on the positive side.[22] It is not the purpose of this study to examine particular countries and the reasons why their shares showed a certain deviation. That would be asking too much of an international comparison; therefore, further analyses will have to be left to more refined and detailed studies of individual countries.

5. CHANGES IN SHARES OF GROSS DOMESTIC CAPITAL FORMATION

A. *Statistics*

Gross domestic capital formation at factor cost has also considerably increased over the decade 1953-1962, in aggregate terms by more than half (56 per cent), because of significant economic growth. The increase in relative terms was not so spectacular, although significant.

The General Tendency

The decennial average percentage of the gross domestic product allocated for capital formation has moved from 18.26 to 21.36, showing quite an important increase of 3.10 per cent of the GDP allocated to gross domestic capital formation (GDCF). This was taken in part from the share of the employees and to a much greater extent from the share of the GDP which had hitherto been in the hands of other groups.

The regression equations of the gross domestic capital formation as shares in the GDP (Y_K) were obtained in the following form:

[22] The closest to the general line on the positive side were the Netherlands, Ireland, and Ecuador. The deviations do not depend only on the level of development and the share but also on the absolute and relative number of employees in the country and other factors. One must bear this in mind and not read into the figures more than they can explain.

1953	$Y_K53 = 7.95 \times 0.135$	$s = 0.26$ (log)
1962	$X_K62 = 7.75 \times 0.155$	$s = 0.25$ (log)

X stands for the GDP per capita in dollars.

The curves of the capital formation shares do not fit as well as those of the employees' share. The standard deviation is .25 to .26.[23]

Thus the functional relationship between growth and gross domestic capital formation is not so close as between growth and the labor share. The reasons are that we are using gross instead of net capital formation;[24] and that the contribution of the rest of the world to capital formation is excluded (which has a different effect on capital formation at various levels of development). We are dealing here with the domestic, not the national product.[25] Also the lag between capital formation and its effect on growth is not taken into account (the gestation period). On the other hand, real capital formation (on the EXPENDITURE side), not the income saved, is the basis of our conclusions. The mixture of productive and nonproductive investment is not differentiated; capital is considered to be homogeneous in quality at all levels of development, which also

[23] The Y_K curves in Chart I are drafted so as to give a more comparable picture. The $100 - Y_K$ picture of the curve will not mislead anyone to believe that the curve is not positively increasing with economic growth (X). For the definition of the gross domestic capital formation (GDCF) and the distinction from the definition of the labor share, see footnotes 7 and 27.

[24] The difference between gross and net capital formation is such that a relatively bigger share of capital is allocated for depreciation allowance in developed countries. Thus gross capital formation in less developed countries is closer to net than in the more developed ones.

[25] This may hold more for the end years of the decade than for the beginning ones, i.e., more for the early 1960s than for the mid-fifties. The difference between the net national income and gross domestic capital formation (both at factor cost) varies according to countries but there is a widening gap between them as we move towards more developed countries. In the mid-fifties the GDP of the United States averaged 120.3 per cent of the national income. This percentage was considerably higher in some developed countries: over 30 per cent above the national income in France, Germany, Luxembourg, Canada, Venezuela.

In the middle range countries the discrepancy was around 20 per cent. (Belgium 26, Netherlands 24, Israel 32, Norway 22, Austria 22, Japan 21, and Australia 21.) In the less developed countries the variation is very great. Some countries showed a positive difference of some 20 per cent (Costa Rica, Ecuador, Jamaica, the Philippines, Greece [115], Cyprus, and Rhodesia-Nyassa, 117). Other countries developed a much smaller difference (Spain 7, Mauritius 10, Panama 4, Ceylon 9, etc.). The transactions with the rest of the world amounted to an equivalent of the net national income in Belgium of 42.9 per cent, in the United Kingdom 30.8, in Denmark 3.79, and Norway 51 per cent. In France it was of smaller influence (20.1) and in Germany and Austria a little greater (25). Greece showed only 13 and Spain 7.7 per cent.

R. Bičanič, "Economic Growth by Economic Sector", paper presented to the International Association on Income and Wealth (1959) (mimeo.).

TABLE VI

Countries ranked by the share of GDCF in GDP in 1962

Japan	38.24	Luxemburg	25.78	Taiwan	20.96	Mauritius	16.96
Israel	31.31	Puerto Rico	24.94	Peru	20.94	Trinidad	16.92
France	31.19	Cyprus	24.48	Rhod. Nyassa	20.41	United K.	16.85
Switzerland	30.06	Sweden	23.30	Belgium	19.46	Ecuador	16.03
Norway	29.52	Greece	23.68	Denmark	19.44	Costa Rica	15.95
Trinidad	28.07	N. Zealand	22.86	Spain	19.30	Korea	15.68
Austria	27.73	Canada	22.45	Panama	18.59	Ceylon	14.20
W. Germany	26.69	Argentina	22.20	Columbia	17.81	Honduras	14.08
Australia	26.18	Jamaica	21.33	Ireland	17.63	Philippines	12.91
Netherlands	25.84	Malta	21.02	U.S.	17.18	Uganda	9.93

assumes equal productivity of capital and equal capital mix. It was not possible to get internationally comparable data for such analytical distinctions.[26] Therefore, it is not surprising that the functional relationship shows a bigger standard deviation than the comparatively more homogeneous labor variable. Nevertheless, the functional relationship test of the equation allows one to draw relevant conclusions.

The general tendency which the equations show is that the share of capital formation increases in the process of development. The gross domestic capital formation among forty countries varies between Japan at 38 per cent and Uganda at less than 10 per cent of the GDP, with 21 per cent as a median (Table VI). In the group of ten countries at the lowest level of development the percentage of GDCF in the GDP turned round the median of 16 per cent; in the group of ten developing countries the median was 21, and in developed countries it amounted to 24.5 per cent. The ten most developed countries showed a somewhat lesser percentage, that is, 22.5.

The general tendency in these empirical figures can be better visualized when the computed data are considered (Table IV). In this case the countries at 100 dollars p.c. development level have a percentage of 15.8 GDP allocated to gross domestic capital formation. Countries at 500 dollars GDP per capita give 20.3 per cent, those at 1500 dollars p.c. 24 per cent, and those at 2500 GDP per capita allocate 26 per cent of the GDP to gross domestic capital formation.

The increment of the shares, however, declined in the process of growth. This increment in countries at lower levels of growth, in the

[26] We are limited by our statistical source, the *UN Yearbook of National Accounts Statistics*.

100 to 200-dollar bracket, represents 1.8 per cent of the GDP p.c. For an increase of 100 dollars in the GDP per capita at the 500 to 600-dollar level, growth of only 0.60 per cent was required; and to reach another 100-dollar increment of the GDCF at the 1000-dollar level of growth, the increment in the share of the GDP amounted to only 0.36 per cent. It is still smaller at 2000-2100 dollars (0.22 per cent); and at 3000 to 3100 dollars in growth, the increment in the capital formation is only one eighth of one per cent (0.13). Thus, in the course of development the increment of the share of the GDCF climbed fast, but it becomes ever smaller, and at high levels of development it is almost a straight line (but not parallel to the axis X).

B. *Policy*

As we have already seen, the relationship between economic growth and gross domestic capital formation is more complicated than that between the labor share and economic growth. Here we shall describe two policies of capital formation, each with two variants, which can be connected with the process of growth.

One policy approach is partial and autonomous, expressing the interests of the main actors in capital formation. The other policy is the overall national policy of capital formation which emerges at different levels of economic growth.

a. *What comes first: maximation of the share of gross domestic capital formation or maximation of economic growth?*

In dealing with the policy approach based on the specific interests of the actors in capital formation, one policy variant is to maximize the share of gross capital formation in the GDP at all costs, treating it as an independent variable. The share increases at a higher rate than the rate of growth.

The other policy approach is where gross capital formation is closely linked to economic growth, thus making the share dependent on this growth. In other words, what matters is the maximization of economic growth as a whole, and the share of gross capital formation is conceived as a variable dependent on it.

In the first case the policy of capital formation advocates limitless capital formation as the top policy priority, to which austerity of consumption is a residual correlate. The main question in growth policy is how much capital should be extracted from the GDP. Where private capitalists are the main accumulators of capital, they advocate a policy of removing all obstacles to domestic capital formation in their own hands by increasing the distributive share. Where the state takes over the task of capital formation, maximization of the share of GDCF ('the investment quota') is considered to have priority over all other considerations in economic policy. In both cases policy instruments concerning product distribution take precedence over those dealing with production.[27]

The policy of maximizing GDCF in the GDP at the expense of consumption leads logically to sharpening of the class conflict between capital formation maximizers, whether private or state, and general consumers, a conflict which in turn leads to the use of force and to political product distribution.

Nevertheless, an increased share of capital formation does not result in a proportionate increase in the gross domestic product, since the capital coefficient does not remain constant in the process of development. Thus, this policy of maximization of capital formation can be partly explained, in the early stage in development when the capital coefficient becomes increasingly heavy, by the changed capital mix during the building of infrastructure. And later, at a higher stage of development, the capital output ratio declines when the infrastructure has been already built. The capital formation becomes more proportionate to the increase in gross product per capita.

However, there is a second element in this tendency toward maximization of capital formation: the indiscriminate policy of pushing towards capital investment, with no regard for its effectiveness or profitability (increase of national power; accelerated building of socialism). This is heavily paid for in the next stage of development.[28]

Another policy approach of promoters of capital formation, occurring

[27] The main difference is that private accumulators suppress consumption in the interest of their private capital accumulation, invested mainly for themselves. The fruits of this investment have, in the short run, to stand the test of the market which may or may not be positive. In the case of state accumulation consumption is suppressed in the public interest, as defined by the state decision makers, but the investment decisions are not tested in the market. Disproportions become evident only in the long run and can have positive or negative consequences, which the time lag makes more meaningful.

[28] Those economists who favor capital growth at all costs have done a disservice to countries accepting their advice that in the initial stages of development no great mistakes can be made in developmental investments since everything ultimately will be welcomed and find a place. These countries have eventually paid heavily for the errors in their consultants' judgment.

in countries where development has already gained momentum, is based on the following considerations: (1) that the volume of capital formation depends almost proportionally on the growth (the size of the GDP p.c.); therefore, it is in the specific interest of the capital accumulators to stimulate the productivity of direct producers by increasing their possibilities of consumption, thus maximizing economic growth as a whole; (2) that increased consumption plays an important role in the creation of demand which, at higher levels of development, induces investment and capital formation.

Therefore they advocate a policy of maximizing overall growth by favoring increase of national power and national solidarity, preaching class harmony, or sharing the burden of progress by present and future generations, etc.

The first, autonomous approach to capital formation was dominant in early periods of capitalist development and still is prevalent in business circles of less developed countries. In developed countries, small and medium business — nurturing ideas of personal entrepreneurship and free competition — still support this policy. Its backbone is free enterprise and individual entrepreneurial decision-making in capital formation.

A similar policy of capital formation exists in countries with a sizable public sector (intending to build socialism or not), but at a modest level of development. It stands for compulsory capital formation, limitations on consumer demand, and arbitrary political decision-making in investment policy, covered by ideological motivation which overrules economic reasoning.

In both cases, since the workers and their organizations are denied a role in the capital formation process, they consider their role to be that of a third party in a capital formation process in which they neither have direct interest nor bear any responsibility.

The second approach to capital formation policy can be found in capitalist countries at a developed level. In big business, managers' rather than owners' autonomy evolves corporation decision-making into management planning on a large scale, merges corporation planning and government policies, and introduces macroeconomic elements into capital formation decisions.

At the same time, following this policy approach the workers and their organizations are considered to bear their part of responsibility for national growth and capital formation policies. In many countries their role in capital formation is institutionalized, be it in government policy ('guidelines' in wage policy), or formalized in union bargaining procedure, or in partnership in management process (workers' co-determination).

The workers' organizations consequently are accepting this view and developing their own policy of growth and capital formation — that the fruits of technological progress should be shared adequately. Their endeavors produce various results.

In developed socialist countries the pressure of facts leads to a policy of capital formation which recognizes its limits in consumers' increased weight (greater elasticity of demand because of greater increase in supply); autonomous capital formation is replicated by induced capital formation; both factors, consumers' role and induced investment decisions, require a greater independence and risk which the state bureaucracy is neither capable nor willing to take. Therefore, autonomy of socialist enterprises and workers' management is a logical outcome.

b. *Does the economic growth limit capital formation or capital formation limit economic growth?*

On the national level, advocating a policy in the interest of a macro-economic entity involves the following dilemma: should the national policy of growth maximize the share of capital formation in the GDP, or should this share determine growth? In the former case growth is considered to be a function of capital formation; in the latter, capital formation is treated as a function of growth. Because in countries at a low level of development there is a shortage of capital, maximizing capital-formation is considered the main task of national growth policy. In the case where GDCF tends to maximize its share in the GDP, the presupposition is that the greater the share, the greater the product. This relationship makes of capital formation an active factor of growth, pulling growth along with it. Therefore maximization of the share is advocated in the interest of national policy, a policy sometimes called the formation of the domestic entrepreneurial class or of 'national' capital, waving the national flag in front of capital formation. If the private sector does not or cannot accumulate capital to the required extent, the government steps in and introduces compulsory saving and capital formation. In socialist countries this function is claimed to be the main justification for nationalization and authoritarian administration of industries and other capital-forming socialist sectors, in spite of the fact that maximation of capital formation means an increase in exploitation of workers, other producers, and consumers. Thus the second assumption has been made: the larger the share of capital formation, the faster the rate of economic growth, which presupposes linear functional relationship, existing as we have already seen only in specific circumstances.[29]

The other approach is that of a domestic policy limiting capital formation according to economic growth. This is the case in developed countries, which try to keep an almost constant proportion between the share accruing to capital formation, and the residual share of general consumption. For this purpose different policy measures and devices are used such as: collective bargaining between labor and capital; progressive rates in income and corporation tax; welfare-state policies, etc. Reverse policy also takes place: if the capital formation is too small, the policy of tax exemption and reduction is advocated, and favorable treatment and subsidies for capital formation are accorded, etc. Thus this linear equilibrium is a result of actions by opposing interest groups in national policies and does not occur automatically.

c. *Changes in the Share of Gross Domestic Capital Formation over the Decade 1953-1962.*

The changes in the share of gross domestic capital formation over the decade have shown a confirmation of the general tendency for gross capital formation to increase. This increase was due to (a) the overall economic growth over the decade; (b) the increase in the share of GDCF in the GDP; (c) the greater development of the country.

At the 100-dollar level the decennial difference in percentages of the GDP was only plus 1 per cent; at 1000 dollars 2.3 per cent (from 20.3 to 22.6 per cent), and at the 2500-dollar level 3.1 per cent (from 22.9 to 26.0). The capital formation line moved faster in 1962 than in 1953 toward increased percentages of capital formation.

The comparison of the two curves shows that the 1962 curve was more rounded at the higher levels of development than the 1953 curve. This is confirmed by the magnitude of the exponents of the corresponding curves, which in 1953 was 0.135 and in 1962, 0.155. Unlike the employees' curve which was flattened over the decade, the curve of the share of the capital formation showed a pronounced rounding. The employees' curve in 1962 as compared with that of 1953 demonstrated a marked movement against the general tendency. The capital formation curve showed a marked movement in favor of the general tendency.

Our conclusion is that over the decade (1953-1962) there was a favorable climate for domestic capital formation which expanded its share, and that this climate was more favorable in more developed than in less

[29] See "The Threshold of Economic Growth", pp. 35 ff. of this book.

developed countries. Both moved toward an increased share of capital formation in the GDP, but the more developed countries moved faster than the less developed ones.

What, then, was of more influence: the policy of capital formation or the policy of overall growth? There is little doubt, taking a static view of product distribution as at the same level of growth, that the policy of increasing the share of capital formation had more success than the policy of overall growth. But if we take a dynamic view when comparing the share to overall growth, the picture changes. The cumulative effect over the decade of dependence of the increase in the share of GDCF on economic development is shown by the developmental elasticity of shares. This elasticity (Table XII) is positive and greater than 1.0 in some developing countries like Argentina, Panama, Ceylon, Philippines, Taiwan, and Korea where the increase in the share was favored more than economic growth and domestic capital formation more expanded than development. There was a moderate but positive elasticity in most of the developed countries like the U.S., the U.K., Switzerland, Germany, France, etc., where the functional relationship was somewhat to the benefit of the capital formation. Negative elasticity in the decade existed in such developed countries as Canada and Finland and also in such developing ones as Spain and Peru. A very negative elasticity developmental coefficient of GDCF shares existed in Costa Rica, Rhodesia-Nyassa, and Uganda, showing that the domestic capital formation was not organically linked to the process of development.

(1) *Deviations of the Capital Formation shares from the General Tendency in GDP Distribution.* — The general tendency in GDP distribution with regard to the share of capital formation shows some characteristic deviations in both the positive and the negative sense. The greatest deviations in the negative sense were shown in some of the most developed countries such as the U.S.A., the United Kingdom, Ireland, Belgium, but also in some less developed countries such as Uganda, the Philippines, and Honduras.

Obviously an important element is missing here: that of international relations, which so greatly influence many countries. The countries showing the largest positive deviation were those which allocated a greater share to capital formation than the general tendency would allow. These countries were Japan (almost double), Israel, France, and Norway, followed by Switzerland and Austria. Trinidad and Taiwan also had a very high positive deviation in capital formation. On the lowest side of the positive deviation were Australia, Luxembourg, Jamaica, the Netherlands, and others.[30]

TABLE VII

Deviation of capital shares in GDP in 1962 (in percentages)

Country	Negative	Country	Positive
U.S.	−34.74	Japan	85.69
Uganda	−32.03	Israel	34.22
U.K.	−29.59	Trinidad	32.81
Denmark	−23.60	France	30.56
Philippines	−21.12	Taiwan	28.7
Honduras	−19.64	Cyprus	23.43
Ireland	−18.47	Norway	21.68
Belgium	−16.65	Peru	21.66
Ceylon	−14.47	Switzerland	20.01
Costa Rica	−13.0	Austria	25.91
Canada	−9.91	Greece	22.00
New Zealand	−8.06	Finland	22.00
Ecuador	−8.06	Rhodesia-Nyassa	18.06
Panama	−6.16	Puerto Rico	13.77
Sweden	−6.07	Malta	13.68
Mauritius	−4.38	F.R. Germany	11.70
Colombia	−4.22	Argentina	10.88
Korea	−2.29	Netherlands	10.53
Spain	−0.41	Jamaica	7.59
		Luxemburg	6.73
		Australia	5.45

(2) *Comparison of Deviations of the shares of Labor and of Capital from the General Tendency.* — Deviations from the general tendency have taken place, as we have already described (Tables V and VII), and have been quite significant in the shares of labor and those of capital. The question arises as to whether one share has deviated in such a way as to strengthen the other deviation or to compensate for it. In other words, were these deviations a phenomenon significant for a country as a whole, or were they expressing conflicting influences in internal distribution of the GDP?

In Table VIII we have divided all countries into four groups according

[30] What was said for the labor share can be also extended to the capital share. See note 20.

to types of deviations. In the first group are the countries which have positive deviations of both labor and capital, i.e., those getting bigger shares than the general tendency indicated. Such countries were the Netherlands, Puerto Rico, Jamaica, etc., although in the case of the Netherlands the deviation of the labor share was just 0.9 per cent and that of capital 10.5 per cent. Nevertheless both show a deviation well above the general tendency, which might have different and conflicting causes (e.g., increase of labor wages, decline in the rural sector). Finland was in the same category and so were some less developed countries such as Malta, Rhodesia-Nyassa, and Taiwan.

Negative deviation for both capital and labor shares took place in some very developed countries such as Canada, New Zealand, Belgium, and Denmark as well as in some less developed ones like Uganda, Korea, or the Philippines.

Of particular interest are countries with opposing deviations. In the second group on our Table VIII are countries [grouped] in which the deviation of labor shares was below the general tendency level and those of capital formation above the general tendency level. This means that the share of labor has not reached the general level of the regression line of forty countries and that the share of capital overstepped it. Switzerland, Australia, Norway, Luxembourg, and Germany were among these countries in 1962.

The other group, which showed a share of capital below the general level and a share of labor above it, consisted of some very developed countries like the United States, Sweden, the United Kingdom; but this group also included Ceylon, Ecuador, and Honduras.

One should not draw hasty conclusions from these figures which indicate that, at the first approximation, such tendencies exist, and that detailed studies country-wide have to give further explanation to these observations.

6. THE THIRD GROUP

Our main concern in this study is with the shares of the employees and of capital formation in the gross domestic product. Therefore, we have put all other groups into one residual lump and named it the Third Group. This group is very heterogeneous: as we said before, it includes peasants and artisans, i.e., all independent owner-operators as well as those living on rent; the leisure classes as well as the consumption of capitalist entrepreneurs, small and big; and also the general government's

TABLE VIII

Percentage deviation of shares of labor and capital in 1962

Labor and Capital positive			Labor negative and Capital positive			Labor positive and Capital negative			Labor and Capital negative		
Country	L	C	Country	L	C	Country	L	C	Country	L	C
Netherlands	0.9	10.5	Switzerland	– 1.8	20.0	U.S.	7.05	–34.7	Canada	– 3.0	–10.0
Puerto Rico	15.2	13.8	Australia	– 3.1	5.5	Sweden	19.7	– 6.1	New Zealand	– 4.2	– 8.1
Finland	9.6	22.0	Norway	– 1.0	21.7	U.K.	20.4	–29.6	Denmark	– 6.0	–23.6
Jamaica	15.4	7.6	Luxemburg	– 9.4	6.7	Ireland	2.0	–18.5	Belgium	– 4.9	–16.7
Malta	14.5	13.7	Germany F.R.	– 3.9	11.7	Panama	33.7	– 6.2	Spain	– 2.3	– 0.4
Rhodesia-N.	24.5	18.1	France	– 8.9	30.6	Costa Rica	30.4	–13.0	Colombia	–28.2	– 4.2
Taiwan	6.6	28.7	Israel	– 3.8	34.2	Mauritius	23.8	– 4.4	Philippines	– 6.6	–21.1
			Austria	– 1.5	25.9	Honduras	42.6	–19.6	Korea	– 5.9	– 2.3
			Trinidad	–20.0	32.8	Ecuador	6.2	– 8.1	Uganda	– 9.5	–32.0
			Japan	– 5.3	85.7	Ceylon	13.6	–14.5			
			Argentina	– 3.3	10.9						
			Cyprus	–46.5	23.4						
			Greece	–18.6	22.1						
			Peru	– 8.4	21.7						

final consumption. In sum, it comprises domestic final consumption of all excluding the employees.[31]

This residual and heterogeneous character of the group prevents us from drawing more than some very limited conclusions in our analysis. The general tendency in the gross domestic product distribution is that the share of the Third Group decreases with economic development: the more developed the country, the smaller the share of the Third Group. In countries at the 100-dollar GDP per capita level, the differential share of the Third Group in 1953 was 49.95 per cent; at 1000 dollars 29.93 per cent, and at 2500 dollars only 19.89 per cent. The corresponding percentages for the year 1962 were 47.54, 28.80, and 19.57 (Table IV).

But as there is also a general tendency in the course of development to slow down the rate of increase of the shares of labor and capital alike, the result points toward a certain consolidation of the share of the Third Group in countries at a higher level of development. Both curves became less and less convex and lean toward a straight line with a span of some 20 per cent between them. This difference of percentages is the residuum between the lines of regression of Y_L and Y_K and represents the share of the Third Group (Chart I). In making this statement we must bear in mind the heterogeneous character of this group. It is likely that the income of owner-operators and other private consumers declines fast but that this decline is compensated for by the increase in the share of the general government's final consumption.

In connection with this observation we can say that the relative consolidation of the Third Group occurs at the higher level of development. Its changeability at lower levels indicates that the increase of both the labor and the capital shares in lower developmental levels occurs at the expense of the Third Group, while at the higher levels, where this group is more consolidated, the increase of the labor share becomes comple-

[31] There is a conceptual difference in the definition of the share of the employees and of capital formation. The former is an institutional and the latter a functional one, i.e., the sector of employees consists of incomes from wages and salaries only and does not represent total incomes of persons earning wages and salaries; it excludes the parts accruing from other activities such as independent activity, income from farming or rent, etc., but includes income which employees invest. This last item is also included in the sector of gross domestic capital formation so is counted double. As data for this specific item are not available, we had no choice but to leave this error in our model. The share of the Third Groups — a residual — would have to be increased by this amount. It would not be quite correct to interpret the share of the employees in the gross domestic product exclusively and totally as the share of the working class. Neither does the gross domestic capital formation stand for the accumulation of capital of the capitalist class. The general government's final consumption excludes income paid to its employees and gross domestic capital formation.

mentary to the decrease of the capital share, and vice versa. This observation makes the issues clearer and the confrontation simpler, but at the same time the mutual and complementary interdependence of shares becomes more evident than before. So far, the escape from this static

TABLE IX

Changes in the share of the group, 1953-1962
(in percentages of the Domestic Product)

Country	Labor	Cap. form.	III Group
United States	0.40	−0.03	−0.37
Switzerland	−1.50	8.72	−7.22
Canada	3.29	−1.93	−1.36
New Zealand	3.41	3.81	−7.22
Australia	1.42	−0.15	−1.27
Sweden	4.20	3.23	−8.43
Norway	3.68	0.19	−3.87
Luxemburg	0.35	1.58	−1.93
Denmark	2.03	0.66	−2.69
United Kingdom	3.98	2.40	−6.38
West Germany	3.65	5.11	−8.76
France	3.87	14.59	−18.46
Netherlands	7.22	8.51	−15.73
Belgium	5.84	4.08	−9.92
Israel	2.98	3.70	−6.68
Austria	−0.39	11.38	−10.99
Puerto Rico	−8.45	7.38	+1.07
Finland	1.01	−7.51	+6.50
Ireland	3.46	0.43	−3.99
Trinidad	−4.63	7.59	−2.96
Japan	4.22	10.37	−14.59
Argentina	−7.28	6.17	+1.11
Cyprus	−2.50	10.85	−8.35
Panama	1.89	7.78	−9.67
Jamaica	0.45	8.07	−8.52
Greece	7.58	8.26	−16.84
Spain	−4.13	1.49	−2.64
Malta	4.23	7.82	−12.05
Colombia	−1.11	2.73	−1.62
Costa Rica	3.44	−5.26	+1.82
Mauritius	−0.97	0.97	0.00
Honduras	13.75	0.53	−14.28
Ecuador	3.32	2.53	−5.85
Rhodesia-N.	13.21	−4.02	−9.19
Peru	6.93	−3.55	−3.38
Ceylon	0.07	3.56	−3.63
Philippines	−1.32	4.07	−2.75
Taiwan	1.85	4.37	−6.22
Korea	8.07	3.73	−11.80
Uganda	1.80	0.59	−2.39

confrontation has been to accelerate growth; the escape is operational only as long as acceleration is possible.

In the course of the decade 1953-1962, the general tendency of the Third Group's share to decline continued, showing a slightly smaller slope of the curve.

Table 9 shows how much the Third Group declined in the decade in particular countries.

We can divide all countries of our model into two main sets, one (including 34 countries) in which the Third Group's share decreased, and the second where it increased. The FIRST set, countries in which the share of the Third Group DECREASED and the shares of both capital and labor increased, we subdivided into two subsets according to which share increased more, that of capital or that of labor. In the third subset we put those countries where the capital share declined but the labor share increased, and in the fourth subset were grouped the countries where the labor share declined and the capital share increased.

The SECOND main set is comprised of countries where the share of the Third Group INCREASED; it too is subdivided into two subsets: one where the labor share declined and the other where the capital share declined.

Thus the following results were obtained: (Table IX).

Reasons for DECLINE of the share of the Third Group over the decade 1953-1962 (34 countries):

(a) There was a greater increase of the labor share than of the capital share (9 countries): Sweden, U.K., Australia, Belgium, Ireland, Trinidad, Honduras, Korea, Uganda.

(b) There was a greater increase of the capital than the labor share (14 countries): New Zealand, France, Germany, Netherlands, Norway, Luxemburg, Israel, Japan, Greece, Ecuador, Panama, Jamaica, Taiwan, Malta, Ceylon.

(c) There was an increase of the share of labor and a decrease of the share of capital formation (4 countries): United States, Canada, Peru, Rhodesia-Nyassa.

(d) There was a decline of the share of labor and an increase of the share of capital-formation (6 countries): Switzerland, Austria, Spain, Cyprus, Colombia, Philippines.

Reasons for INCREASE of the share of the Third Group over the decade in 6 countries out of forty:

(a) There was a decline of labor share in Finland, Argentina, Puerto Rico, and Mauritius.

(b) The capital share declined in Costa Rica only.

In some countries the decline in the share of the Third Group was so great that it represented a major structural change of wide implications. The countries where the decline was more than 8 per cent were the following: in Europe, France (−18.5), Netherlands (−15.7), Austria (−11), Belgium (−10), Germany (−8.8), Sweden (−8.4); in the Mediterranean they were Greece (−16.8), Cyprus and Malta; in Asia, Japan (−14.6), and Korea (−11.8); in Latin America, they were Honduras (−14.3), Panama, and Jamaica; in Africa, Rhodesia-Nyassa.[32]

7. DEVELOPMENTAL ELASTICITIES OF GDP SHARES

An analysis of the developmental elasticities will give further insight into the change of shares in the gross domestic product during economic development.

We are dealing here with developmental coefficients of elasticity of the shares of employees and of gross domestic capital formation in the gross domestic product. The coefficient of developmental elasticity indicates

[32] It is not the purpose of this empirical study to give theoretical explanations of why the shares of labor and capital formation change as they do. Nevertheless, empirical evidence is such that it contradicts some theories based on the constancy or on fixed proportions of the shares of labor or of capital. The P. Douglas theory of constancy of the labor share was based on empirical studies of some developed countries for which long-term series were available (U.S., Canada, Sweden, etc.). That the theory is not generally valid is evident when data for countries at various levels of development are introduced into analysis. Moreover, the validity of the theory can be questioned for highly developed countries even for such a short period as a decade.

Another more recent theory of constancy of shares is that of S. Lebergott. He maintains that the GDP shares to capital and to wages are constant because they are functional to the quantity and price ratios of these factors. ("Price of capital service must bear a constant long-term proportionality to that of labor.") This, according to the theory, applies to a competitive economy and assumes a neutral technical progress at constant rates and stable interest rates, both of which assume a constant capital coefficient. But if these assumptions do not hold, and they actually do not, then the whole theory of proportionality of the labor and capital shares cannot stand.

N. Kaldor's theory of three fixed proportions assumes a constancy in a steadily-growing economy, it is not valid since it cannot be proved that either the capital output ratio or the capital investment share is constant.

It seems to us that the GDP sharing cannot be explained by microeconomic behavior, the entrepreneur's endeavoring to keep the fixed proportion between his direct costs and prices of GDP shares. The main factors in sharing are significant structural changes in the process of development, disequilibria in labor demand and supply, and above all changes in the capital output ratios over a span of time. Finally, the organized capital market which economists would like to see operating does not exist in more than a dozen countries. The capital market is still more imperfect than the commodities market.

how much the shares of the GDP change as functions of the GDP per capita change at a certain point of economic development. This coefficient of elasticity is defined as a first derivation of our regression equations (Table X).

TABLE X

Developmental elasticities of labor and capital shares

GDP per capita	Coefficients of elasticity				Elasticity ratios		
X	$E_{L\ 53}$	$E_{L\ 62}$	$E_{K\ 53}$	$E_{K\ 62}$	$E_{L\ 62:53}$	$E_{K\ 62:53}$	Sum
50	0.09553	0.08263	0.03658	0.04398	0.865	1.202	2.067
100	0.05302	0.04499	0.02009	0.02448	0.849	1.219	2.067
500	0.01351	0.01096	0.00500	0.00628	0.811	1.257	2.069
1000	0.00750	0.00597	0.00274	0.00350	0.796	1.274	2.070
1500	0.00531	0.00418	0.00193	0.00248	0.787	1.284	2.071
2000	0.00416	0.00325	0.00151	0.00195	0.781	1.292	2.072
2500	0.00344	0.00267	0.00124	0.00161	0.776	1.297	2.073
3000	0.00295	0.00228	0.00106	0.00138	0.772	1.302	2.074

On the basis of these formulas we have computed the developmental elasticities of shares for different levels of growth.

Developmental Elasticities

$$E_{L62} = 2.56\ X^{-0.877}$$
$$E_{K62} = 1.20\ X^{-0.845}$$
$$E_{L53} = 2.65\ X^{-0.849}$$
$$E_{K53} = 1.08\ X^{-0.865}$$

The coefficients are small because the scales on the axis X and Y are so different. The variable X ranges from 1 to almost 3,000 while that of axis Y ends with 100.

In our analysis we shall examine:

(a) the overall developmental elasticities of the shares of labor and capital formation which represent the structural relationship. We consider that the elasticities depend on the institutional frame of the developmental process.

(b) changes that occur in elasticities of labor and capital formation shares at different levels of development.

(c) the comparison of changes of these elasticities over the decade 1953-1962.

(d) the distribution of these changes in elasticities over the range of countries at different levels of development.

Looking at the developmental elasticity coefficients, we can say that the labor shares show on the whole a comparatively greater elasticity than capital formation shares. The elasticity coefficients of the labor share were in 1962 greater than those of capital formation and varied between 0.082 and 0.002, while those of the capital formation share were much smaller, showing a span from 0.044 to 0.001 between the levels of the most and the least developed countries (Table X). The fact that the labor shares were, from the developmental point of view, more elastic by half than the capital formation shares contradicts the opinion of several economists. The employees' share of the gross domestic product reacts more strongly than that of capital formation to the change in the level of development. Or, in other words, the share of labor in the gross domestic product increases in the process of development faster than the share of capital formation.

The general tendency is that elasticity of both shares decreases in the course of development as we move from the less developed to the more developed countries. Countries at a lower level of development have a greater developmental elasticity coefficient than those at higher levels of development. In other words, the product distribution in the former is more subject than in the latter to the influence of the developmental variable, indicating a greater institutional stability (rigidity) in developed countries than in less developed ones.

The range of developmental elasticity of labor shares in the GDP is very wide, more elastic at low levels of development and very inelastic in the countries at a higher developmental level. The labor share for 1962 at the 50-dollar-per-capita level of development shows an elasticity coefficient of 0.0826 while that at the 2500-dollar level is negligible, 0.0027. A similar tendency exists with the elasticity of capital formation shares. Their elasticity at the lowest level of development is 0.0440, while at the high point of 2500 dollars it falls to the 0.0014 coefficient. (Table X, cols. 3 and 5.)

The difference in elasticity of the capital formation shares in the course of development demonstrates that the less developed countries are more dependent than the more developed ones on the developmental variable in changes of capital formation. The latter have a more rigid share of capital formation.

Comparing both elasticity coefficients, we come to the conclusion that at all levels of development the labor share is more elastic than the capital share (elasticity from ratio 1.88 to 1.65, Table V).[33] In other words, structural changes in the gross product distribution depend on development; this dependence is more pronounced in the changes of the share of employees than in the share of capital formation. Development works more in favor of the increase of the labor share than of the capital share of the GDP.

The picture changes when we proceed to the analysis of the developmental elasticities over the decade 1953-1962. The decennial change in the developmental elasticity of the labor share was downward, i.e., their overall elasticity was greater in 1953 than in 1962. The share of labor became less elastic over the decade, i.e., more rigid on the whole, and responded less flexibly to the developmental variable. At the lowest level of development the decennial ratio of elasticity coefficients moved from 0.095 to 0.082 (ratio 0.87) and on the highest level from 0.003 to 0.002 (ratio 0.077). In the course of this decade the share of labor in the GDP became less dependent on economic development, which is the same as saying that labor was in a position to get a progressively smaller part of the GDP.

The share of capital formation showed the opposite course in the decennial change of developmental elasticity. Here the elasticity increased considerably over the decade in countries at all levels of development. Shares which capital formation took from the GDP became more dependent on the level of development at the end of the decade than they were in the beginning.

The ratio of the annual elasticity coefficients for 1962 and 1953 is as follows (Table V):

[33] The contention that the labor share of the GDP is less elastic than the capital share cannot be confirmed as a general tendency by our evidence. On the contrary, our evidence shows that it is considerably more elastic than the capital share in the process of development. Moreover, in the labor share the income of government employees is included, which certainly represents a more inelastic element than the labor force in the business sector, which therefore has to be considered still more elastic. This can explain the preponderance of growth movement over cyclical changes. But the fact that over the decade of prosperity the capital share has increased and the labor share decreased supports the theory of anti-cyclical changes in the labor share and the amplifying cyclical movements in the capital formation ones. (B. Kravis, T. Scitovsky, S. Goldberg).

It is also likely that there is an effective lag in the share of the employees both during the prosperity stage and in the period of inflationary pressure, as stated by Phelps Brown. In this case one should have expected the increased pressure by workers' organizations to eliminate the lag in the subsequent period which materialized after 1962. On the other hand, this lag is counteracted by the character of the shares; the labor share has an immediate effect on the market of consumer goods while the capital formation share primarily influences the capital market goods.

$$r_L = \frac{e_{L\,62}}{e_{L\,53}} = \frac{2.55\ x^{-0.88}}{2.67\ x_{-0.85}} = 0.96\ x^{-0.032}$$

$$r_K = \frac{e_{K\,62}}{e_{K\,53}} = \frac{1.196\ x^{-0.85}}{0.918\ x^{-0.91}} = 1.31\ x^{0.016}$$

The ratio in the case of labor is close to 1, which means practically no change, but the changes in the labor share elasticity diminished more as the level of development increased. The exponent over x is negative and very small.

The capital formation shares increased their overall elasticity during the decade. Although the exponent is very small, it is positive and twice as large as that of labor shares. The ratio of capital share elasticities increases with development. The exponent over x is positive (+0.016). This again proves that during the decade the labor shares in the GDP have become less elastic and less dependent on the developmental process, while the capital formation shares have become considerably more elastic and more influenced by the developmental process.

The developmental elasticities of the shares of labor and capital formation in the GDP are demonstrated in the chart showing their change on a log-log line. This chart (No. II) shows the movement over the decade of the labor share toward less elasticity, and the movement of the capital formation share toward more elasticity. The movements came close together.

Thus the decennial trend worked against the general tendency. The share of labor, which is generally more elastic in relation to development than the share of capital formation, became less elastic. And the share of capital formation, which is generally less elastic than the share of labor, became more elastic. All four lines run almost parallel on the log-log line.

Can we draw from this the conclusion that the change in both shares is becoming subject to similar tendencies or that both shares are moving toward each other under the influence of the same developmental forces? At the moment it would be premature to make any forecasts.[34] The change in the elasticity ratios increased. This increase was not equally spread over the forty countries of our sample. The developmental elasticity

[34] The available data for international comparison in the *YNAS* do not yet give sufficient information about why the developmental coefficients of both shares, labor and capital formation, change. Nevertheless, there is enough material for some interpretation.

coefficients became greater (the capital formation more elastic) in the course of the decade in the more developed countries than in the less developed ones. Or, in simple terms, developed countries spent more on domestic capital formation in 1962 than in 1953. The less developed ones also spent more but not as much more as the developed ones. The capital formation of the more developed countries made greater gain from development in the decade 1953-1962 than that of countries at a lower level of development.

The decennial movement shows that the labor share is less elastic than that of the share of capital formation. While the first can be considered as proved, the second is our hypothesis based on the movements in 1962 compared with 1953.

The year 1962 was, in the world economy, a year of great expansion in accordance with which rates of elasticity of the capital formation share rose from 1.67 to 2.18, if 1953 is taken as 1. The ratio of the developmental elasticity coefficient of the labor share, on the other hand, declined from 1 (in 1953) to 0.79, and further down to 0.68, according to the level of development, for the year 1962.

The general tendency of the developmental elasticity of the labor share to be subject to a smaller change, i.e., more rigid the more developed the country, seems to confirm the view that cyclical changes influence the labor share in less developed countries more than they do in the relatively developed ones.

The opposite is demonstrated when changes in the elasticity of the capital share over the decade are analyzed. Here, the change is greater on the upper level of development and less pronounced on the lower level, a fact which could be explained by a greater cyclical influence of the process of development on capital formation at higher growth levels. We are not assuming here that phases of cyclical movements spread simultaneously all over the world. We are simply stating what changes take place according to the results of the cross-section analysis.

APPENDIX: GAIN FROM GROWTH AND GAIN FROM DISTRIBUTION

An attempt is made here to measure gain from growth and gain from distribution by a specific method.

Gains from growth in our research will here be measured by units of the area under the curves obtained by regression equations showing the share of labor and the share of capital formation in the GDP of 40

TABLE XI

Developmental elasticity of shares of labor in the GDP in the decade 1953-1962

Positive		Negative	
Very elastic	Little elastic	Little elastic	Very elastic
$l_L > 1$	$1 < l_L > 0$	$-1 > l_L < 0$	$-1 > l_L$
Costa Rica	U.S.	Switzerland	Uganda*
Honduras	Canada	Austria	
Ecuador	New Zealand	Trinidad	
Rhodesia-Nyassa	Australia	Puerto Rico	
Peru	Sweden	Philippines	
Korea	Norway	Argentina	
	Luxemburg	Mauritius	
	Denmark	Cyprus	
	U.K.	Spain	
	Germany	Colombia	
	France		
	Netherlands		
	Belgium		
	Israel		
	Finland		
	Ireland		
	Japan		
	Panama		
	Jamaica		
	Greece		
	Malta		
	Ceylon		
	Taiwan		

* Decline in the GDP; increase in the labor share.

CHART II Labor gain (P_L)

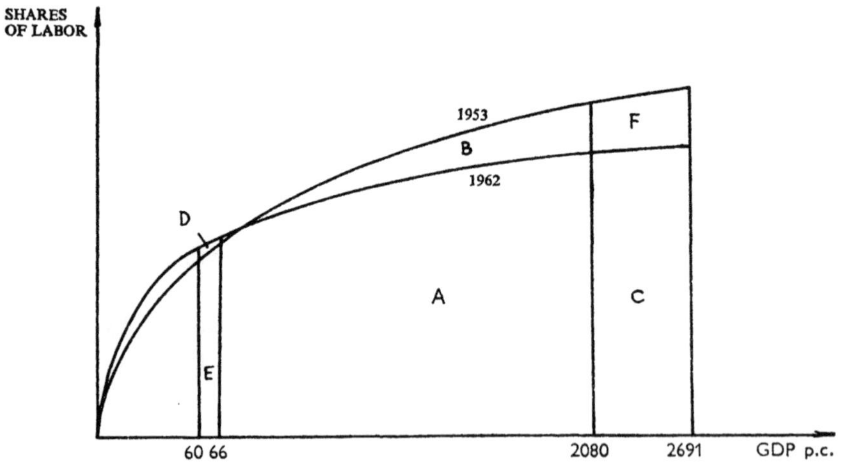

countries. Computed integrals of the curve will be called SHARE VALUES OF GDP. The units of measurement will be SHARE UNIT OF GROWTH (SUG), which will have the dimensions Y, Y_L or Y_K and H, where Y stands for gross domestic product, Y_L and Y_K for shares of labor and capital formation in terms of money, and H for the number of inhabitants of each country.

CHART III CAPITAL FORMATION GAIN (P_K)

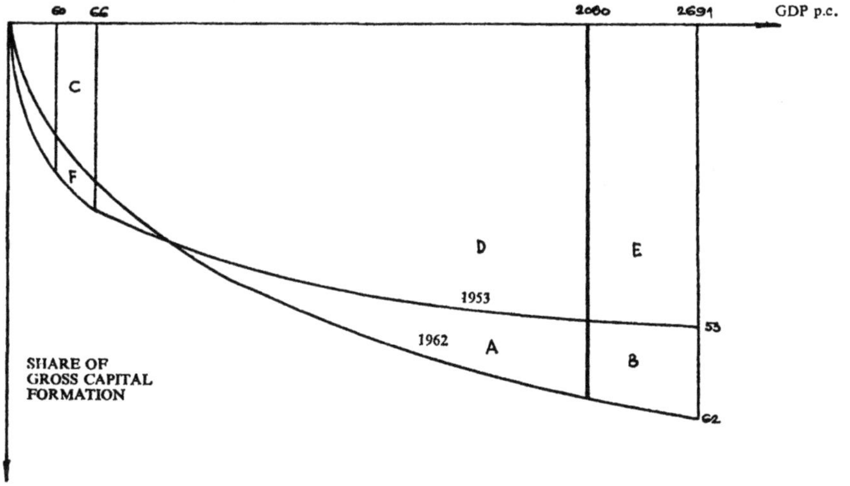

There will be three kinds of gain:

(a) TOTAL EFFECTIVE GAIN FROM GROWTH, obtained by computing the difference between the 1953 and the 1962 curves within the corresponding initial and end countries;

(b) GAIN FROM GROWTH, representing the gain which is derived from growth under condition that there is no change in distribution (i.e. in shares), only changes in values of x;

(c) GAIN FROM DISTRIBUTION, which represents the difference between the areas under corresponding 1953 and 1962 curves. Gain from distribution will be that part of gain which results from changes in the shares of growth. This represents gain under the assumption that the values of x have not changed, but only the values of y.

i = smallest value, e = largest value of the GDP p.a. of 40 countries.

$$P_{L62} = \int_i^e Y_{L62}\, dx = 20.82 \frac{1}{1.123}\, x^{1.123} \Big/_{60}^{2691} = 129.950$$

$$P_{L53} = \int_i^e Y_{L53}\, dx = 17.61 \frac{1}{1.151}\, x^{1.151} \Big/_{66}^{2080} = 98.970$$

$A = 18.540\,(2080^{1.123} - 66^{1.123}) = 96.642$
$B = 15.300\,(2080^{1.151} - 66^{1.151}) = 98.972$
$C = 18.540\,(2691^{1.123} - 2080^{1.123}) = 33.103$
$D = 18.540\,(66^{1.123} - 60^{1.123}) = 208$
$E = 15.300\,(66^{1.151} - 60^{1.151}) = 198$
$F = 15.300\,(2691^{1.151} - 2080^{1.151}) = 34.802$

$$P_{K62} = \int_i^e Y_{K62}\,dx = 7.75\ x^{\,0.155} = 7.75 \frac{1}{1.155}\ x^{\,1.155} \Big/_{60}^{2691} =$$

$$= 6.71\ x^{\,1.155} \Big/_{60}^{2691} = 60.650$$

$$P_{K53} = \int_i^e Y_{K53}\,dx = 7.00\ x^{\,1.135} \Big/_{66}^{2080} = 40.020$$

$A = 44.764$
$B = 15.802$
$C = 88$
$D = 40.016$
$E = 13.913$
$F = 83$

TABLE XII

Developmental elasticity of shares of GD capital formation in the decade 1953-1962

Positive		Negative	
Very elastic	Little elastic	Little elastic	Very elastic
$l_K > 1$	$1 < l_K > 0$	$-1 > l_K < 0$	$-1 > l_K$
Argentina	U.S.	Canada	Costa Rica
Panama	Switzerland	Denmark	Rhodesia-Nyassa
Malta	New Zealand	Finland	Uganda
Cyprus	Australia	Spain	
Ceylon	Sweden	Peru	
Philippines	Norway		
Taiwan	Luxemburg		
Korea	Denmark		
	U.K.		
	Germany		
	France		
	Netherlands		
	Belgium		
	Israel		
	Austria		
	Puerto Rico		
	Ireland		
	Trinidad		
	Japan		
	Jamaica		

Two more terms will be introduced:

EFFECTIVE GAIN, that is, the gain that has actually materialized in results (*lucrum emergens*);

POTENTIAL GAIN, that is, the gain which would have occurred under given exponents if growth had been extended beyond the actual limit, but which has not actually occurred (*lucrum cessans*).

The actual figures obtained are the following:

TABLE XIII

Total gain from growth (in SUG units)

	L	K	Total
1. Share value of GDP in 1953	98,970	40,020	138,990
Percentage	71.2	28.8	100.0
2. Share value of GDP in 1962	129,950	60,650	190,600
Percentage	68.2	31.8	100.0
3. Total effective growth gain	30,980	20,630	51,610
4. Percentage of gain	31.0	51.5	37.1
5. Gain from growth	33,310	14,000	47,310
6. %	33.4	35.0	34.0
7. Gain from distribution	2,330	6,630	4,300
8. %	2.4	16.5	3.1
9. Potential loss because of distribution	1,700		
10. Relation between growth gain and distribution gain	8:(−1)	2:1	11:1

Gain from total growth of labor share was obtained mainly in countries with a higher level of development and amounted to 33,400 SUG-s or one third of the 1953 SUG value of the labor share. Effective growth amounted to 30,980 SUG units, but this was offset by the negative movement in distribution gain (−2.330 of labor). There was also a potential loss of 1,700 SUG units by labor representing the amount they would have received had their distribution rate remained unchanged.

The relationship between gain from total growth, and effective and potential negative growth (loss) from distribution showed an 8:(−1) ratio. This shows that LABOR HAD 8 TIMES GREATER INCREASE OF GAIN FROM GROWTH THAN LOSS FROM DISTRIBUTION (Table XIII, column L).

Gross capital formation in the GDP had a total effective gain of 20,630 SUG units.[35] In 1962 this represented a 51.5 per cent gain over 1953. This gain was derived from both sources, i.e. GAIN FROM GROWTH AND GAIN FROM DISTRIBUTION (Table XIII, column K). This increase, too,

[35] We wish to stress again that we are dealing here with the gross capital formation in real terms and not with the income or share of the capitalist class or with its saving.

was due mainly to the large increase of the GDP in the higher growth range countries. The extension in the lower side is almost insignificant.

The SUG value of gross capital formation in 1962, gained from growth, was 35 per cent more than in 1953. The gain from distribution was positive also, and amounted to one half of the gain from growth (16.5 per cent). Thus capital formation gained also from change in distribution, and was four times less than labor (8:2) interested in growth as it was in distribution.

Indeed, a comparison between the gains of labor and of capital formation brings us to some significant conclusions.

The total effective gain from growth amounted to a much higher percentage (51.5:31.0) for capital formation than for labor. In other words, the behavior of capital formation brought a considerably greater total effective gain from growth expressed in relative terms than the behavior of labor (Table XIII, ads. 3 and 4).

In absolute values of SUG units, labor's gain was greater than that of capital formation (3:2, Table XIII, row 3). This was due much more to the gain from growth than it was to the gain from distribution (2.4:1.0, Table XIII, rows 5 and 6). Speaking in absolute terms, labor managed to increase its share more than capital formation did by 10,350 SUG units. In relative terms, however, they kept the same percentage of their SUG values, which means that their behavior brought both sides a relatively equal gain from growth (33.4 and 35.0 per cent).

The gain from distribution showed a different picture. Labor gained considerably more from growth than it lost from changes in distribution (8:1). Capital formation was in a different position. It gained comparatively four times more from distribution than it did from growth when compared to labor.

From this, we can draw four conclusions as to the tendencies of GDP distribution: (a) that the behavior of capital formation was much more effective in gains than distribution from labor; (b) that labor showed the opposite tendency. It was much more effective in obtaining gains from growth than from distribution.[36] The relationship can be expressed as 16.5:(−2.4) per cent.

(c) An almost equal proportion of gain from growth is still kept between the two elements. Can it perhaps be explained by a policy of equilibrium in sharing the fruits of growth? It remains to be answered

[36] This could perhaps be an explanation of the changed attitude of the Italian, French and British trade union movements towards growth policies and planning in the 1960's, from a negative to a positive approach.

why the gains from growth have kept in proportion and capital formation transferred gain from labor (2,400 SUG units) and also from the Third Group (4,200 SUG units). Are there long-term reasons of developmental change behind this, greater requirements of capital for growth, or political reasons of pressure groups? Or are they caused by some short term factors (different cyclical phases)?

(d) Finally, we have to link growth of the GDP to the share of the GDP which went to capital formation, which will also show the effect of capital formation on growth of the GDP. This can be measured by a kind of marginal capital coefficient, stating the ratio between growth of the GDP and increase in the capital formation of the first and last years of the decade. The ratio is 3:1, which can be generally accepted, although it is a little too high for a marginal capital coefficient.[37]

One has to bear in mind that the proportionate rate of capital formation does not mean a proportionate rate of growth. Capital formed not only increases in mass but also in quality, i.e. in the change in its longevity, in alterations in the capital mix towards more productive sectors carrying more weight and, above all, in technological progress. All this makes the economy grow faster than would be proportionate to the capital formed. The capital coefficient is not constant, but becomes more productive in the course of development.

[37] Total increase of the GDP in SUG units is $(X_2\text{-}X_1)$. 100 = 61,700. Capital formation grew by 20,630. The specific marginal capital coefficient was therefore 2.98.

V

HOW NOT TO DEVELOP A COUNTRY: AN ESSAY IN ECONOMIC PATHOLOGY

There have been many policies for economic development[1] made by many people for many countries. In such an affluent situation we have undertaken a rather different approach and set ourselves the task of studying how not to develop a country. Not only is this not quite so negative as it might seem at first, but we hope that it may also produce some positive conclusions.

We are more concerned here with the PROCESS of development than with its preconditions or final objectives.

Assuming that development is a 'good thing'[2] and that the rulers of a country have decided to undertake developmental action, how does the process run? Based on the experience of a number of countries we would venture to generalize and condense it into the following stages on the economic policy level:

(a) The economics of Overlord;
(b) The economics of Overstrain;
(c) The economics of Underground;
(d) The economics of Overchange.

[1] We propose to distinguish these related macroeconomic terms; ECONOMIC GROWTH is usually defined as increase of real output, or real income aggregate or per head over a period of time. Though generally accepted this is not very satisfactory. We would prefer to consider it as an increase in the capacity to produce, i.e. increase in capital of which national income per head is only one external measurement. Thus we would introduce three-dimensional growth: growth in height, or increase of real capital per head; growth in width or increase of economic interdependence; and growth in depth, or increase in the quality of capital. We would define economic development as ECONOMIC GROWTH by conscious, human action, directed from one level to another, higher level of equilibrium (or quasi equilibrium) by autonomous means. The former is a concept of general economics, while the latter is a term of economic policy. Cf. R. Bićanić, "Economic Growth Development and Planning in Socialist Countries", in: E. Nelson (ed.), *Economic Growth, Rationale, Problems, Cases* (Univ. of Texas Press, 1960), p. 171.

[2] For controversial approaches to growth see UNESCO *Report of the Expert Working Group on Social Prerequisites to Economic Growth* (1963), p. 171.

All these four stages show the pathological side of development and could be called the 'black cycle' of developmental policy.

At first development is a Mission. The rulers are overwhelmed with the epics of their program of Developmental Action. We call this period of economic policy the ECONOMICS OF OVERLORD.

The second stage starts when the strain of development begins to be felt and serious problems to accumulate. Development is now no longer a mission but a Profession. This we call the ECONOMICS OF OVERSTRAIN.

When the strain of the policy of development becomes too great there is a reaction at many points among the population, and people try to satisfy their wants by other means. Now the policy of development has become a policy of pressure. This stage we call THE ECONOMICS OF UNDERGROUND.

Finally a stage begins where the developmental policy has run down to such an extent that a new concept of policy is necessary, as a result of which everything is expected to change. This new approach we call THE ECONOMICS OF OVERCHANGE.

At this stage the 'black cycle' is complete. Does it begin anew and repeat itself? Or does it take a new path? It is difficult to generalize. In any case this developmental cycle gives us enough material to contribute a fragment to a more general theory of development process.

We shall describe the policies followed in these stages, for though they sometimes escape the attention of the theorists and model makers of development, they are a constant worry to practical men, sometimes even reducing them to despair in the daily life of their developmental activity. Our description will follow the simplest economic model of action[3] consisting of aims, actors, instruments and environment.

1. THE ECONOMICS OF OVERLORD

The actors in this developmental policy are the political rulers of the country. Fascinated by their overwhelming and heroic task, they are impelled to develop their country according to the best they know, and to proclaim the highest of intentions. For this end they demand perfect obedience from the subjects concerned, and either formally or *de facto* introduce an authoritarian regime for the benefit of the people. The people's life must be changed, but the risks and difficulties of changing an entire way of life, "new, innovating and opposed in some way to

[3] J. Tinbergen, *Economic Policy, Principles and Design*, pp. 6-24.

existing social norms or approved forms of behaviour",[4] without alternative choice or reinsurance, are not taken into account by the Developers who, if their plan is resisted, call the people conservative.

So that Development may be securely under the control of the Developers a social mechanism has to be introduced or at least streamlined — a centralized, administrative and bureaucratic mechanism, led by politicians and based on experts. The more centralized it is, the more efficient it is supposed to be. But these experts may well be conservative technocrats, as so many experts are, believing in the unquestionable superiority of their own special art, though more in the imitative than in the creative side of it. If native experts are lacking or are inexperienced, or if their ideas of how to develop their country differ from those of the politicians with regard to aims, instruments and tempo, then such experts are regarded as a brake on Development, and foreign experts who command more initial respect are called in to help the Overlords. These experts are expected to be a miraculous composition of the genius, the ascetic and the apostle, all at the same time, while they may well be just second-best men whom their own country can spare to send out to develop a foreign country. After many useless efforts to persuade the Overlords to take what they consider to be rational action, they acquiesce, working conscientiously from 9 a.m. to 5 p.m. applying the best experience of their own country to a foreign environment, with a break for tea twice a day or for coffee several times a day. No wonder misunderstandings soon arise on both sides.

In order to remove many-sided opposition to Development a monopoly of authority has to be created which will assure success. In order to ensure that the chosen project will appear the best one, people who have different projects will have to be silenced, and a monopoly of information created, followed by a monopoly of education and supported by an extensive interpretation of the concept of state secrets.

To insure the best allocation of resources as the central developers see it, technical, economic and locational rules have to be replaced by a monopoly of decision-making, subordinating to it the technical preparation and calculations of projects. Such authoritarian and centralistic decision-making is bound to become voluntaristic.

The magnitude and grandeur of the task is supposed to justify all

[4] B. Hoselitz, "Economic Growth and Development", *American Economic Review* (1956), Suppl. p. 37. "Sociological Approach to Economic Development" (Milano, Centro nazionale di Prevenzione e difese sociale, Atti del Congresso Internazionale di studi sul Problema delle Aree Arretirate, 1955, pp. 755-778).

measures, excuse all errors and provide benefits for all in the end. The Developers know best — like the eighteenth-century monarchs — that what is good for Development is also good for the people, and here the technocrats and bureaucrats agree with the politocrats about this general motor of growth.

The aims of Development are left pretty vague. Nothing less is required than the maximum developmental growth of everything in the minimum time. This slogan, so appealing to politicians, is readily taken up by bureaucrats, for whom to maximize means to stop thinking, just to follow 'the line' to the maximum instead of trying to find out where the optimum may be; optimization calls for judgment, risk and responsibility which every good bureaucrat abhors. That the difference between maximum development and optimum growth consists, in fact, of effective waste does not occur to the Developers at this stage of development.

Developmental maximization in Overlord economics is based on the following assumptions:

(a) unlimited demand for capital goods, which means a high positive income elasticity of demand for capital goods,
(b) an unlimited supply of labor, and a high income elasticity of demand of labor (The paradoxical situation is solved by making the life of the peasants more difficult than that of proletarianized labor.),
(c) an unlimited demand for consumer goods which means a high income elasticity of demand for such goods. This means that ever greater numbers of groups of consumer goods acquire high elasticity coefficients like luxury goods. Even demand for modest consumer goods (i.e. for textiles) reaches a big income coefficient of elasticity (e.g. 2 or 3 for cotton goods).

The model of such development is not quite consistent but it is hoped to achieve consistency by stirring popular *elan* and official enthusiasm.

The means to achieve such a policy are as great an accumulation as possible of all resources which the government may be able to lay hands on for Development. This may in some fields, in fact, go so far as to represent disinvestment and reduction of personal consumption as a form of sacrifice for Development. On the other hand it will leave out saving, which the central administration is not able to accomplish. It also means deflection of many resources from places where they could be utilized with better effect for economic growth than when taken for the central Development scheme.

Development being the domineering priority, current production tends to be neglected — there is lack of maintenance and replacement of fixed capital, a shortage of spare parts and a deficiency of raw materials and fuel. This is particularly the case in economic activities with a heavy capital coefficient which 'can wait', such as agriculture, transport and housing. Therefore local, current production may supply for Development less than the expected means, making necessary increasing reliance on foreign aid. Foreign aid is preferred for use, for it comes in concentrated quantities to the central government, it can be used for purchases abroad, and it does not have to be paid for, at least at the moment.

Maximization of development also requires that the developmental policy should become the only mobilizing factor in society. All means must be mobilized for the 'big push forward' or the 'great leap ahead', and whatever is not part of this plan for Development is considered useless and must be dropped. A great expectation of social gains is projected into the Future. The cost-benefit relationship is neglected — who would bother about such shopkeeper's preoccupations in the Great Design!

When only modest results are attained in Development then 'conspicuous production' is introduced[5] — showpieces of what things will look like in the end. These not only have a propaganda value, but also a cumulative self-deceptive effect. The symbolical meaning of some favorite top-priority project is taken as representative of total Development, while in fact it is just an economic oasis.

Statistical reports become substitutes for real progress. Statistics are the opium of the Developers. The economics of growth soon turn into the logistics of reporting. To be safe one has to find out what the Overlords would like to hear and report accordingly. This has a cumulative effect of self-persuasion, because in the course of time all begin to believe in such reports, until a crisis brings them down to the ground — or to the underground.

2. THE ECONOMICS OF OVERSTRAIN

The economics of Overlord lead to the economics of Overstrain. In this stage of development the actors, the aims and the instruments are the same. But they have all become somewhat ineffective because the environment has been transformed into a network of bottlenecks. Thus the

[5] The term 'conspicuous production' served me well to describe investments for the purpose of investment only, or investment in order to make an impression on the population. R. Aron, ed. *Colloques de Rheinfelden* (Paris, 1960), p. 148.

fascination of Creation has been turned into the routine of the machine.

The pressure caused by the voluntaristic policy of unlimited development has created bottlenecks everywhere, which means inelasticities between various sectors and within one and the same sector. The determinates of growth have remained the same but the parameters of behavior have changed; the set of equations is the same but the values aiming at equilibrium differ greatly from those expected — if, indeed, the system of equations is at all soluble.

The policy of least resistance appears to be to concentrate all the attention of the actors and instruments on the development of propulsive sectors, leaving everything else aside, and to strengthen this policy through isolating each sector from the other by firm institutional frames to increase pressure, which prevents multipliers from operating. This makes the strain still greater and turns it into overstrain.

We now have a situation in which new problems emerge while the old ones have not been solved. Thus the policy begins to look like that of digging holes one by one to put into them the earth left from previously dug holes.

To the problems of a dual economy which has both traditional, stagnant and new, developing sectors, fresh divisions now appear within the developing sector itself. Under the strain of unlimited growth it splits into two or even more sectors. In one of such sectors the elasticity is high, and in the other it is low. In this short essay we cannot do more than enumerate the forms which this splitting may take: The labor sector is split between skilled and unskilled; demand for goods into demand for consumer goods and demand for capital goods; over-capitalization in one sector, undersupply of capital in the other; inflation here, deflation there; exports moving differently from imports; waste in the middle of poverty, growth and decay in the same sector at the same time.

The strains so created, unnoticeable or underestimated in the early developmental *élan*, begin to be felt to an ever increasing degree; inspiration turns into perspiration. The first sector where this strain usually becomes obvious is that of labor. Once the infrastructure has been built with an unlimited amount of unskilled labor (welcomed in some socialist countries because of the ideological urge to create a working class), there is less demand for unskilled labor and increasing need for skilled. Thus the tension: underemployment in the sector of unskilled labor, and shortage in the skilled labor sector, particularly of trained experts — a high elasticity of demand for skilled workers and a low elasticity of demand for unskilled even turning negative but still low in absolute terms. This problem leads almost to a freezing of the division between the two sectors of labor. The situation is aggravated by agricultural underemployment, and the attempt to solve the latter creates overemployment either in industry or, more often, in public administration; the pressure of agricultural underemployment leads to a transfer of population.[6]

The second strain to be felt is that of the inelasticity of demand for consumer goods, and growing elasticity of demand for capital goods. Demand for consumer goods is compressed more and more until it approaches the point of IRREDUCIBLE demand where the elasticity approaches zero. This leads to a consumers' revolt which strains the whole social fabric until it ultimately bursts at the seams.[7] On the other hand demand for capital goods approaches the saturation point, which means that the demand for capital goods approaches infinite elasticity in monetary terms. The demand transgresses the volume of physical production and also that of the receptivity of the economy for further capital goods for a period of time (length of the gestation period, bottlenecks, etc.).

There are two more points of constriction here. The first is overcapitalization in one sector and undersupply of capital in the other. The second is inflation in the investment sector and deflation in other sectors. The economics of Overlord cause overstrain in the investment sector. Some obvious examples of the tendency to maximal investment overreaching optimal investment are: the construction of industry for conspicuous production; making of products which no one will buy of their own free will or which are double or more the price of imported goods; industries built in places where there are no raw materials; railways which do not have enough goods to transport to use their capacity; purchase of expensive agricultural machinery which nobody uses, etc.

On the other hand there is undersupply of capital, where just a small investment would give realization to great capacities to produce. These small investments are not made because the decision makers, centralized in agencies dealing with investment, do not care about such 'trifles' and

[6] The opinion expressed by some economists that growth increases by transferring population from the agricultural sector to that of industrial industries is almost naive, as it assumes the existence of an unlimited supply of capital in a true neo-classical way. The problem lies not in transfer of population, but in shortage of capital for such a transfer.

[7] One has to remember the consumer revolt in Western Europe in the late 1940's and those in Eastern Europe in 1956. In both cases government policies favored consumption increase after the crisis.

the people on the spot have no means at their disposal, their means having been taken away from them by compulsory saving at the Center.[8]

Thus cross-elasticities of demand are great while the supply is made inelastic by institutional factors (another sector, another branch of industry which is not given administratively high enough priority by the Developers, etc.).

An overambitious investment program necessarily leads to inflation. As it is easier to supply money than provide physical investment goods there is a tendency to identify real capital formation with monetary expenditure in investment projects. An inflationary gap is the obvious result, making the prices of capital goods soar while consumer goods follow at a slower pace. There are other consequences of overinvestment: The range of priorities is greatly upset, changing the optimum level, and the period of gestation is prolonged thus leaving a greater part of the volume of investments frozen for a period of time. Thus we arrive at the paradox: had we spent less we could have built more.[9]

Overstrain of development aggravates the balance of payments, since the export sector and the import sector behave differently under the strain, which also deteriorates their terms of trade.

The utility of imported capital goods is in fact evaluated in Development programs at its total use value (in the T. Barna sense).[10] The comparative market prices of such goods are difficult to establish. The Developers, eager to develop fast, are willing to pay higher prices than usual.

On the other hand exports are considered to have the function of earners of foreign currency to pay for the import of capital goods. Therefore the mass of currency earned matters more than the level of the market price of homogeneous raw materials and agricultural products, and there is underselling. This different bargaining position for imports and exports leads to all sorts of pressures, ending in an increase in price for imported goods and a decline in price of exported goods. The greater the developmental strain inside the country the faster the movement in opposite directions.

[8] There is so far no book which has better described the implications of centralized planning than J. Kornai, *Overcentralization in Economic Organization* (Oxford University Press, 1959).

[9] Cf. R. Bićanić, "Economic Growth under Centralized and Decentralized Planning", *Economic Development and Cultural Change*, No. 1 (1957), pp. 69-70.

[10] For the full cost concept of T. Barna's see *Journal of Statistical Society*, CXL (1952).

3. THE ECONOMICS OF THE UNDERGROUND

The economics of Overstrain leads in turn to the economics of the Underground.[11] Underground economics develop when aims (wants) are covered by other than legal means, by non-institutionalized actors acting in non-transparent conditions in the same environment in which overground activity is taking place.

The strain is such that interdependence withers and the bounds of legality snap. The continuous economic process can no longer stand the monopolistic control of goods and services. Contacts are established between customers and sellers in an illegal way by piercing the legal and institutional barriers which the economics of Overstrain have set up. This is done in order to ease the strain and establish direct contact, making the economy to a certain extent interdependent again.

The economics of the Underground are the economics of disintegration; the actors act in their self-interest, but the 'elite' is rather debased and no social objectives are set or redefined. Such economics lead to blocking development and to the deflection of economic growth into other channels. These deviations occur when overstrain pushes economic activity with such intensity that in order to satisfy its accepted wants it breaks the existing developmental legal and institutional frame. The contradictions between the official developmental policy and the activities of different social groups is a symptom of disorganization of Developmental institutions, a lack of a consensus of values, whose extent is measured by the failure of different members of the society to have a common understanding of the Developmental issues. The greater the pull between the developmental policy and the interests of different social groups, the greater the disregard for risk and personal integrity; the result is a general confusion of values, involving wilfulness, arbitrariness, violation and crime.[12]

If the strain becomes so great that the developmental tasks cannot be fulfilled by 'normal' efforts, and if people are forced to fulfill the targets of Development, the frontier between what is permitted and what is illicit becomes so blurred that even what would normally be within people's capacity is no longer feasable. Official bottlenecks are broken by self-help, be it by circumventing, avoiding, or breaking the law. Developmental activity may be generally accepted, and given public lip-

[11] The term was first used by S. J. Kurovski in his article "The Model and the Aims of the National Economy", *Zycie gospodarcze*, No. 7 (Warsaw, 1957).

[12] B. Hoselitz, *op. cit.*, pp. 37-40.

service, but in private self-help is practiced and not considered defamatory.

These underground economics are the black or grey counterpart to F. Pérroux's economics of pressure, gift and exchange. Action is motivated by formalization and deinstitutionalization of conflict-cooperation exchange.[13]

Thus the economics of the Underground assume the existence of two kinds of economic activity — one normative, formalized and institutionalized, the other actual, deinstitutionalized, fluid.

The law no longer has the meaning of general will. Its significance is relative and obedience selective. Everything can be done at a price, provided one is not caught by the law enforcers. Developmental policy started by upsetting the then existing traditional set of social values, and now the developmental policy itself has to meet the reaction of social groups to the set of values that it has established. There are two different phenomena — one based on an old and the other on a new set of values — which sometimes, but not necessarily, combine.

This also occurs when the developers have been given common consent at the beginning of their action, or credit by expectation or through fear, and then the Development policy began to create a feeling of frustration among social groups, or even among factions of the Developers themselves. There are three main causes for such situations: (a) groups of the population or the general public may disapprove of the aims of development because of opposed interests, lack of information, or lack of time for adjustment; (b) some social groups may not trust the actors, their ability or their honesty; (c) the means of the Developmental policy may not be considered effective enough to attain the aims of development, or may be impossible to carry out, i.e. sacrifices are out of proportion to gains.

The economics of the Underground are based on those sectors isolated by the economics of Overstrain which are further split into narrow sections within each of the different sectors, and individualized into isolated markets or service mechanisms. In fact there are in the same environment numerous isolated markets: two markets for each commodity under pressure, superimposed upon each other but each with a different group of actors and different instruments of action (price formation, technique of trading, time and size of market, etc.). Contact is non-transparent (secret, illegal), limited to packets of small quantities of readily divisible goods and services, and a small number of customers for each operation;

[13] F. Pérroux, *Economie et Société* (Paris, 1960), pp. 13-16, 83-96.

thus the black market has a highly monopolistic or monopsonistic character in spite of its overall deconcentration.

The process operates somewhat like a hydraulic pump — small changes in quantity or price in the wide vessel of legal flow, and big changes in the narrow vessel of black market flow. Instead of cross-elasticities of demand in sectors of different strain (as happened in the economics of Overstrain), the main role is now taken over by the price elasticity of demand for the same commodity.

Social contacts are heterogeneous and isolated, with various competing values for the same commodity. Thus there are for different persons different values of goods and services for which there is greater demand than supply; these values are rigid in one part of the sector, flexible in the other.

In underground economics there is a low price elasticity of demand for 'black' goods and service, i.e. they have a monopolistic price. At the same time there is a very high income elasticity of demand; this demand has the character of a demand for luxury goods. The price elasticity and the income elasticity of supply are highly inelastic.

In the formalized, official market the price elasticity of demand is very low, as is the income elasticity of demand; i.e. changes in quantity are restricted by factors other than changes in income. The demand for all goods assumes the character of a demand for prime necessities. The price elasticity of supply is moderately elastic, and the income elasticity of supply very small.

Every level of economic development has its specific underground economics as it has its own notion of luxury.[14] In our case from the developmental point of view the environment is the same, the aims are the same, but the actors and the means are different. Among the actors appears a whole legion of strongly motivated intermediaries, marginal individuals ready to take risks in a small sector of activity or in a commodity which they can handle more effectively than can the official economic agents. Nevertheless concentration is taking place. The range goes from tolerated intermediaries and individual interventionists to the

[14] In China there were two movements which expressed the dangers of underground economics. The first was the 'wu fan' or the 'Five Anti-Movements' in 1952, concerning the economic malpractices of private businessmen, typical of all as a whole — tax evasion, bribery of state employees, fraud, theft of state economic secrets, and pilfering of state property. The second was the 'zan fan' or the 'Three Anti-Campaigns of Purification of the State, Economic and Government Personnel at all Administrative Levels from those Backsliders who lost the Revolutionary Enthusiasm' — the abuses here were corruption, waste and bureaucratization.

VIP and BLAT in the Soviet Union, and from lobbying pressure groups to gangster groups and widely organized crime in the U.S.A., and includes various sects and secret activities in Asia and the Mediterranean. Socialist countries are also not free from it.[15]

(1) The most obvious case of underground activity in developmental economics is DISLOYAL COMPETITION among actors selling and buying goods of developmental priority under different conditions than they handle goods of the rest of the economy. Conflict arises between the new developmental regulations and established trade customs.

(2) TAX EVASION is another field of underground activity. A sudden introduction of increased taxes for development purposes creates a widespread practice of tax evasion which inexperienced administration cannot cope with. The more developed a country, the less opportunity for tax evasion.[16]

(3) The BLACK MARKET of goods and services is the most widespread example of underground economics. The black market is defined as "illegal activity among business and professional men which covers all types of profiteering in the sale of commodities under price or quantity control". Nevertheless, it takes at least two to make a black market. It also includes dealings with services, foreign currency under government control, imposing conditions of sale, trading without license, obtaining goods without proper authority, etc.[17]

(4) Also common is CORRUPTION in public administration by politicians

[15] In socialist countries at least some estimates of waste by underground activities are available. In 1955 in agriculture one quarter of the crops was lost in many collective and state farms. *Pravda* 24.6 (1955). The Economic Commission for Europe estimated that on a weighted average some 20 per cent of the crops were lost in the *sovhozes* and *kolkhozes*. *U.N.-E.C.E. Economic Survey of Europe in 1955*, p. 191.

[16] At the VII Conference of the International Association for Research in Income and Wealth in 1957, estimates of tax evasion were given for some European countries. It amounted to 10 per cent for Sweden, 20 per cent for Denmark and 5 to 100 per cent for Belgium. Further south the figures were greater, e.g. for Greece, between 50 and 75 per cent. The class structure of tax evasion was also significant. In Belgium the tax evasion of wage earners was around 5 per cent, of the salaried 5-10 percent, trades 56 and business up to 100 per cent. The lawyers' evasion amounted to 75 per cent and the worst were the medical doctors, who paid one third of what they should have paid. (Evasion 200 per cent).

"A South American industrial oligarch told a visitor: 'Our country's growth is based on not paying taxes. If we paid the government would spend it on foolishness like the army ...'".

[17] An attempt at systematization of the matter of black market was made with considerable success by B. M. Clinnard, *The Black Market* (New York, 1958). At present it is estimated that smugglers control some 20 per cent of the Latin American imports, i.e. well over 1 billion U.S. dollars, of which by conservative estimates in Argentina some 300 million and in Brazil 400 million dollars.

and bureaucrats, the use of public authority for personal interests, grants of privileges, subsidies, etc.[18]

(5) Other underground activities include the THEFT AND PILFERING of public property, bribery, embezzlement, all that has been called ECONOMIC CRIME in some states.

(6) Almost every Development policy emphasizes the necessity to import foreign capital for development purposes. On the other hand not much is said about the reverse movement — that of EXPORT OF CAPITAL from developing and underdeveloped countries. Illicit export of capital is carried out not only by big business, but also by politicians and high government officials.[19] Only a part of this is business speculation; the major part is meant as security for people who do not believe in the stability of their public positions. This export of capital is a significant and sensitive part of underground economics.

Recently brought to attention was the re-export of foreign aid funds from certain underdeveloped countries, funds which found a short way to the 'Swiss and Manhattan banks'.[20]

[18] For more recent research in this problem in the U.S.A. see E. L. McKitrick, "The Study of Corruption", *Political Science Quarterly* (Dec. 1957).

The historical study of corruption as a factor in capital formation is most complete in W. Sombart's *Der moderne Kapitalismus*, I (Berlin, 1922), pp. 581-715.

Recently R. Wraith and E. Simpkin published a book, *Corruption in Developing Countries* (London, 1963), dealing mostly with African countries. It is "about the poisoning of public life in so many developing countries by the endemic corruption, bribery, and nepotism that have followed so swiftly, and contrast so sadly with the apparent idealism of the political struggle for independence". The authors make a comparison with eighteenth-century Britain and its problems of corruption.

In one Asian country a prime minister (a career soldier), considered worth 143 million U.S. dollars died. "The investigating committee published an interim report disclosing that it had unearthed 20 million dollars in various bank accounts ... his commercial empire included a controlling interest in at least 15 specially privileged companies. Among them: the only merchant bank allowed to import gold; the only sales agency for the government plywood monopoly; a brewery with a heavy share of the government beer monopoly; two companies with concessions to print and sell tickets for the national lottery; a construction firm with major government contracts. He also owned a commercial fishing boat, some 50 cars, 30 villas and a 3,000 acre farm. The committee said that to date it had traced 17,8 million dollars of government money to his estate. The money came from a special government account known as the "Fund for Secret Work" (*Time*, July 17, 1964).

[19] The author of this paper found to his surprise that during the Second World War the British government was able to block no less than 27,000 active accounts of Yugoslav citizens with British banks, which in fact represented illicit export of capital from the then undeveloped Yugoslavia. The greatest exporter of capital from prewar Yugoslavia was the dictator King Alexander himself.

[20] In the most recent report of the Bank for International Settlements (issued June 8, 1964), it is stated: "... It would appear that on balance Europe was a substantial net

(7) Still another manifestation of underground economics is THE TWO PLANS TECHNIQUE. Socialist countries have some forms of underground economics similar to those of other developed and underdeveloped countries, but out of their specific economic system some specific forms of underground economics appear. The visible phenomena of such underground activities in socialist countries of the Soviet type are: planned versus spontaneous growth, (e.g. development of agricultural production in the *kolkhozes* as against growth of production on the individual plots of the *kolkhozniks*); deviations from the normative official planning in Soviet enterprises culminating in the making of two plans, one official for 'those upstairs', and another internal for operational use; the constant preoccupation of the planning authorities to redress the balance of planning proportions, the increased rigor of legislation against black marketeers and 'white collar crimes'; transactions on the 'left hand' etc. The problems of underground economics are the constant preoccupation of the authorities in all socialist countries.[21]

Generally speaking there are many other forms of underground economic activity, for the imagination of strongly motivated underground actors is more inventive than the classifying capacity of scholars.

4. THE ECONOMICS OF OVERCHANGE

When in the course of time the Overstrain caused by the Overlords has pushed an ever greater part of economic activity Underground, it becomes evident that the existing Development policy will not long be able to operate. There are so many strains on the system, and so many exceptions to it, that the Development policy as such does not function and the situation is ripe for a change. Then change becomes the slogan of the day. Everybody talks of changes and all measures of development tend to be explained and justified, and all errors excused — by the magic of

importer of capital from non-U.S. sources, particularly the less-developed countries." Two things point to this. The first is that the net capital imports of the less developed countries were surely much less than the gross amount of foreign capital they received ... There must therefore have been a considerable gross outflow of funds from these countries. The second factor is that, on the basis of U.S. balance of payment figures, not more than about half of Europe's capital receipts ... can be attributed directly to U.S. sources. Hence it would appear that the inflow of capital into the less-developed countries, mostly from the U.S., has been to a significant extent offset by an outflow from them, mostly to Europe." (The figures given refer to 1961 and 1963.) Bank for International Settlements, *Thirty-Fourth Annual Report* (Basle, 1964), pp. 27-28.

[21] For socialist countries cf. R. Bićanić, "Economic Growth etc.", *Development and Planning in Socialist Countries*, pp. 178-184.

the word 'Change'. Less attention is given to the question: What is a change? Or, better to say, when can a change be considered a change from a developmental point of view? But the process of rationalization of the magic of change should not be neglected.

In this paper we do not intend to develop a whole theory of social changes or one of revolutions. We are confining ourselves to a more limited subject — change from the developmental point of view, or redefinition of development. Some changes are useful for development; that is, they influence development in a positive way in one, two, or all three of its dimensions — the height, width and depth of growth. Other changes are not useful; these may be either neutral or actually damaging to Development as such. Such useless or exaggerated changes from the developmental point of view we will call Overchanges in Development.

Let us deal first with the problem of CHANGE, and then go on to OVERCHANGE. We shall once again follow the simple model of economic policy and define change as the substitution of a new model of development for an existing one by the alteration of one or more of its elements — the actors, aims and means within an environment.

Three elements give six possible combinations which we present in the table below, together with an explanation of what concrete types of change we have been able to distinguish, and how to classify them.

Actors	Aims	Means	Example of types of change in developmental policy
n	n	n	conservative, no developmental change at all
n	n	ch	liberalistic
n	ch	n	gradualistic
ch	n	n	personal regime, military dictatorship
ch	n	ch	fascist
ch	ch	n	reformist
n	ch	ch	revisionist
ch	ch	ch	revolutionary change in development

n = no change; ch = change.

When none of the elements in the model change in the course of development we would call the situation CONSERVATIVE. The actors do not change, and both the aims and the instruments remain the same. Growth is meant to be spontaneous, and no development takes place.

When the actors and aims do not alter and the instruments do, we would classify the situation as a LIBERALISTIC type of change.

Unchanged actors, when they purport to achieve new ends by old means, would be classified as GRADUALISTIC.

If the change affects only the actors, but the ends and means remain the same, we would call this only a change in the PERSONAL REGIME of an authoritarian system.

That change which consists of the achievement of unchanged ends by new actors and new means is simply a deceiving type of FASCISM.

The example of how to use old means by new actors for new ends is given by the REFORMISTS.

Old actors trying to achieve new aims with new means represent a REVISION of the developmental policy.

New actors who use new means for new ends produce a REVOLUTIONARY CHANGE in the developmental sense.

Classification made on this level does not take into account the magnitude of the change, its quality or quantity, its intensity, or its speed and elasticity, though only these can provide a true and specific meaning for Change. Here we can do no more than note the elements of change. But it is convenient to do so in order to deal generally with all shades in the developmental process. Further study of the classification would throw more light on the subject.

All these types of change have taken place in some of the countries carrying out the policy of development, but it is beyond the scope of this article to analyze what is existing or old, and what is new. These words may have very different meaning and content — political, national, class, social, group, economic, etc. The range of change is very wide — it may be very modest, but it may also extend to a revolutionary situation.

Nevertheless one observation is necessary: In developmental policy very few people will risk being called defenders of the existing situation. Most of them will pretend to be for change, since development always implies change. Thus another test is necessary to qualify the change. This is, whether the actors pursuing their aims with their instruments have actually succeeded in changing the environment. By introducing a fourth element into our type of model we arrive at twelve groups of developmental changes. Thus change of actors, or ends, or means alone does not suffice; the real test of change is the alteration of environment.[22]

[22] It is a widespread escapist practice that when the developers are not able to make effective changes in the environment they pass some radical law or present long-term perspective plans with little concern for the likelihood of fulfillment.

CONCLUSION

By demonstrating the 'black cycle' of socio-economic development — Overlord — Overstrain — Underground — Overchange — our intention was to draw attention to the most usual manifestations of blockages in developmental policy. We did this by centering attention on what NOT to do in development.

Our essential conclusions are:

(1) authoritarian and centralized activity of Overlords is not the surest and quickest way to achieve optimum economic development. For the sake of development it is essential to keep the Overlords under the popular control of those whose activities and life development they mean to better; i.e. abolish the conception of Overlords of Development altogether;

(2) the economy should not be overstrained by concentrating too many means of development on the officially proclaimed leading sectors, and thus blocking the process of growing economic interdependence;

(3) the lines of communication within an economy should be kept free in order to prevent the development of underground activities;

(4) any changes made should be for the sake of optimal growth; change for change's sake is to be avoided.

In conclusion, one must take care that forced maximal Development does not block optimal growth.

AGRICULTURE

VI

LACK OF INSTITUTIONAL FLEXIBILITY IN AGRICULTURE

1. SOME THEORETICAL CONCEPTS

(a) A SOCIAL INSTITUTION may be called flexible if an external disturbance causes adjustments or adaptations of its constituent elements (structural or functional) over time, without changing the fundamental social relations of the institution. If there is no change we speak of inflexibility or rigidity. An institution lacks flexibility if its resistance to change is such that the external disturbances do not cause any alterations in its constituent elements; or if the change, when it occurs, alters the identity of the institution by changing fundamental elements, the strain in this case causing it to break rather than bend. Dealing with flexibility, or with lack of it, we have always to look for an outside force which tries to induce changes in the institution.[1] By ADJUSTMENT we mean changes in the functions of the institution with no changes in structure. By ADAPTATION we mean an alteration of the structure of an institution caused by outside influences.

(b) There is a difference between functional and structural changes considered to be lesser changes on the one hand, and FUNDAMENTAL changes which bring a qualitative difference in essential social relations among human beings on the other. For example (1) If a peasant holding acquires more land, and the family members work it by increasing their labor efforts (increase in function), such a change will be a flexible one. (2) If they acquire so much land that the family labor is not sufficient to work it and hired labor must be permanently employed, the social change is fundamental, and the holding can no longer be considered a peasant family holding. (3) But if for working the extended land the family buys machines (and does not hire labor), then there is no fundamental social

[1] For considerations regarding a similar concept of flexibility limited to price mechanism cf. O. Lange, *Price Flexibility and Employment* (= *Cowles Commission Monographs*, No. 8) (1944), pp. 2, 3, 91.

change, and the holding remains a family one. In the second case we have to deal with a rigid institution; in the first with a flexible adjustable one; and in the third with a flexible and adaptable one (i.e. change in structure).[2]

The fundamental elements of an institution can be varied, and are dependent on the character of the institution. Malinowski, dealing with cultural changes, distinguished several functions, such as those covering essential physiological needs, personal elements, instrumental, technical, institutional, normative, operative elements, etc. He maintained that changes of one element lead to changes in others.[3] To Marx the fundamental element was the change of technology (development of production forces) which brought about institutional changes (the production relations).

(c) The persistence of non-financial elements. Under financial elements we understand here results of economic activity aiming at profit in terms of money. Lack of flexibility regarding the profit motive thus means a situation where a change in agricultural institutions, motivated by profit expectation, is expected to occur, but such a change does not in fact take place. In extreme cases the institution disappears or fundamentally changes its social character, but neither adjusts nor adapts itself to the profit motive.

2. POPULATION AND INSTITUTION IN AGRICULTURE

The institutional approach in agriculture is of such importance that even the definition of agriculture has an institutional character. Many household auxiliary and ancillary activities which in a more fully developed economy belong to another group of economic activities (manufacturing, transportation, building, etc.), in a lesser developed society are still considered as agricultural activities. Thus what is agricultural activity depends on the institutional development of agricultural organization.[4]

[2] Regarding differences between fundamental and structural changes see J. Tinbergen, *Economic Policy* (1956), pp. 4, 5, 149, 186. His definition of fundamentals could be differently classified. Marx called changes in production relations fundamental social changes.

[3] B. Malinowski, *The Dynamics of Cultural Change* (1945), pp. 105-109. For a criticism of the functionalist theory cf. R. Fletcher, "Functionalism as a Social Theory", *The Sociological Review*, vol. 4, No. 1, vii (1955). Regarding social change cf. W. F. Ogburn, *Social Change*; R. Manheim, *Man and Society in the Age of Transition*; U.N.E.S.C.O., *Social Change and Social Tension*; T. Parsons and I. Smelser, *Economy and Society*.

[4] *Measurement of Income Originating in Agriculture*, E.C.A.F.E., E. CN. 11 STAT. (Conf. 3/3, 1953), U.N.-E.C.O.S.O.C.

'Agriculture' here stands for joint economic activities of primary, secondary, and tertiary industries, integrated in agricultural organizations in a society with undeveloped division of labor.

Agricultural institutions are influenced and ultimately, even fundamentally, changed by many non-financial elements. Population pressure is one of the non-profit motivated forces which may change the character of agricultural institutions. Childbirth is certainly a phenomenon where the profit motive is not the moving factor. On the other hand the number of family members remaining on family land, or leaving it, is flexible and depends on both financial and non-financial considerations. We are dealing here with only one restricted aspect of the problem and are interested in the degree of flexibility or inflexibility[5] of agricultural institutions caused by movements of population according to social status. Sex differentiation also plays an important role in institutional flexibility. As there is a general tendency for the agricultural population to decrease in developed countries, the question is — who leaves agriculture first?

Most inflexible is the male owner-operator; then comes the female owner-operator. The number of owner-operators of holdings has increased where land reform has taken place and where population pressure leads to the dismemberment of rural holdings. Hired labor is next in inflexibility, and here again male agricultural workers are more mobile than female. In some lesser developed countries, however, there is an increase of male hired labor, showing a tendency for the extension of labor (and not machine) using capitalistic development in agriculture. There is an increase of female hired labor in some well-developed countries (possibly as a consequence of the Second World War) although on the whole female hired labor decreases more rapidly than male. Unpaid family members are the least inflexible and move away from agriculture fastest.

The figures in Table I support the following tendencies: (a) a relative decrease of agricultural population; (b) an institutional resistance to change, tending to weaken the family holding, with the owner-operator showing comparatively the greatest immobility and the family members the greatest mobility; (c) a tendency to deproletarianization of agriculture, fast reducing the amount of hired labor. This last institutional change is a development which has been taking place ever since the second half of the nineteenth century in European countries, and which gradually spreads to other regions as economic development spreads. In England

[5] The term 'mobility' is used here for movements of individuals and 'flexibility' for changes in institutions.

TABLE I

Active agricultural population by social status
(percentages of annual change)

		Owner-operator			Unpaid family members			Hired labour			Total		
		Male	Female	Total	Male	Female	Total	Male	Female	Total	Male	Female	Total
Japan	1947-50	+1.1	+8.1	+2.0	−4.5	−2.3	−2.9	+3.3	+5.0	+4.0	−1.0	−1.2	1.1
Egypt	1937-47	—	—	−0.1	—	—	3.0	—	—	0.32	—	—	0.15
Mexico	1940-50	—	—	+10.8	—	—	−3.5	—	—	−2.5	—	—	+2.6
Yugoslavia	1931-53	—	—	+1.0	—	—	−0.3	—	—	−2.8	—	—	+0.1
Portugal	1940-50	−0.2	−1.3	−0.3	−2.1	−4.7	+0.2	+4.4	+9.2	+5.1	+0.6	+0.7	+0.6
Belgium	1930-47	−0.8	−1.4	−1.4	−1.9	−3.6	−2.6	−3.0	−4.5	−3.2	−1.6	−3.3	−2.0
W. Germany	1946-50	−2.1	−7.6	−3.2	−0.5	+1.5	−1.2	−7.3	−5.1	−6.6	−3.8	−0.5	−2.1
Ireland	1936-51	−0.4	−1.6	−0.6	−1.7	−3.2	−2.0	−2.5	—	−2.5	−1.3	−2.4	−1.5
Gr. Britain	1931-51	−0.5	−0.6	−0.5	−4.6	−1.0	−4.2	−0.1	+6.2	+0.2	−0.84	+2.8	−0.4
Sweden	1945-50	−1.0	−1.8	−1.0	−6.1	+5.5	−3.9	−4.0	—	−0.40	−2.9	+3.8	−2.5
Denmark	1940-53	+0.5	−3.8	+0.3	—	+0.8	+0.8	−2.1	−2.9	−2.3	−1.0	−0.5	−0.9
Norway	1930-50	+0.1	−1.3	0.0	−1.3	—	−1.3	−1.0	−3.2	−1.2	−0.4	−1.7	−0.7
Finland	1940-50	−0.2	−2.4	−0.6	−4.9	−2.1	−3.2	+3.0	−6.7	+1.2	−1.4	−3.0	−2.1
Canada	1941-51	−1.2	−4.3	−1.3	−5.0	+53.0	−4.3	−0.9	−4.7	−0.6	−1.9	+9.0	1.8
U.S.A.	1940-50	−1.6	−2.4	−1.6	−3.8	+4.1	−2.3	−2.5	+3.3	−2.3	−2.4	+1.8	−2.1

between 1871 and 1951 the index number of owner-operators rose from 100 to 112; relatives working on the farm decreased to the very low figure of 21, and the workers to almost a half, only 55. In Italy the number of owners increased between 1871 and 1931 from 100 to 106, the share-croppers increased to 118, and hired labor fell to 54. The same tendency is seen in France between 1896 and 1946 where per 100 holdings using hired labor the number of owners increased to 130 and that of workers fell to 85. In the U.S.A. between 1910 and 1950 the number of agricultural workers fell to 57, and that of farmers to 64.

In the most recent years, 1950-1955, the mobility of workers and family labor in Europe has been somewhat reversed, and workers have been moving out of agriculture faster than family members. This is due to the increasingly strong 'pull out' factor of full employment in industry, which is even stronger than the already powerful 'push out' factor of agricultural mechanization.[6] This is also the case in countries with a quickly developing industrialization, i.e. those in eastern Europe, in spite of land reforms which were carried out on a large scale. Many agricultural workers in Yugoslavia after 1945 preferred to get employment in factories rather than remain on the land which they had got by land reform.

In the Soviet Union, on the other hand, in spite of accelerated mechanization there had to be a mobilization of 2 per cent of the agricultural youth of the *kolkhozes* per year, to be transferred compulsorily to industry between 1940 and 1955. There are no published data of occupations by social status in the U.S.S.R. But the number of *kolkhoz* homesteads reached its peak in 1950 (20.5 million) and is gradually falling (19.7 million in 1955). In 1940 it was only 18.7 million. At the same time the percentage of *kolkhoz* peasantry fell from 57.9 in 1937 to 41.2 in 1955 when there were 82 million. The numbers of *sovkhoz* workers increased in 1940-1945 from 1.8 million to 2.8 million and that of the M.T.S. workers from 537,000 to 3,120,000. In 1953 the members of the tractor brigades (some 1.8 million people) were transferred from the status of *kolkhozniks* to that of M.T.S. workers.[7]

There are little data for long-term comparisons of the very complex social status of agricultural population in under-developed countries, but

[6] *U.N.-E.C.E., Economic Survey of Europe in 1955*, p. 170.

[7] *Narodnoe Khozhyaystvo S.S.S.R.*, pp. 19, 128, 134, 138, 188. For changes in Asian people's democratic countries compare E. F. Kovalev (ed.), *Agrarnie preobrazovania v narodno-demokratiheskih stranach Azii* [Agricultural Transformations in the People's Democratic Countries of Asia] (Moscow, 1957).

it may be expected that this will follow the tendencies of mobility shown in the developed countries. In India the change from 1931 to 1951 was in the same direction, as the figures of labor force show (in millions):[8]

	1931	1951	±
Non-cultivating owners	2.45	2.04	−0.41
Cultivating landowners	51.3	79.9	+28.6
Agricultural laborers	28.0	20.1	−7.9

3. ENTRY AND EXIT

Population problems cannot be considered as changes affecting a mass of individuals. People live in social groups and population pressure manifests itself through tensions in and between social groups. Most of the agricultural social organizations are production and consumption units at the same time. These organizations are subject to many changes, and alterations in their personal structures come with many other changes — instrumental, operational, technical, normative, etc. Thus the problem is much too complex to be reduced to the system of land tenure.[9]

We shall deal here only with extreme cases, those of fundamental inflexibility causing an increase or decrease in the number of units; enumerating briefly the causes of the entry and exit. These depend to a great extent on socio-economic structure and its development.

(a) In a TRIBAL society the land is allocated to the new entrants (mainly newly-wed couples) by the tribal head, from the common land, and the new household is included in the tribal economy.[10] Exit is also regulated

[8] *Studies in Indian Agricultural Economics*, p. 226.

[9] For some recent international comparisons of agricultural institutions mostly connected with land tenure, see Colin Clark, *Conditions of Economic Progress*, 3rd ed. (1955); U.N. *Land Reforms*; W. and S. Woytinsky, *World Population and Production*; Sir John Russell, *World Population and World Food Supplies*; K. Parsons, Penn and Raup, *Land Tenure* (1956). Particularly for Europe: E.C.E.-F.A.O., *European Agriculture* (1955); Folk Dovring, *Land and Labour in Europe 1900-1950* (1956); F.A.O., *The State of Food and Agriculture* (1955); Rene Dumont, *Les Systèmes agricoles* (1956).

[10] In the Bantu reserves in South Africa every newly-wed member of the tribe normally gets about 0.4 hectare of land as his homestead, and around 4 hectares of the arable land which represents about one-eighth of the total tribal land. Seven-eighths of the tribal land is used for common pastures. For each wife an appropriate amount of land is added. The cultivable land is given to the male as his personal holding, which returns to the tribe when he dies. Nowadays there is some expectation on the part of the wife and children that the land of the deceased will be reallocated to them. D. Hobart Houghton, *The Tomlinson Report* (A summary of the finding and recommendations in the Tomlinson Commission Report, Johannesburg, 1956); *The Pattern*

by tribal customs and relates to death or expulsion from the tribe. In shifting agriculture, and in tribal or village organizations where there is a periodic redistribution of land, entry is still less important, as all holdings are quite uniform and non-stimulative, being equal and able to operate within the customary tribal economy.

(b) In a FAMILY economy, particularly that of a joint family, most often the family holding is perpetuated, as there is no change in continuity of the family holding when individual members of the family die. The exit of the family unit takes place only if the family dies out. Inheritance of land is the method of entrance. In countries where real division of land is the law there is great rigidity; farm holdings having to be split with almost every new generation.[11] In countries where there is no real division but where consolidated farms as a whole are inherited there is more flexibility and less entry and exit of farms as such than in the previous case.

(c) New entry can be made by purchase of land or farm, and this is the normal way in capitalistically developed countries which consider farming as a specialized occupation, trade, or enterprise. In this type of land tenure, the family cycle is not connected with changes in property, as there is a BUSINESS continuity of the holding. In the commercial farm type there is a discontinuity between the farm and the family, and each has a specific institutional structure of its own. In some countries there is an astounding rigidity of agricultural holdings (in particular, Austrian agriculture shows such rigidity of size with practically no changes since the First World War).

Exit of production units is due to many factors, including the natural death of the owner, migration from land, partition among successors, and sale of parts of the land or of the whole farm.

INHERITANCE means change of property without new capital investment, although the adequate paying out of other successors having some other occupation by those remaining on the land means a steady outflow of

---

of Race Policy in South Africa, Digest of South African Affairs, IV (1956), State Information Office, Pretoria. For still stronger tribal relations in a more primitive agriculture in Kenya see S. and K. Aronovich, *Crisis in Kenya* (1946); C. K. Meek, *Land, Law and Custom, in the Colonies*, pp. 76ff.; Colonial Office, *Land and Population in East Africa*, H.M.S.O. (1952); East Africa Royal Commission Report, *Land and Population in East Africa (1953-1955)*.

[11] The old Tchayanov-Marxist controversy over whether the size of land adjusts itself to the size of family or vice versa, is thus resolved, as neither is an independent variable. In modern agriculture, where the role of land and manpower is being reduced, and capital investment is of ever-increasing importance, they depend on a larger system of equations, where many 'push-and-pull', 'in-and-out', factors play their role.

capital from agriculture. On the other hand, purchase of land from others than farmers can mean considerable flow of capital into agriculture.[12] Where there is concentration of land there is a net number of exits, as the statistics of the U.S.A. and Great Britain show.[13] This drift out of agriculture refers mainly to small family farms which could not adjust themselves to new conditions and disappeared as independent units.

(d) In many countries of Europe, Asia, and Latin America, LAND REFORM secured the entry of many new small production units, by force of law dismembering the old estates and large farms. In some countries where much of this took place the number of production units increased by 20 or 30 or even 44 per cent (Mexico). The effect was mainly to level out differences in size. In fact, land reform where land was actually divided speeded up two basically different and historically opposite trends. One was the process of decomposition of feudal or semi-feudal estates which were inefficient but still resisted change, and of giving the land to more efficient peasant smallholders. The other gave land to those victims of capitalistic development, the agricultural laborers and small peasants, for whom the concentration of land into ever fewer hands meant being crushed and deprived of their own land. Political pressure and social justice required that they should be given land, especially in countries where no other means of existence were available.

(e) COLLECTIVIZATION of land in Soviet-type countries resulted in institutional change — the exit, as independent units, of millions of peasant holdings, reduced from the status of production units to the status of households (consumption units). Thus, for ideological reasons, there was an impatient anticipation of the process of concentration of land by force of the State. This measure did not examine the flexibility of peasant holdings with regard to new economic and technical possibilities, but assumed their utter rigidity and inability to adapt themselves even when full employment of their resources had not been achieved. The result was that the anticipated economies of scale were offset by other factors, such as lack of personal initiative and efficiency in work, lack of flexibility on the part of the centralized management to adjust means of production to their full use. As this administrative change lacked material economic basis, collectivization was carried out by coercion and arbitrary

[12] An expanded research of national accounts by sectors, with the agricultural sector properly defined, would be of great help in establishing the flows of current and capital transactions in and out of agriculture.

[13] The number of farms in the U.S.A. decreased from 1950 to 1957 by 802,000 or 14 per cent, and in the United Kingdom from 1951 to 1957 by 94,000 (also 14 per cent).

measures and the whole system became degressive and inefficient and had to be changed.[14]

The next institutional normative change in the U.S.S.R. was the concentrating of about three *kolkhozes* into one, thus increasing the possibilities of economy of scale. But once more the administrative rigidity of centralized planning did not allow production to increase up to the possible levels, and after 1953, further organizational changes were found to be necessary to increase the flexibility of the *kolkhozes*, i.e. stimulation of producers by increase of prices, gradual relaxation and abolition of compulsory deliveries to the State, and the paying of more attention to peasants' material interest in general. On the other hand the peasant *kolkhozniks* showed great tenacity; they changed the fundamental character of the plots of land which they had received under the new agrarian policy, so that instead of subsidiary self-subsistence production they were turned to commercial production of a more intensive type than the *kolkhozes* themselves.

(f) In the POST-COLLECTIVIZATION period in countries which almost entirely abandoned the Soviet type of collectivization, i.e. Yugoslavia and Poland, the peasants re-entered agricultural activity organized in family holdings as producers and consumers. A regeneration of agricultural production became evident after the collectives were allowed to disband. The policy at first was to increase production by letting the peasants make the fullest possible use of their own productive capabilities, helping them by allocating more investment funds to agriculture, and trying to supplement by organizing co-operatives where the limits of small family holdings had been reached. On the other hand, priority has been given to the technological leap in the effort to bring agricultural production up to modern standards on the large socialist estates run by workers' management. The whole system is liberated from administrative rigidity and a flexible system of land ownership exists, with free establishment of family holdings (free entry — although it is limited in Yugoslavia to a maximum of ten hectares of cultivable land per family holding), and a flexible system of marketing (free market prices and free sale of products).

[14] Cf. for Poland, statement of M. Jaworski, U.N.-E.C.E., *op. cit.* (1956), and of E. Lipinski, in E.C.E., *Economic Bulletin for Europe*, No. 3 (1957), p. 31. The final judgment on *kolkhozes* in Yugoslavia, expressed by the National Assembly in 1957 was that experiment showed negative results; loss of interest by agricultural producers in their work, and decay of agricultural production. Therefore "nobody thinks any longer of collectivization of agriculture in Yugoslavia" (S. Komar) — Federative Peoples' Assembly, *The State of Agriculture and Co-operation, and the Perspective for Their Development* (Beograd, 1957).

(g) HUMAN VACUUM IN AGRICULTURE. A new development in European agriculture is a mass movement of people, particularly young people, from agriculture. This movement, the obviously complex causes of which should be more closely examined, shows that in many countries there is a rural exodus even where economic conditions in a narrow sense do not justify it. In France in 1955 50 per cent of the owners of holdings of more than 30 hectares were considered to be without successors, and in those below 10 hectares the percentage was as high as 30 per cent. In Western Germany there is a tendency towards an ageing male agricultural population, and in Norway there are no sons remaining on land in many peasant families.[15] Recently in some of the most fertile parts of Croatia (the Danubian plain) as well as in the most mountainous parts (Lika) the same phenomenon became evident. This kind of movement is very strong in the U.S.A. Even in Texas the age of 47 per cent of all farm operators is sixty-five years or more.

Further investigation might show how far all this is a consequence of war losses which are only now becoming apparent, and how far it is a consequence of the pull-out factor of industrial full employment, or of other psychological factors such as improved general education, and also how far modernization of agriculture has justified it economically. In any case this vacuum caused by the shortage of young people is bound to show itself in the near future in great institutional changes in the agriculture of countries where it occurs.

4. PRESERVATION OF THE PEASANT WAY OF LIFE

Agricultural inflexibility is often linked to the preservation of the 'peasant way of life' based on tradition and past rationality of techniques, where agriculture is considered as an art rather than an economic activity based on scientific research and accountancy.

No doubt, peasant farmers and other types of agricultural population show many cases of non-rational conservatism. But there are also cases where other people's rationality based on different *principium rationis* is imposed upon the agricultural population which then rejects it. The reason for this rejection may appear conservative at first glance but may prove to be quite rational from the point of view of the peasant. Allegations of conservatism are sometimes too easily accepted, be it for reasons of preventing changes from taking place, or not admitting that things

15 U.N.-E.C.E., *op. cit.* (1955), p. 141.

have already changed. Such allegations may serve also as a pretext for justifying imposition by force of changes against the interests of the agricultural population, or as an excuse for the failure of inadequate policies.

More intensive research is needed to investigate 'the way of life' and the 'conservatism' of the agricultural population. Perhaps a definition stripped of the emotional and romantic shell might be that of a large number of different services supplied by, and organized on, an agricultural family or village basis:[16] economic (productive, consumptive, transport, distributive, etc.), protective, administrative, religious, health, educational, recreational, etc. It seems the village community movement is based on such multiple services, rationalized, modernized, and multiplied, taking advantage of the non-utilized resources lying idle in the village.[17]

Studying the process of the reduction of functions of peasant families in Yugoslavia, we noticed the rigidity of some of them (with a low coefficient of variation) and the greater flexibility of others. Comparatively most inflexible were the biological functions of the family (number of family members, percentage of the population in matrimonial status, etc.). All functions connected with the problem of expanding monetary economy showed greater flexibility. Most flexible were those connected with a higher standard of living (spread of electricity and expenditure for various services — medical, cultural, etc.).[18] The variation coefficients in the first group were around 0.18, in the second near 0.28, and in the third from 0.47 to 0.72.

Pride and prejudice, honor and prestige in the environment could be transferred to economic language where conspicuous consumption plays a great role, but CONSPICUOUS PRODUCTION in traditional and modern ways should not be overlooked either. There are many instances where economic investment in capital goods was made with very little economic calculation but more for reasons of prestige — to have a good team of horses even though uneconomical on a small holding, or to have a stable or barn bigger than a neighbor's, is the counterpart on the production side of such conspicuous consumption as a large and expensive house,

[16] For some recent definitions of peasant family holdings cf. O. Howald *Schweizerische Zeitschrift für Volkwirtschaft und Statistik* (1957), p. 151; F. G. Friedman (ed.) *The Peasant, a Symposium concerning the Peasant Way and View of Life*, Nos. 1-8 (1954-1957).

[17] D. Ensminger, *A Guide to Community Development* (1957), pp. 65-92; V. T. Krishnamachari, *Community Development in India*, pp. 66-82; H. D. Malaviya, *Village Panchayats in India*, pp. 272-276, 280-283.

[18] R. Bićanić, *Reduction of Family Functions in Peasant Families*, Conference on Use of Statistical Methods in Sociological Research (Beograd, 1957).

family festivities (weddings especially), rich national costume, radio, television, motor scooter, etc.[19]

In connection with institutional inflexibility we shall deal in this paper with two cases of the 'way of life'. One is the prejudice of growing one's own food, and the other is the desire to have one's own implements and machines.

(a) Growing one's own food is one of the fundamental principles of subsistence agriculture. Even when the economic calculus shows an evident loss, the peasant family will still grow its own food however uneconomical it may be. The result is that some kinds of staple food are grown where much more rewarding crops could be cultivated, be it for economic or for natural reasons. These crops are preserved only for reasons of peasant prejudice based on the family institution as a consumption unit as closed as possible. Since the turn of the twentieth century western European agriculture has moved away from this type of agriculture, and concentrated mainly on livestock and dairy intensive farming, relying for the supply of cereals on imports from abroad. Nevertheless in some countries the policy of growing one's own bread has become again, on the national level, the main bulwark of agricultural policy. Large subsidies given to staple food production, in order to make it adjustable to national needs under the existing institutional framework, represent the extension of the peasant prejudice from peasant family to national level for various reasons (strategic, full employment, etc.).

In the U.S.A. where there is excess production of grain, grain producers are paid for not producing certain kinds (i.e. wheat, maize, rice). This policy of making individually profitable the idleness of resources, however well justified it may appear from a national point of view, is difficult to understand from an international standpoint in a world where so many people are unable to satisfy their hunger, or even to produce their own food.

In the Soviet Union the policy of growing one's own grain led to the imposition of compulsory deliveries of grain all over the Union, with the effect that the more intensive and advanced areas, such as the Baltic republics with intensive dairy farming, had to return partly to grain

[19] For reasons of ideological prestige horses were replaced by tractors in the first days after the revolution in eastern Europe in many co-operatives where horses could have done the work more economically for many years to come. In an effort to keep the younger generation on the land in some countries, e.g. Sweden and Austria, the farmers were advised by experts to buy tractors or cars where mechanization was plainly uneconomical, in order to persuade the sons to stay on the father's farm. U.N.-E.C.E., *op. cit.*

production in order to satisfy the policy of compulsory deliveries of grain. The rigidity of the system of compulsory deliveries caused a retardation in the production of livestock and dairy products, and even a general recession of agricultural production in zones which had long ago passed this phase of agricultural development.[20]

(b) Peasant families desire to own their own implements and machines even when their capacity oversteps the organizational framework of the peasant family holding. This means an excessive investment in an agriculture which is otherwise poor in capital. This over-investment then leads to under-employment of capital goods when there is a great shortage of capital in other machines or other means of production. For example, the capital investment in agriculture in Yugoslavia is 600 dollars per hectare and in the U.S.A. 300 dollars per hectare (including land value). The investment in Yugoslavia is so much the larger mainly because of the great density of agricultural population (42 male agricultural workers against 4 in the U.S.A. per 100 hectares of cultivated land). It is also caused by the particularly large number of small family holdings, each wanting its own means of production and its own house. The use of the means of production has to adapt itself to the relatively stiff relations of ownership and lack of other opportunities.

The number of ploughs in Yugoslavia in the private sector (i.e. peasant family holdings) is particularly large. In 1957 there were 2,320,000 holdings with 1,400,000 ploughs, or 60 ploughs per 100 holdings. But the area under plough was 6,960,000 hectares. Counting as optimum utilization one plough per 10 hectares (which is very low), 700,000 ploughs would be enough to work this area if rational overall principles of distribution could be applied. Thus there was an apparent over-capitalization in ploughs of 50 per cent — i.e. half the existing ploughs, rationally distributed, could do the work for which twice the number is used today. A similar (very general) comparison for India (counting the area sown more than once as double) shows that on 100 holdings there are 75 ploughs, and that counting 10 hectares per plough some 13.5 million ploughs would be sufficient. Therefore, 59 per cent of the ploughs could apparently be considered in excess.[21]

There can, however, be quite a different approach to this problem than the macroeconomic one, namely the microeconomic approach of the peasant who wishes to have the equipment of his own choice; to have it

[20] In the report of Mr. Khrushchev of 17 June 1958 a change to a more flexible system of compulsory deliveries in this respect was proposed and subsequently introduced. *Pravda* (21 June and 1 July, 1958).

[21] The quality of the ploughs is here not taken into account.

at the time most favorable for his work; to be independent of other people's services, and not to have to pay excessive prices for such services. On these grounds it may pay to have one's own plough even in such general situations as previously described.

Some years ago Colin Clark estimated that the investment in tractors in Great Britain was carried to excess. Britain had the greatest density of tractors in the world per 100 acres of arable land, 2.5 times more than U.S.A., and 3.5 times more than France or Denmark. Clark attributed this mainly to the British taxation system which enables farmers to spend part of their taxable income on the purchase of machinery rather than pay it to the treasury, as this expenditure is exempt from taxation.[22]

Unused, excess capacity exists also in the U.S.A. in land, in machinery, and in tractors. There is even a surplus agricultural population, as we shall see later.

There is excess, unused capacity, due to institutional rigidity in the Soviet Union. This was officially admitted in 1958 when the Machine Tractor Stations were abolished. It was then said that there were too many people engaged in them, doubling the administrative line of the *kolkhozes*, often one M.T.S. serving just one *kolkhoz*.[23] Expenditure for the superfluous personnel amounted to 4.8 mrd. roubles a year, as they worked only seasonally and had to be paid all the year round. Altogether, on an average, one quarter of all M.T.S. (i.e. 2,250 M.T.S.) served up to no more than 5 *kolkhozes* each in 1955. M.T.S. machines had to work from 10 to 100 kilometres away from their stations, and depreciation of machines was premature causing excess expenditure for repairs. Allocation of inappropriate types of machine was not infrequent. The M.T.S. had full monopoly of large machines; they were expensive and did not serve the *kolkhozes* at the right time, nor with the proper service. Yet the stations had adverse balances which had to be met on the State budget. Khrushchev estimated that the *kolkhozes* could use machines much better, and do the same amount of work with 80 per cent of those used by the M.T.S.

This institutional change could not be carried out for many years because of administrative rigidity, caused by the ideological stiffness of the agricultural policy makers. The reasons given were that it would mean a retreat from state ownership to the lower, co-operative level of socialist property.[24]

[22] *Manchester Guardian* (25 May 1955).
[23] Mr. Khrushchev's speech, *Izvestia* (1 March 1958).
[24] J. Stalin, *Economic Problems of Socialism*, pp. 96-104.

In Yugoslavia experience with M.T.S. was so unsatisfactory that they were abolished in 1950.

5. INSTITUTIONAL INFLUENCE ON THE AGRICULTURAL TERMS OF TRADE

It is too often assumed that agricultural producers face a market of perfect competition because they are, to a very great extent, small producers who cannot influence the market prices by the small quantities which they offer for sale,[25] and that for this reason their production is not influenced by prices, though it is admitted without controversy that they buy goods at the monopolistic price level.[26] These statements only partly correspond to facts, as the inability to influence prices by producers occurs also where monopsonistic tendencies are prevalent, as is the case in many agricultural markets. Monopolistic and monopsonistic dominations depend on the size of the markets, and are observable even on small local markets. The technique of trade should not prevent us from noticing the essence of this kind of imperfect competition. Improved competition already represents a higher level of economic development.

In a capitalist developed country, with sufficient capital available, large storage facilities, a developed transportation system, and a fairly large and transparent market, the monopsonistic tendencies are not so obvious. Nevertheless agricultural protective organizations in this field, such as sales co-operatives, public warehouses, credit and market control, etc., are the best proof of the existence of such monopsonistic pressures though they are partly neutralized or checked.[27] The recent spread of

[25] We are far away from perfect competition in agriculture as this definition shows: "... in an adjusted agriculture individual farms would be producing the products in which they had greatest comparative advantages, farms would be of such size that unit production costs were at a minimum, inputs would be used in such combinations and amounts that marginal costs equalled marginal revenues, and both quantities of resources used in agriculture and the volume of farm input would be such that market prices enabled earnings of labour and capital in farming to be comparable with those outside of agriculture, non-monetary factors taken into account". G. E. Grandew, "Alternatives to Orthodox Programs and Goals of Agricultural Adjustment", *Journal of Farm Economics* (1957), p. 1634.

[26] *Policy for Commercial Agriculture*, Report of the Sub-Committee on Agricultural policy to the Joint Economic Committee Congress of the U.S.A. (10 Feb. 1958), pp. 3, 12, 17.

[27] Cf. in particular the striking analogy which Vining finds between the workers' trade unions, and the farmers' organizations' practices in the U.S.A. Vining's main idea is that farmers there should get stability of income through organization as workers get it through their trade unions, and big business in monopolies. He defines stability as a fixed relationship between two calculations. He compares mandatory

contract farming in the U.S.A., Sweden, and the U.K., etc., certainly strengthens the monopsonistic tendencies. It somewhat freezes the demand over a certain period, giving the farmer certainty and eliminating risk. The agricultural producer prefers to renounce for a limited time his managerial function of manoeuvring on the market as a seller, in order to concentrate on combining the factors of production. He gains more stability in his money income together with the possibility of making larger and more expensive investments. The managerial decision-making and risk-bearing is then taken over by big business ('agri-business') capitalist corporations operating on a large scale.[28]

The purchase of agricultural products for the 'ever normal granary', strategic stock-piles, emergency reserves, communal feeding, foreign aid, etc., provide other institutional forms of agricultural trade which relieve monopsonistic pressures by increasing the demand for agricultural products.

There is strong criticism in America of the present American agricultural policy. Price support is criticized in that it benefits only large farmers, in that it discourages the 'natural movement' of farm population out of agriculture (the 'natural' principle being: get bigger, get better, or get out), in that it increases the government cost of storing and acquiring surpluses (amounting already to 7.3 milliard dollars), and in that higher prices cause loss of foreign markets.[29] From 1932 to 1956, 22.5 milliard dollars were spent for agriculture (net cost) of which one half went to stabilize prices and incomes. This amounts at present to about 2 milliard dollars a year.[30] The efforts to get land out of production through the

co-operative marketing to the T.U. closed shop; collective bargaining of farm co-operative and industrial management in setting up commodity prices, to T.U. bargain ing for wages; the parity principle to the escalator clause in labor clause contracts; rules on the assignment of allotment acreage to the seniority rule. Surplus production and surplus acreage for him are similar to labor unemployment or idle resources in industry. Rutledge Vining, "Parity, Price and the Farm Problem", *A.E.R.* (Supplement 1958), pp. 343ff.

[28] Such a farmer was wittily called an aggricultural foreman by D. F. Capstick at the Conference of South-western Economists (Dallas [U.S.A.], 1958).

[29] For recent discussion of the problems of American agricultural policy see particularly *American Economic Review* (Suppl. 1958). Address, articles, and discussion of J. D. Black, W. Wells, R. Vining, E. J. Wooking, etc. The Compendium Policy for Commercial Agriculture connected with the U.S. Congress Hearings (16-20 Dec., 1957); *Journal of Farm Economics* (Dec. 1957), articles by J. D. Black, J. Brandon, E. O. Heady, etc. Committee for Economic Development, *Toward a Realistic Farm Policy*, U.S. Congress Joint Economic Committee, *Policy for Commercial Agriculture* (Papers, Hearings, Report of the Sub-committee) (1957).

[30] U.S. Department of Agriculture, *Realized Cost of Agriculture and Related Program* (March 1957).

Soil Bank mechanism cost the Federal budget in 1957 1 milliard dollars for 83,000 conservation reserve contracts. Nevertheless the aggregate net income of farm operators declined from the peak year of 1949 to 1956 by 34 per cent, but as there were fewer farms, the decline *per capita* was only 6 per cent, while the overall increase of income per head in the U.S.A. amounted to 37 per cent. Thus the still greater flexibility of incomes than of farms made life for those remaining on the land possible at only a little under the previous level. Those going out (about 1½ million farms and 3 million people) found employment outside agriculture more profitable.[31] The policy did not achieve the adjustment of demand to production. Private demand for agricultural products was not expanded and therefore surplus stocks increased. In order to get rid of them a double price system has been introduced for exports, and great quantities sold or given away as aid or grants. The acreage decreased, but more intensive farming of these parts under cultivation actually increased the total volume of production.[32] Rigidity of soil allotment was offset by flexibility in capital. Moreover the more flexible and non-restricted crops (barley, sorghum, and soybeans) were substituted for restricted crops and their production greatly increased. Most critics agree on one thing, that the basic problem is that of institutional inflexibility. "All of the people now in commercial agriculture using all of the land, machinery and other resources they are now using, could not earn reasonable incomes at free market prices for their products."[33]

One is impressed by the fact that the main practical proposals for new agricultural policy measures are restrictive, limiting production, and nationalistic in character, solving the problem within national frontiers rather than by expansion of demand and of production. One is tempted to ask what kind of income and price levels would be reached if a break

[31] T. S. Schultz is of the opinion that the main cause of the maladjustment of agriculture in the U.S.A. is not the unsatisfactory allocation of land but the labor force which is still too large, although it has sunk to a bare 12 per cent of the active population, having been reduced by 3 million since 1940. T. S. Schultz "Economic Prospects of Primary Products", p. 22, *Round-table of the International Economics Association* (Rio de Janeiro, 1957). I am indebted to Prof. Schultz for giving me this paper before it was published.

[32] According to Dr. B. T. Shaw, American agriculture produced in 1957 about 40 per cent more from the same acreage as in 1939. Wheat production is 27 per cent more on 17 per cent less land, maize 32 per cent more on 17 per cent less land, and the cotton acreage though reduced by 45 per cent yielded 95 per cent as much cotton as in 1939. A similar trend is shown by Dr. F. Wahlen in western Europe, where the area was reduced, the labor force cut by one-fifth and at the same time the volume of production rose by 20 per cent.

[33] Committee for Economic Development, *op. cit.*

through the existing price-cum-income monopolistic circle could be achieved, and full use of productive resources envisaged for agriculture.[34] There are some experts who think that in order to achieve income parity at the present aggregate income level in the U.S.A., the agricultural population would have to be halved (from 22 to 10 million, and the number of farms reduced to almost one-third, from 4.9 to 2.2 million). If such a tremendous change be the price of achieving stable income, what would be the price of achieving full use of productive capacity?[35]

In under-developed countries the monopsonistic tendencies are much more highly developed, and their institutional character more visible. The markets with strong imperfect competition are most obvious on the lowest level of the local (village) market. The barriers to the entry of new buyers to the market are often limited by custom, local or central government regulations, and also by the position of monopsonistic buyers sometimes strengthened by government pressure for taxes in money, particularly in the colonies. The personnel for this trade often represents an extension of tribal or village organization, where the local chiefs assume this position of monopsonistic buyers of agricultural products. On the other hand some marginal individuals or traders' *élites*, strongly bound by their loyalties, form potent monopsonistic and monopolistic groups, based on social deviance.[36] The narrow markets loosely integrated, the deficiency of storage in the hands of the producers, the consumers, and the dealers, and the shortage of capital restrain to some extent the monopsonistic tendency. On the other hand it is strengthened by restrictive trade practices, the transportation bottleneck and many institutional elements such as lack of sellers' organizations and the splitting of solidarity for non-economic reasons (different tribes, racial groups, villages, nationalities, etc.). The trader-cum-moneylender is often in complete control of an area's contact with the outside world, controlling even the post and letter writing where there is a high degree of illiteracy. The very rigid institutional elements on the lowest level show a gradual weakening as one approaches the higher level of market organization, where capital-

[34] Such an experienced expert as L. H. Bean estimates America's capacity to produce in agriculture by referring to a possible increase in acreage of 40 per cent and of production of 50 per cent. "Agricultural Capacity", *America's Needs and Resources* (1955) pp. 810-812.

[35] J. A. Baker, "Full Flexibility will not Solve the Farm Income Problem", *Policy for Commercial Agriculture* (Papers submitted), p. 466.

[36] For the most recent description of this behavior see B. Hoselitz, *Sociological Approach to Economic Development*, Atti del Congresso Internazionale di Studi sul Problema delle Aree Arretrate (1956), pp. 755-778. See also Hoselitz, "Economic Growth and Development", *American Economic Review* (Suppl. 1956), p. 37.

istic market practices prevail over the rigidity of local markets.[37] Institutional rigidity enables those in control of the market to impose prices which are arbitrary and which depend on their 'free will' and irrational interests. The result is an unstable system of prices sometimes showing several hundred per cent differences over very short distances or periods of time.

Our survey of price variations in Croatia in 1939 after the harvest established that prices paid to the peasants for wheat on local markets differed from 70 to 165 dinars, and for maize from 90 to 202 dinars per 100 Kg.[38] The position is aggravated by a great number of intermediaries, whose gains are always borne by the weakest link in the chain, the small peasant producer. Thus the greatest exploitation of the peasant producers takes place even before their goods reach the market operations of wholesale commerce.

In Soviet-type countries the trade in agricultural products was rigidly institutionalized, except for the *kolkhoz* market. The State purchasing agencies, operating under administrative rules, were in administrative and economic control of the institutionalized markets, with planned or government fixed prices and 'hard' norms of deliveries for each kind of institution (compulsory deliveries, payments in kind, M.T.S. services, State contractual deliveries, State purchases) and the income was distributed according to rigid administrative rules, different for each kind of institution. The results of this institutionally and ideologically rigid Soviet price policy was that "up to 1953 the purchasing prices for the most important products were low, they did not repay the labour and material costs, and did not secure the minimum conditions for the development of social production".[39] The slow increase of agricultural production in the socialist sector was the consequence of this inflexibility.

The rigidity imposed upon the agricultural producers, who were firmly organized into *kolkhozes*, had grave consequences. The producers were not interested in increasing production. Livestock production in particular lagged behind total agricultural production, and there was price discrimination against the *kolkhozes*. The goods sold to the *kolkhozes* were sold at retail prices, while the *sovkhozes* made their purchases at whole-

[37] For a description of such local monopolistic and monopsonistic markets see *All India Rural Credit Survey*, vol. III (the General Report 1954), pp. 100-106. For West Africa cf. P. T. Bauer, *West African Trade*, pts. 3 and 7. For pre-war Yugoslavia see R. Bićanić, *Kako Zivi Narod* [How People Live], pp. 39, 69-84.

[38] R. Bićanić and others, *Najnuznije narodne potrebe* (1940), pp. 46-53.

[39] Khrushchev report to the Central Committee of the C.P.S.U., *Pravda* (17 June 1958).

sale prices. There were some unexpected results. There was an increasing difference between the biological harvest on the fields and the harvest in the barns. On an average, most of the difference managed to leak between field and barn. On the other hand, the *kolkhozniks'* plots which were institutionally considered as complementary sources of *kolkhoznik* family food, grew into a major source of marketable food. The peasant families, reduced to small plots of land comprising only 4.3 per cent of the total sown area, showed such vitality that their spontaneous production achieved a faster rate of growth than the planned production of the common *kolkhoz* fields. *Kolkhoznik* plots were responsible for as much as 45 per cent of the total production of potatoes and vegetables, 46 per cent of the cattle (56 per cent of the cows), 40 per cent of the pigs, and 83 per cent of the goats.[40] Also, compulsory deliveries to the state by *kolkhozniks* from their plots amounted to 19 per cent of all meat, 16 per cent of milk, and 11 per cent of wool. These deliveries were abolished from 1 January 1958. Dividends and money income of the *kolkhozniks* from the common land brought them in 1957 43 milliard roubles and sales on the *kolkhoz* market 37 milliard roubles.[41] The total volume of trade in food increased from 1940 to 1955 in the State and co-operative shops by 43 per cent, and in the *kolkhoz* market by 68 per cent. The prices increased in the former by 41 per cent, and in the latter by only 11 per cent.[42]

Institutional rigidity on one hand stimulated the peasants to find an outlet for individual activity on the other.[43] The rigid institutional set-up of prices and volume of production leads to the appearance of non-normative markets. They are both linked, like a system of double flasks in hydromechanics. The greater the rigidity of one part of the institutional framework, the greater the pressure for flexibility in another market. One cannot help remembering the dictum of A. G. B. Fisher: "The more stabilization the less stability".[44]

[40] F.A.O., *op. cit.* (1957), p. 116.

[41] U.N.-E.C.E., *op. cit.*, pp. i, 10, 2.25-26.

[42] Calculated from data of retail trade, food and indices of prices, *Narodne hozhyaystvo S.S.S.R.* (1956), pp. 201, 207, 210, 215.

[43] One is inclined to ask oneself what increase of agricultural production in the U.S.S.R. would take place, particularly in the critical livestock and dairy, fruit and vegetable production, if, say, the *kolkhozniks'* plots were to be doubled to 8.6 per cent of the total sown area, or from 0.3 to 0.6 hectares per family. What a release of administratively blocked production forces this flexibility could represent.

[44] "The more we provide a formal stability in this way (i.e. piecemeal) for selected industries, the more we concentrate the necessity for flexibility upon the other sectors of the economy left outside. Fluctuations which apart from efforts to impose partial

Following the large expansion of sown areas of new virgin fields in Kazakhstan and Siberia the main interest of Soviet agricultural policy turned to intensification. For this purpose the rigidity in agriculture has had to be softened, and considerable reforms for the improvement of unsuccessful institutions carried out. The new system of prices and deliveries to the State, introduced in July 1958, means a considerable weakening of institutional differences, and a strengthening of the uniformity of the price system for products bought and sold by *kolkhozes*.[45] The principle is accepted that agricultural products should not be sold at less than cost, and the prices should enable the *kolkozes* to accumulate funds for their own investments as well as for their contributions to investment in heavy industry. Prices must be stable and flexible at the same time, depending on the outcome of the harvest. The principle of direct material interest of the *kolkhozes* and the individual *kolkozniks* is stressed, and the *kolkhozes* are left to sell on the *kolkhoz* markets all produce which the State does not take. Nevertheless, compulsory quotas of deliveries are all centrally planned and the prices fixed according to zones of production. The price leadership of the *sovkhozes* is established, although in 1956 only 28 per cent of all *sovkhozes* had positive financial balances.[46] On the whole the reform is directed toward strengthening the market forces, but it can develop in many different ways, increasing the role of *kolkhozes* or tuning them into *sovkhozes*.

In conclusion I should like to say a few words on the perspectives for agricultural institutional development. In several papers the institutional set-up of agriculture in under-developed countries was considered in opposition to that of developed ones, and subsistence and family farming opposed to commercial agricultural enterprise. Are we right in doing this? Is it really a case of EITHER ... OR?

Does not history teach us about multi-institutional frameworks of agriculture? Cannot both types exist side by side, each performing a different economic function? Cannot the labor-intensive family farm with its scarcity of land exist alongside the capital intensive, large agricultural estate which I believe would be better socialized?

There is full scope in the modern development of agricultural technique for both types: for the large-scale commercial agricultural enterprise

stability in the selected industries might have been quite manageable are therefore likely to be converted into violent *convulsions*." A. G. B. Fisher, *Economic Progress and Social Security*, p. 202.

45 Khrushchev, *op. cit.*

46 S. Nedelia, *Finansy S.S.S.R.*, p. 35.

feeding great numbers of the population, and for the small family holding dedicated to family subsistence, part-time farming, and the supplementing of family income, using the surplus labor and leisure time of the family members. Let us look at it with no limitations of national frontiers. There may be areas so short of land and so thickly populated that there would be no room for large estates, and others so richly endowed with fertile land that only a small part need be devoted to subsistence farming, the major part supplying the wide world with its main foods and fodder.

The strongly market increase of part-time farming in advanced capitalist countries, and the irresistible trend towards strengthening the production on *kolkhozniks'* plots in Soviet-type countries, are evidently part of the same general tendency imposed by modern technological development. It seems to be of a more permanent character than is sometimes envisaged. What will happen in the future industrial society, when the expectation of life is extended to over seventy years of age, and the working hours shortened to 30 or less per week? Will the workers' leisure be exhausted in horse or dog races, and in watching football games, that most frustrating way of spending leisure in the lonely crowds of industrial agglomerations in both capitalist and socialist countries?

Is not modern civilization moving in the direction of multi-institutional agricultural organization? We have to bear in mind that the process of industrialization of agriculture is simultaneous with the movement of urban populations from towns to suburbs, and from suburbia to conurbia and to exurbia — back to nature. Thus what used to be a romantic dream of integrated peasant culture may turn into the general pattern of life of the humanity of our atomic age, removing the difference between town and country, and between agriculture and industry. I feel deeply that we should give some thought to these ideas in the country of India, which gave the world the great teacher of integrated humanity, Mahatma Gandhi.

VII

AGRICULTURAL TURNING POINTS IN ECONOMIC DEVELOPMENT

Long-term changes which we call turning points in economic development, are of particular importance in agriculture because of its very complex nature and because the developmental process is such that some factors operate over long stretches of time while others are of rather short duration. This is all the more true where awareness of the reversal of developmental factors is lacking. Such lack often leads to errors both in managerial decisions on the micro-level and in agricultural and general economic policy decisions on the macro-level.

Turning points in agriculture are also periods of sudden change outside agriculture, encompassing a faster rate of change in the national division of labor than the rate of change in the agriculture as such; isolating it, in their minds, from other sectors of the national economy, policy-makers are often unaware of the increased importance for agriculture, at this stage, of general economic policies, and thus have difficulty in shaping an adequate policy for its optimal benefit. This is all the more true for international aspects of agricultural policies.

As a rule concrete agricultural policy does not follow the requirements of long-term economic logic. There is a lagging behind these requirements, which is shorter or longer depending on the complex interaction of both objective situations and subjective factors. Sometimes a lag may exist a decade or a generation or more before the impact of changes is felt or appropriate measures are taken.[1] On the other hand, hasty anticipation of long-term unverified changes can also induce premature measures in economic policy, thereby causing great damage to agriculture.

In this paper we have reduced our observations to three basic factors

[1] Dovring estimates that the backlog may take about one generation, allowing for adjustment of numbers of the agricultural population to the technical need for labor. He ascribes to this lagging a margin of underemployment and the continuation of the disparity of incomes between agricultural and non-agricultural populations. (F. Dovring, "The Share of Agriculture in a Growing Population", *Monthly Bulletin of Agricultural Economics and Statistics*, FAO, No. 8-9, Rome, 1959, p. 9.)

in agricultural development — labor, land, and capital — and have tried to see what are the logical consequences for agricultural policy of turning points in these three. Changes within these have not, however, been isolated but have been examined within the framework of the national economy, thus emphasizing the meaning of turning points for agricultural policy as part of the general economic policy of a country. For analytical purposes these factors have been defined as independent variables.[2]

Since we are trying to study the process on a comparative basis in order to find trends in general developmental policy applicable to very different countries, the study has necessarily remained on a rather high level of abstraction.

1. LABOR

The population factor, in long-term agricultural policy, is usually considered as mainly a question of man-to-land ratio, i.e., the absolute number of men engaged in, or living from, agriculture. Or, it is presented as the problem of surplus population measured as a percentage of the AGRICULTURAL in the total population, be it of the entire or only of the economically active population.[3] This relative number is considered most important in framing agricultural policy when economic development is discussed or developmental policies are planned. Consequently the absolute figures have been removed from the main focus of interest.

Our particular approach to agricultural policy in this study is to take both and to examine the relationship between changes in the absolute number of the agricultural population and changes in the relative number

[2] Several assumptions necessarily underlie our analysis. One is the homogeneity over time and space of an agriculturally active population. One could argue that the American farmer of today has little in common in regard to skill, labor productivity, physical effort and standard of living with his ancestor of a hundred years ago, or with the Yugoslav peasant of today. On the other hand, we are dealing with human beings as such occupied in agriculture, counting the number of persons active in agriculture (which we consider to be equal human beings). Land is also assumed to be homogeneous and is aggregated into one magnitude as area under cultivation (or agricultural land minus uncultivated pastures and meadows). Differences in quality of land and yield over time and space are disregarded and land is aggregated with regard to one dimension — its surface. Such factors as irrigation, double or treble annual crops, terraces, etc., are not taken into account and no separation is made of horticulture from agriculture. Consequently, capital is also expressed in homogeneous money terms and its homogeneity is preserved by using the conversion rates based on relative prices in international comparisons.

[3] Cf. "Three Concepts of Agricultural Overpopulation", p. 200 of this book.

in relation to the total population (Table I). The absolute figures show how many people gain their livelihood in a country by working in agriculture. The percentages show to what extent the division of labor has progressed. Here we are interested in only two groups: the agricultural and the non-agricultural populations.

For most countries the empirical data give quite a symmetrically shaped parabola (Chart I). We have also marked the years at which certain points of the curves were reached. If the curve is sharp it means that the change of absolute population numbers took place faster than the change in the division of labor (e.g., in the U.S.A.). If the curve is flat it shows that the division of labor was faster than the changes in absolute figures of population, i.e., that the population has been absorbed in non-agricultural occupations at a very great rate, as in Sweden.

As far as labor is concerned, a turning point in agricultural development is reached when the agricultural population stops increasing in absolute figures and begins to decline.[4] Taking into consideration both this point and the relative importance of total agricultural population in a country, we may divide development into three main stages: one, when the agricultural population INCREASES IN ABSOLUTE TERMS and DECREASES RELATIVELY; second, when the population ROUNDS THE TURNING POINT, i.e., almost stagnates absolutely and continues to fall relatively; and third, when the population in agriculture DECREASES IN BOTH ABSOLUTE AND RELATIVE TERMS. All three stages happen under conditions where the total population of the country is increasing (Chart I). Three stages of agricultural policy rationally correspond to these three stages, those of LIFE PARITY, of PRICE PARITY, and of INCOME PARITY.

We shall not analyze the period of development that occurs when the agricultural population increases both in numbers and in percentage. Such a period is characterized by the agricultural population increasing more rapidly than the non-agricultural, the latter being unable to absorb the increase of the former.[5] (See Appendices I and II.)

[4] What to us is a movement of agricultural population around a turning point, F. Dovring has called a relative stability of agricultural population, thus laying no emphasis on its dynamic character. He gives the following causes of this relative stability: (1) the degree to which urban occupations exercise a 'pull' on rural workers; (2) sociological and psychological factors; and (3) the internal transformation of agriculture as an industry, which is also closely connected with the changes in the urban sector. F. Dovring, *op. cit.*, p. 8.

[5] S. Kutznets in his collection of long-term series of changes in economic development found only two countries among 28 which showed a simultaneous increase of the absolute and the relative number of agricultural population and both were at the turn of the twentieth century (India, 1881-1931, and Yugoslavia, 1895-1921). We have

In India and Indonesia agricultural population increased both in absolute and relative terms between the 1930's and the 1960's; therefore they have not yet reached the turning point. Countries such as Thailand and Turkey show a small decrease in percentages of agricultural population, although the absolute number is still increasing. This could be interpreted that the first group is rather far from the turning point while the second is approaching it.[6]

Great Britain reached the turning point in agricultural population as early as 1820, Sweden in 1880, France in 1900, the U.S.A. in 1910, and Italy in 1920, while Germany did not reach that level of development in agriculturally active population until 1925, the same year as Denmark. Finland got to it in 1930 while Yugoslavia developed to this point in 1948 and the Soviet Union as a whole in 1956, with 41 per cent of the active population in agriculture. It is significant that the turning point was reached in different countries at various levels of percentage of the agricultural population in the total population (varying from 31 to 60 per cent) and at different national income level per head (from 132 dollars to over 500 dollars). This definitely has some connection with development but implies that further research for other variables influencing the developmental process is necessary.

We have said that in the first stage, agricultural population is decreasing slowly in relative terms but shows an increase in absolute figures. There are continually more men in agriculture, which suffers from an abundance of labor. There is little opportunity for other kinds of work (slow relative change). Income per head from extra-agricultural activity is greater than from agriculture, but the opportunities for outside jobs are limited. Chances to increase the market for agricultural produce develop slowly and are small because of other limiting factors (e.g., lack of capital). Thus subsistence economy (LIFE PARITY) is the rule, with maximization of physical volume of production per hectare a common goal.[7] The main

added Mexico, and note that at an earlier date there were more countries at this stage of development. S. Kuznets, "Quantitative Aspects of the Economic Growth of Nations", *Economic Development and Cultural Change*, Supplement to Vol. V, No. 4 (1957), pp. 28-31. Nevertheless there are some short periods when agricultural population increased in absolute terms and stagnated, and even increased in absolute terms also in other countries.

[6] On the basis of such figures some predictions could be made regarding the time when the turning point in agricultural population would be likely to appear.

[7] By life parity policy we mean efforts to keep agricultural population alive according to some established standards of existence within the institutional framework of a subsistence economy. This minimum of existence may become an objective of government policies too, as few governments would admit that they did not take measures to

CHART I

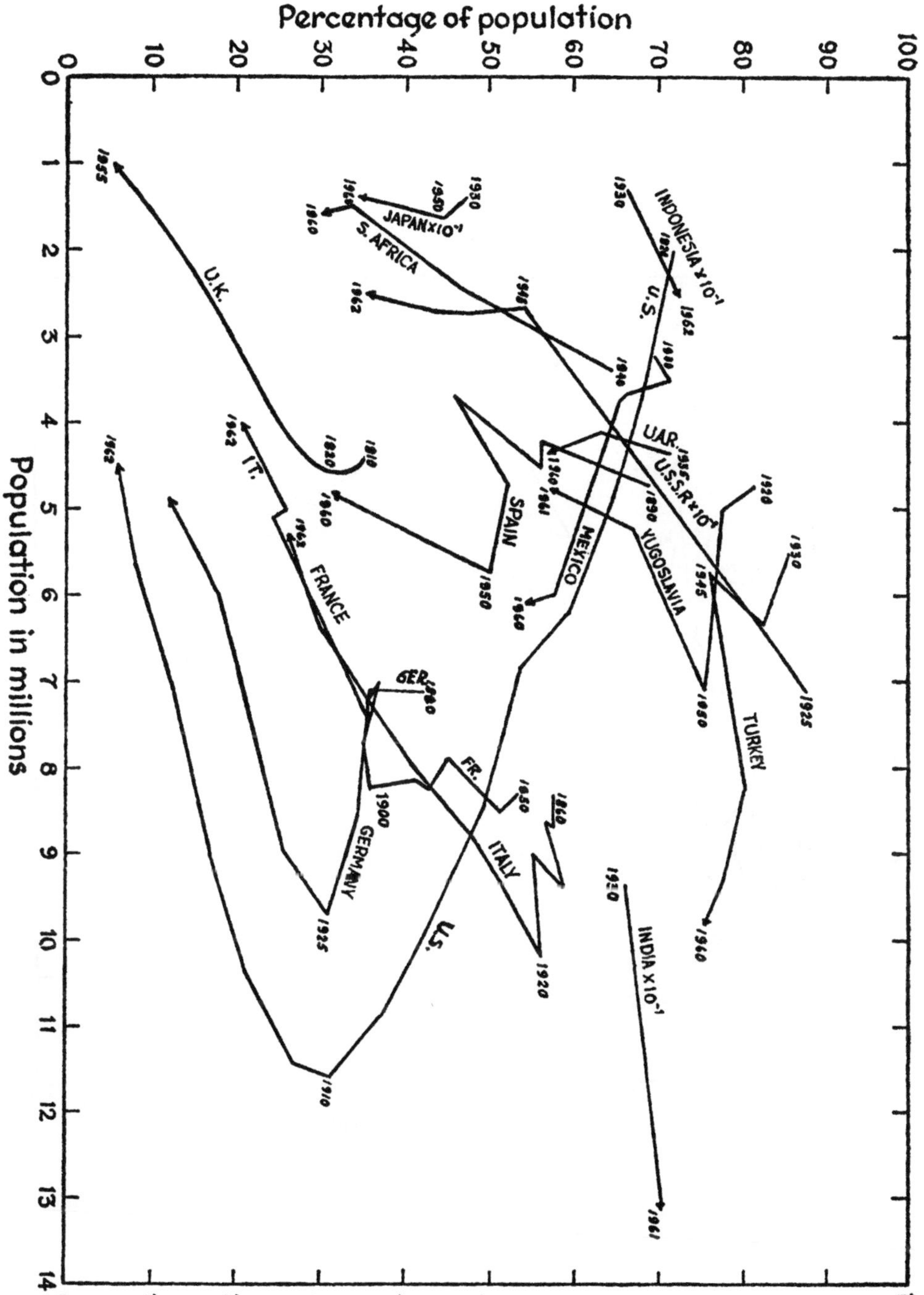

Percentage of population
Population in millions
0
10
20
30
40
50
60
70
80
90
100
1
2
3
4
5
6
7
8
9
10
11
12
13
14
INDONESIA x 10⁻¹
JAPAN x 10⁻¹
S. AFRICA
U.K.
U.S.
U.A.R.
U.S.S.R x 10⁻¹
SPAIN
MEXICO
YUGOSLAVIA
TURKEY
IT.
FRANCE
GER.
FR.
GERMANY
ITALY
INDIA x 10⁻¹

CHART II

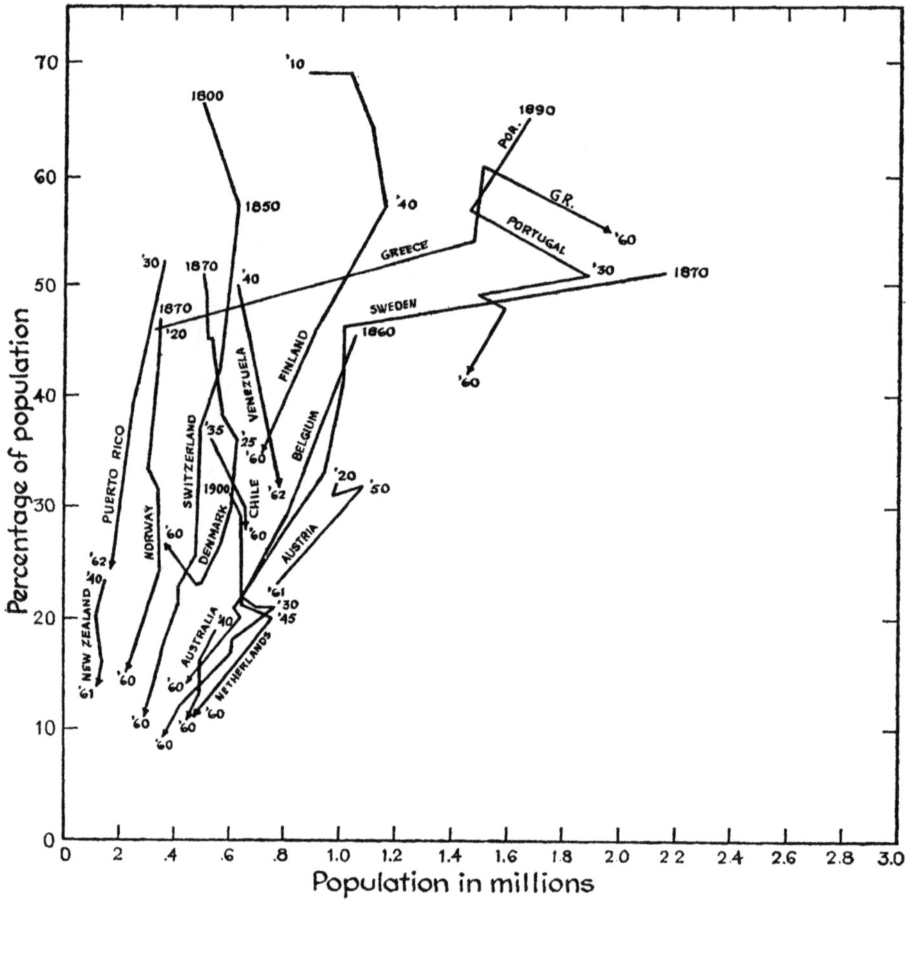
Percentage of population
Population in millions
GREECE
SWEDEN
PORTUGAL
POR.
GR.
FINLAND
VENEZUELA
SWITZERLAND
DENMARK
CHILE
BELGIUM
AUSTRIA
PUERTO RICO
NORWAY
NEW ZEALAND
AUSTRALIA
NETHERLANDS

function of the agricultural operator is to be the organizer of production for the needs of his family.

The price of land is determined far more by population pressure than by yield or income. Dismemberment of family holdings is a process which accompanies the struggle for existence. There is competition for land between the small peasant or landless laborers and big landowners, which usually ends in some kind of land reform.

When there is such agricultural overpopulation, to use as much labor as possible is considered to lead to progress; thus labor intensive farming is not only an outcome but is seen as the way to development. The immobility of labor at this stage results in under-employment or concealed employment. Family existence has priority over business calculation, and the peasant way of life over technical progress.

Pressure of agricultural overpopulation occupies the minds of the policy makers: the result is concealed under-employment in agriculture combined with overt undernourishment. The improvement of techniques on the basis of labor intensive farming is the main aim. Agricultural credit is still in the form of consumption credit, or at best is used to acquire land from the small number of those who leave it or are willing to sell it and take their mobilized capital out of agriculture; therefore land is overpriced. Moneylending and exploitation of the peasant are the dominating phenomena on the market, with extra-economic conditions prevailing. The terms of trade between agriculture and the rest of the economy are unfavorable for the peasant because of the imperfect market. This is the stage when the most exploited person is the peasant producer who is on the boundary between natural subsistence and money economy. Conflicts between the big landowner and the small peasant increase. Government taxes are a cherished instrument for squeezing agricultural products as a 'surplus' out of the peasants' subsistence farming at the expense of their standard of living.

As during the course of development population pressure grows less in absolute terms, and as the relative decrease of those working on the land gradually opens up markets for agricultural products among the non-agricultural population, the position of agriculture in the national economy changes.

The SECOND stage, rounding the turning point, occurs when agricultural population stops increasing and begins to decrease in absolute terms but

---

prevent their citizens from dying of hunger. Such a policy has been carried out also on an international level (e.g., Freedom from Hunger Campaign of FAO).

falls relatively at an accelerated pace, opening the market for agricultural products at a rate faster than the decline in agricultural population. This also means that the market for agricultural produce is increasing faster than the need for subsistence of the agricultural producers themselves, which has a favorable upward effect on the prices for agricultural products. The greater demand on the market sharpens the conflict between the traditional subsistence and the progressive mercantile farming, and this has a shattering initial effect on the established (traditional) moral values of peasant society as well. The increased division of labor provides an outlet for the poor, the young, the enterprising, and the outcasts by securing an opportunity for employment outside agriculture and outside the village. At this stage mercantile agriculture prevails. Development depends on the terms under which agricultural products are sold on the market, or means of production and consumption goods bought and labor hired. Thus the problem of price scissors (PRICE PARITY) dominates agricultural policy.

The agricultural population is ceasing to grow in absolute figures and a slow decline begins. This is accompanied by a fast labor intake from agriculture by other sections of the economy. It is the period of rapid industrialization and of de-agrarianization of the village. Labor is required for industry and has to be obtained by non-agricultural occupations offering higher wages or incomes than in agriculture, by recruitment and schooling, even by creating an antagonistic semi-feudal attitude towards peasant life and labor and squeezing out a labor force by administrative measures, even forced labor.

The opportunities for poor agriculturalists outside the village initiate a process of deproletarianization of agriculture. But at the same time the increased market for agricultural produce created by the division of labor means that the demand becomes greater than the established institutional framework of agricultural production can supply. Therefore another policy becomes necessary, that of stimulating the agricultural producer by government policy. Thus agro-industrial price scissors (price parity) become the second main preoccupation of agricultural policy, or in other words, agricultural policy must stimulate agricultural production by increasing the economic inducements and not by using administrative measures of forcible exploitation. As ever larger quantities of products are required than the surpluses from subsistence farming can supply, the squeezing out of produce by administrative means is no longer necessary nor effective, be it by tax, compulsory deliveries, money-lending, or inducement to change the habits of the village consumers (vodka, women's fashions, conspicuous consumption and production, etc.). The dependence of agricultural output on purchased inputs and hired labor dictates the rate of economic development, and instability of the relationship between the two determines the pace of progress. The cost-benefit relationship imposes the maximization of output per production unit (holding, estate). The operator's most sensitive function is that of a commercial manager.

In the THIRD stage, when the agricultural population declines both in absolute and in relative terms, agricultural development is dominated by an ever increasing shortage of labor which is now more and more finding an outlet in non-agricultural occupations. Both the increase in the agricultural population, and failure to succeed in commercial farming because of lack of land or capital or managerial ability, lead to the proletarianization of the greater part of the peasants. A shortage of labor in agriculture occurs which makes the use of modern machinery and other equipment essential in order to be able to work the land at all. It is no longer a problem of how to produce more or better or cheaper than with human labor. Labor becomes unobtainable for work in agriculture. The situation is now to produce with the help of the machine or not to produce at all. This is made more difficult by the deterioration of the labor force in quality due to rural exodus. In order to put a brake on rural exodus an income parity policy between agricultural and non-agricultural population is required.

Capital intensive agriculture is the obvious outcome. The exodus from agriculture goes parallel with an increased concentration of land in larger farms, which process runs simultaneously with capital and land concentration due to technological changes. This speeds up the process of substitution of labor by capital in agriculture. The gradual depopulation of agriculture is linked to a triple change: agriculture is deproletarianized, and there is a change in the quality of labor because of its feminization and senilization, since the able-bodied male laborers and unpaid grown-up family members leave agriculture first. At the same time there is an increasing technological burden put on those who remain on the land. Thus agricultural labor has to be transformed from a traditional way of life into an occupation which leans heavily on vocational training and the ability to introduce innovations. The increase of the market makes the demand for agricultural products more urgent, and this changes the role of the agricultural operator. He becomes a technical operator rather than a commercial leader.

Structural changes go hand in hand with the absolute decline of the

CHART III

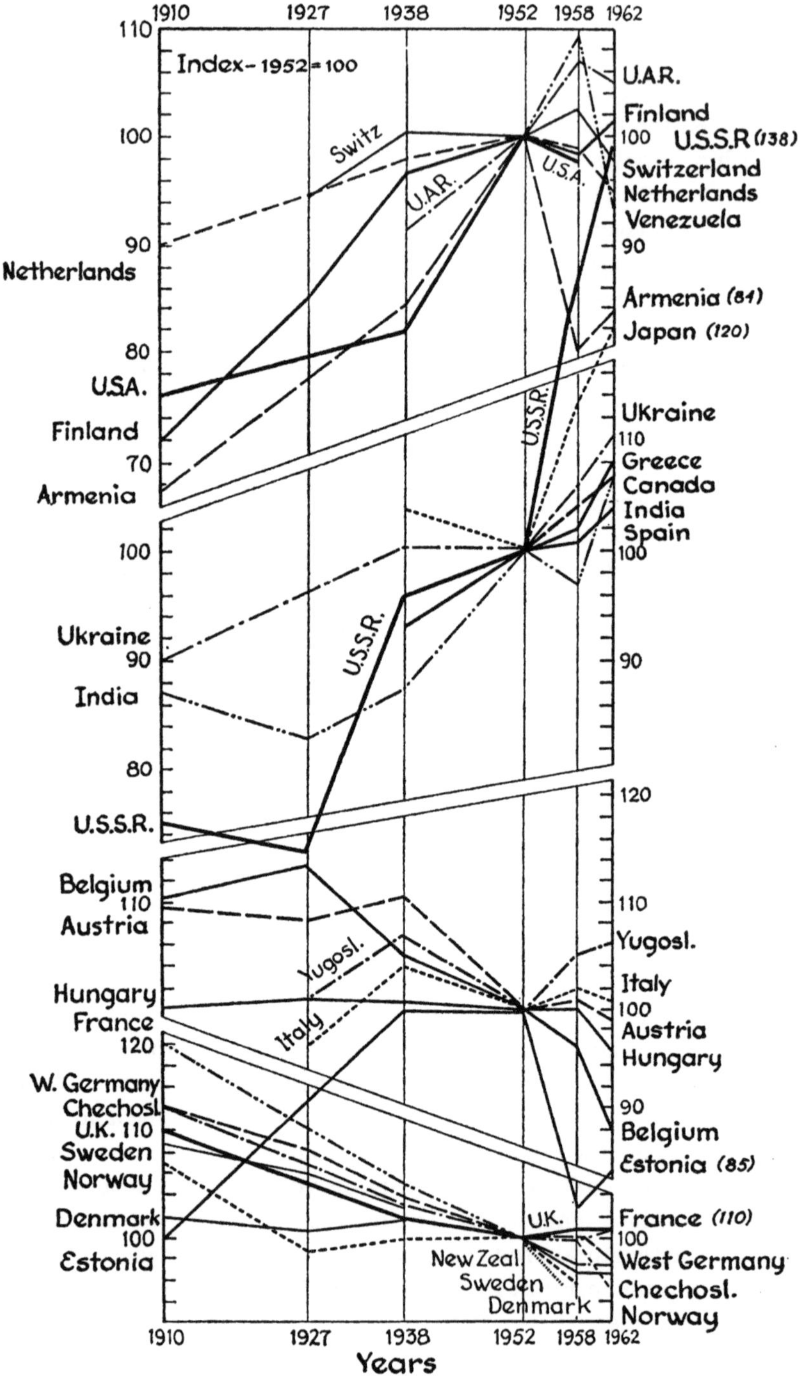
1910 1927 1938 1952 1958 1962
Index - 1952 = 100
110
100
90
80
70
Netherlands
U.S.A.
Finland
Armenia
Switz
U.A.R.
U.S.A.
U.S.S.R.
U.A.R.
Finland
100 U.S.S.R (138)
Switzerland
Netherlands
Venezuela
90
Armenia (81)
Japan (120)
Ukraine
110
Greece
Canada
India
Spain
100
90
Ukraine
India
U.S.S.R.
80
120
U.S.S.R.
Belgium
110
Austria
Hungary
France
Yugosl.
Italy
110
Yugosl.
Italy
100
Austria
Hungary
90
Belgium
Estonia (85)
120
W. Germany
Chechosl.
U.K. 110
Sweden
Norway
Denmark
100
Estonia
U.K.
New Zeal.
Sweden
Denmark
France (110)
100
West Germany
Chechosl.
Norway
1910 1927 1938 1952 1958 1962
Years

agricultural population, and those operators who remain on the land get steadily bigger, until a new wave of technical innovations sweeps the relatively smaller ones away.[8] This gradual process splits agriculture into an ever smaller number of capital intensive large commercial farms and a great number of labor intensive small family farms giving full- or part-time occupation to their owners. Rural exodus becomes so intensive that a policy of INCOME PARITY between agricultural and non-agricultural occupations appears as a dominant instrument in agricultural policy, so as to slow down the drain from the land.[9] Price parity alone no longer meets the requirements of agricultural production.[10] Income parity is necessarily linked to this third stage, i.e., where agricultural population declines absolutely and relatively. In this situation it can happen that the rural exodus is faster than the application of technological progress and substitution of men by machines, and therefore there is great danger of depriving agriculture of sufficient labor. To stem this exodus administrative measures are not effective enough; income parity of agricultural and non-agricultural population is one of the most effective instruments of

[8] In his budget speech, 25th January 1965, the American President L. B. Johnson said that of 3.4 million farmers at present existing in the U.S.A., only one million can be expected to gain a decent living from farming even with continued Government assistance. And that in a country where agriculturally active population represents 5 per cent of the total. The aims of French agricultural policy is to reduce agricultural farmers by one million. The annual decline in the V. French plan is supposed to be 110,000 thousands or from 5.2 million to 3.9 in five years. During the 7-year plan some 6.5 to 7 million people more than planned left agriculture in the U.S.S.R. (A. Nove-J. Matko, *Times*, London, March 3, 1966). For most of the European countries, cf. U.N.-E.C.E.-F.A.O., *Towards a Capital Intensive Agriculture* (Geneva, 1961), table XIV. For changes in the mobility of agricultural populations by groups, cf. our paper "Lack of Institutional Flexibility in Agriculture" (*Proceedings of the Tenth Conference of Agricultural Economists*, Mysore, 1958). Various groups of agricultural population differ in their exodus from agriculture. Active population declines before total agricultural population shows this trend, and male actives before the others. The first to leave are hired workers, then the group of unpaid family labor, i.e., members of the farmers' families, and the last to show an absolute decline in absolute numbers are the independent owner-operators.

[9] Production per man in agriculture (in value terms) in the 1950's was less than one third of that in manufacturing in the following countries: Yugoslavia (15%), Austria (22%), France (32%). It was approximately one half in West Germany, Italy, Canada, Norway, and the United States. It reached almost parity level in the Netherlands, Belgium, and Denmark, while it was 15% higher than in manufacturing in the U.K. (115%). (U.N.-E.C.E., *Some Factors in Economic Growth in Europe in the 1950s*, Geneva, 1965, II, p. 36).

[10] There is a substantial difference between the income and the price parity policy. The former is based on the product dimension while the latter is measured by the institutional dimension (income of the production unit).

the policy to retain people on land. Today even some socialist countries which have rounded the turning point are compelled to introduce a policy of income parity; a decade ago this would have seemed quite unthinkable.

In every country that has rounded the turning point the number of people active in agriculture is actually the same at two different years before and after the turning point, but at different levels of economic development. The U.S.A. had an agricultural population of the same size in 1961 as in the 1860's. But at the earlier date the real income per head of the total population was 232 dollars (1934 value) and one hundred years later, in 1960, it was 2,300, or ten times greater. France had the same numbers active in agriculture in 1940 as in 1860, with the real national product per head being 143 dollars in 1860 and 366 dollars in 1940. Yugoslavia had the same active population in agriculture in 1961 as it had in the early twenties of this century, i.e., *more than forty years ago*, etc. The second fact we wish to emphasize is that the greatest producer of agricultural products, the United States, speaking in absolute figures, now has a smaller agriculturally active population (5.7 million) than some much smaller countries, say Italy, Mexico, Romania, or Yugoslavia. The same applies to an even greater extent to the U.K., which has the same area as Yugoslavia but its agricultural population equals one fourth of the latter, although its total population is more than two and one half times larger than that of Yugoslavia.

The relative number of active agricultural population has declined in the course of the last 50 years in the U.K. from 27 to 4.6 per cent, in the last hundred years in the U.S.A. from 60 to 9, and in the last 60 years in Italy from 60 to 30 per cent. In Yugoslavia the decline in 40 years was from 79 to 57 per cent.

The speed of depopulation of agriculture and the deterioration of its quality is a general phenomenon in North America and Europe, including some socialist countries (Czechoslovakia, East Germany, Soviet Union, Yugoslavia, etc.).

Maximization of output per man thus becomes the main goal of agricultural policy, which gradually makes agricultural development less and less dependent on ever more expensive and rare human labor.

2. LAND

The most important turning point regarding land is that when the agricultural area begins to decrease in absolute terms, fewer hectares of land are cultivated than before.[11]

The statistical observation of empirical data show that many developed countries have passed the turning point, i.e., that the agricultural land has passed its peak and is decreasing, while many others, mainly underdeveloped countries and countries with large uncultivated spaces, have not yet reached that stage. A more detailed analysis shows the following picture. Tables II, III, IV show the countries in which the turning point

[11] The maximal area in France was attained for arable land in 1862; it declined in one hundred years to 70 per cent of this maximum, or by 7.5 million hectares. In 1862 it comprised 49 per cent of the total area of France and in 1962 only 35 per cent. Vineyards also reached their peak in 1862 (at 2,321,000 hectares) and had declined, by 1962, to 900,000 hectares; only less than one half remained. The French *landes*, too, mainly nonfertile land, reached the maximum in the 1840's, then decreased until 1910, and from that year again showed an increase, that is submarginal *landes* which were brought into cultivation were once more abandoned. Meadows and pastures as well as forests showed a steady increase, the latter of 2 million hectares. There was an increase of noncultivated areas, i.e., it rose from 3.2 to 4.2 million hectares in one hundred years. (*Annuaire statistique abregé*, vol. I, 1943, p. 43.)

In Belgium agricultural land reached its peak in 1880 at 1,984 thousand hectares and fell till 1963 to 1,685 thousands or by 300,000 hectares. This represents a decline of 15 per cent. And arable land showed a decrease from 1,601 to 946 thousand hectares between 1869 and 1963. This decrease by 665 thousand hectares represents 42 per cent of the arable area in the turning point year. At the same time the meadows and pastures increased from 366,000 to 739,000 hectares or almost doubled.

In the U.K. the total tilled area (crops and fallow) reached its peak in 1869 and from that year to 1962 declined by 3 million acres or 21 per cent. The area under clover continued to increase from 1866 to 1962 when it almost doubled (increased by 82 per cent), while the permanent pastures increased to 1914 after which a decrease began which lasted until 1944. After the Second World War pastureland increased again for ten years, i.e., until 1955, when another decline began. The turning points in permanent pastures were the following figures for the areas in corresponding years:

Years	Permanent pastures — thousand acres	Rough grazing — thousand acres
1866	11,149	12,087 (1891)
1914	17,606	14,619
1944	10,809	16,278
1955	12,284	16,161
1964	11,302	17,242

Nevertheless the total cultivated area showed a decline of 4.2 million acres, that is, fell from 58 to 51 per cent of the total statutory surface of the U.K. The peak of the cultivated area was reached in 1891 at 32.9 million acres, and in 1962 there were not more than 28.7 million acres under cultivation. Land is dealt with under conditions of continuous increase of the volume of production although the size of the cultivated area is changing. (U.K. source: Official agricultural statistics of the U.K.).

In the United States the farm land increased steadily until 1950 when it reached its

in arable land and in cultivated area has occurred.[12] The turning point in cultivated area was reached in Belgium in 1880, in the United Kingdom in 1891, in France in 1910, and in Sweden during the First World War (1915). Just before the Second World War (1938) the turning point in cultivated land took place in various European countries such as Switzerland, Italy, Hungary and Finland, and after this war in the Netherlands and Norway (1947). The United States attained the peak of cultivated land in farms in 1950, and Denmark and Yugoslavia in 1958. Austria and Czechoslovakia experienced it before 1924.

But as the term 'cultivated land' is differently defined over time and in different states, we produced also statistics related to the turning point

---

peak. This peak had already been reached for crop land in 1935 and for grass land around 1945. From 1935 to 1959 crop land fell from 416 to 392 million acres. (*Historical Statistics of the U.S.*, Table j. 49-64).

In Sweden crop land reached the turning point in 1920, and from that time till 1962 was reduced by 13 per cent or almost one half million hectares. Natural grass land reached the turning point as long ago as 1870 and was reduced by more than one million hectares to the benefit of crop land, forest land and wooded grazing ground. (*Historical Statistics of Sweden*, II, 1959, p. 33.)

Socialist countries are not exempt from this evolution. A significant movement can be recorded in the U.S.S.R. While the total area is still increasing (from 1953-1963 by 40 per cent or by 61 million hectares), the increase is the greatest in Kazakhstan (index 340 for 1963, taking 1953 as 100). The increase is much smaller in the Ukraine (11 per cent). A reverse movement has taken place in some other Soviet republics, particularly the Baltic and the Central Asian republics, as well as some European districts of the Russian Republic. E.g., Estonia has shown a decline in cultivated area in the same decade by 12 per cent and Armenia even by 18 per cent, or 100,000 hectares. (*Narodnoe hosyaystvo v.* 1962 *godu*).

[12] Before we enter into analysis of the statistical material we would like to make the following comments: Statistical data of land utilization are not of a very high reliability, especially when dealing with international comparisons in long-term time series. The definitions vary from one country to another, particularly with regard to non-arable lands, the greatest difficulty presenting the distinction between meadows, permanent grazing land, pastures, temporary grazing land, etc. Nevertheless, these categories are of great importance when intensity of agriculture is examined. Moreover, the definitions change in one and the same country over time. Our sources are mainly national statistics as presented to the international agencies such as the International Agricultural Institute for the pre-1945 years, and the F.A.O. for after the 1945 period. Our observation units are countries considered each as one homogeneous entity, which of course is not the case, particularly when land area is concerned. Quality of land is very different and yields of crops vary. Land can, to a small extent, be made homogeneous, as it is immobile, unlike labor and most forms of capital, and its accessibility depends on nonagricultural factors such as means of transportation. Heterogeneity of land areas within one and the same state will certainly cause the appearance of the turning points in areas under cultivation at different times. In our study we have made abstractions of such cases. They may be very important in large countries and in those where geographical and pedological conditions differ greatly. These reserves should be taken into account when reading the statistical tables.

CHART IV

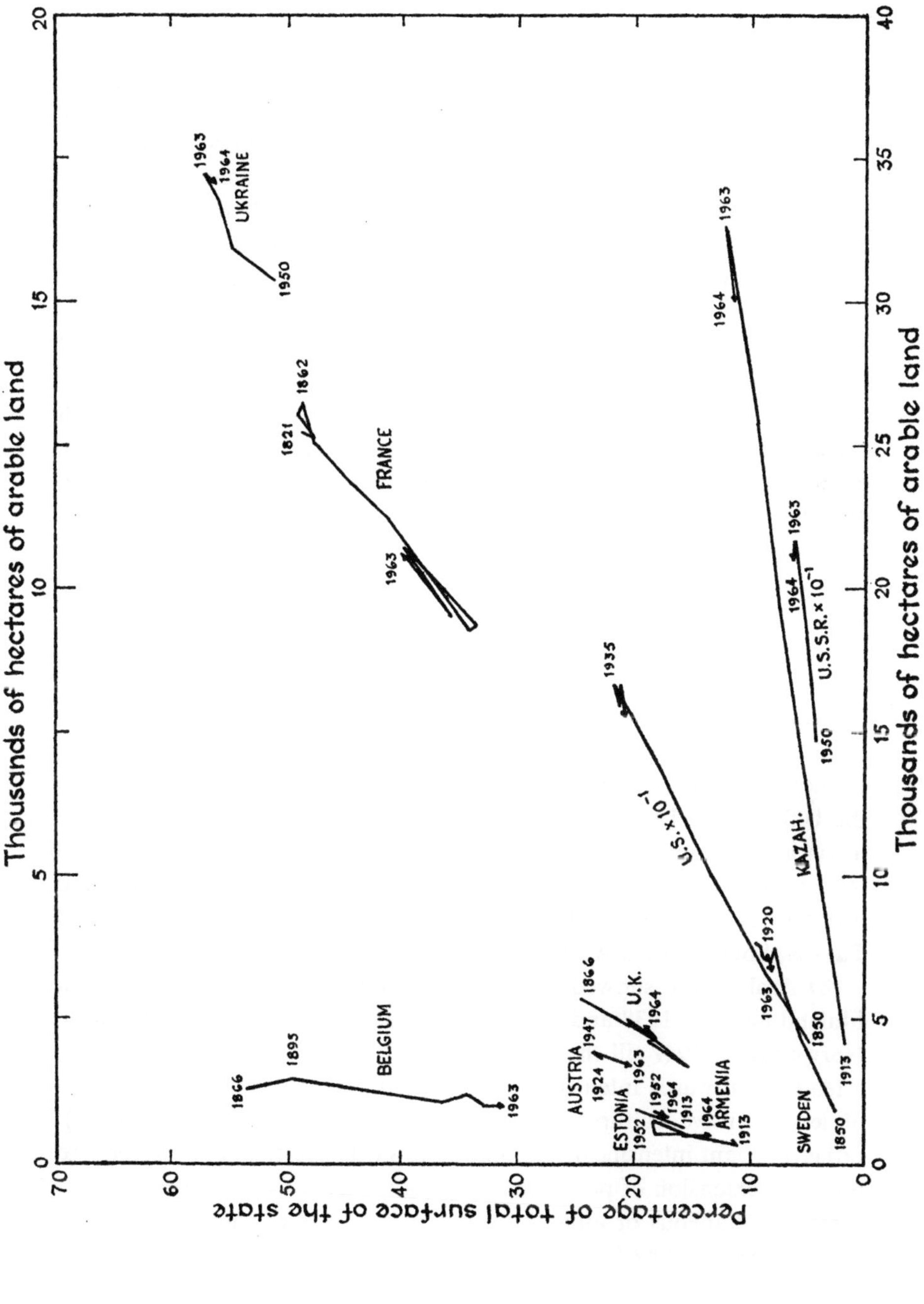
Thousands of hectares of arable land
Thousands of hectares of arable land
Percentage of total surface of the state
UKRAINE
FRANCE
BELGIUM
AUSTRIA
ESTONIA
ARMENIA
U.K.
SWEDEN
KAZAH.
U.S. x 10⁻¹
U.S.S.R. x 10⁻¹

in a comparatively more homogeneous category than that of arable land and/or land under crops. Turning points in arable land occurred in France in 1862, in Belgium in 1866, in Great Britain in 1869; Sweden experienced it in 1920, Austria in 1938, the Netherlands, Hungary and New Zealand immediately after the Second World War (1947), Italy in 1954, and U.A.R. in 1957. In 1956, Venezuela witnessed decrease in arable land. Other countries in our table have not yet reached the turning point and their lands under crops or plough are still increasing. The change was small, i.e., less than 10 per cent increase in Greece, Spain and Japan and also Canada, but a large change in cultivated areas (more than 10 per cent since 1924) occurred in India, the Philippines, Peru, Syria, Tunisia, Australia, New Zealand, South Africa, in our set of observed countries.

Having taken the turning points as points of discrimination for both the cultivated areas and those under crops, we can make a comparison of both and draw some analytical conclusions regarding the state of agriculture in different countries. We can distinguish five different situations (Table IV, Chart III): (a) Before both categories of land reach the turning point, i.e., both areas increase. (b) Arable land increases while cultivated land begins to decrease. (c) Cultivated land still increases but arable land decreases. (d) Turning points in both categories of land occur simultaneously. (e) Land under crops and all cultivated land decrease.

(a) The first situation occurred among our observed countries, e.g., in France until 1862, and in Belgium until 1866, in the U.K. until 1869, in the U.S.A. until 1935, and in Italy and Finland until 1938. Land is still increasing in both categories, but faster in arable land than in cultivated land, in Bulgaria, Greece, Spain, Argentina, and Canada. Cultivable land increases faster than arable land in the Philippines, and Syria and Tunisia, South Africa, Australia, the U.S.S.R. and India.

(b) Arable land showed an increase, and cultivable land a decrease in Finland between 1938 and 1963, in Italy between 1938 and 1954, and in Norway from 1947 till the present day. This situation indicated mainly a tendency towards intensification of agriculture but not of substitution of less intensive cultures (pastures) by more intensive (e.g., cereals); rather it meant intensification pointing towards livestock production and therefore extension of permanent grazing lands.

(c) Simultaneous or almost turning points in both categories of land was reached in Sweden in 1915-1920, the Netherlands in 1947, and Denmark in 1958.

CHART V

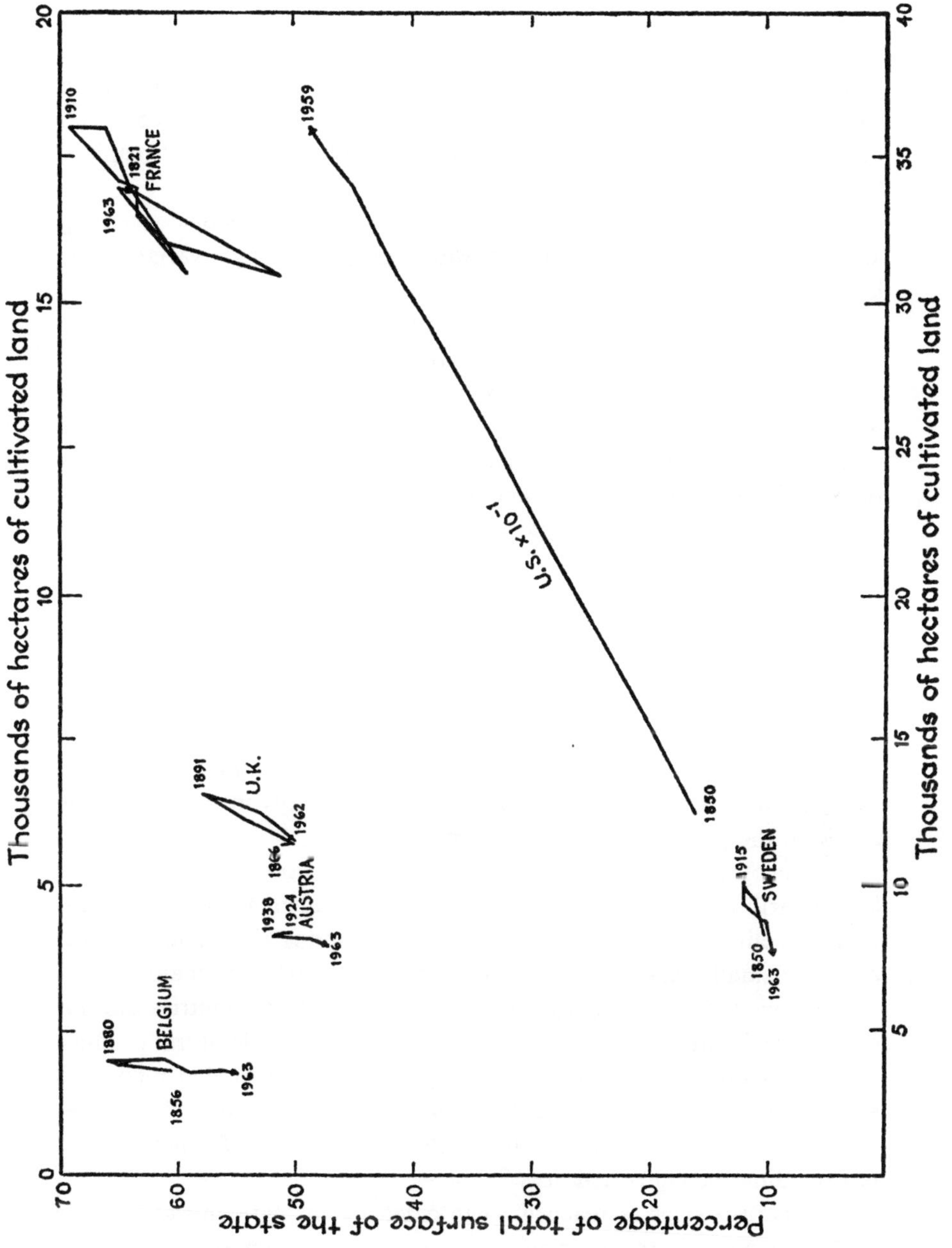
Thousands of hectares of cultivated land
Thousands of hectares of cultivated land
Percentage of total surface of the state
FRANCE
1910
1821
1963
U.S. x10⁻¹
1959
1850
U.K.
1891
1962
1866
AUSTRIA
1938
1924
1963
SWEDEN
1915
1850
1963
BELGIUM
1880
1856
1963
0
5
10
15
20
25
30
35
40
70
60
50
40
30
20
10

(d) Decline in both areas, arable and cultivated, is shown in the following countries which we observed: in Belgium (since 1880), the United Kingdom (since 1891), France (since 1910), Sweden (since 1920), Austria and Switzerland (since 1938), the United States (since 1950), Italy (since 1954) and Denmark (since 1958). This indicates that in these countries other factors became more important in agriculture than land (capital, technical progress, foreign trade, etc.).

We are taking this analysis as a basis for a logical conclusion concerning an ideal type of agricultural policy with regard to a single variable: the land under cultivation.

We shall distinguish three different situations. One is before the turning point is reached, the second occurs around the turning point, and the third when the tendency to diminish the cultivated area prevails. This whole analysis concerns the process of development, i.e., both the increase and the decrease of the cultivated area happen under conditions of continuously increasing volume of production.

In the FIRST situation, expansion of agriculture prevails. The main factor of production is land. Extension of the area under cultivation is the main concern of agricultural policy, and is supposed to solve all the main problems. The cultivated area is increased by bringing under cultivation new, idle, or fallow land, by cutting forests, draining marshes, irrigating dry lands, cultivating parts of pastures, making terraces, and fighting erosion.

This is the period of the opening up of a country at individual as well as at social cost, of building roads, canals, railways in order to have access to the potentially cultivable area.

The encouragement to expand cultivated areas varies from giving free land, distributing communal lands for farming, and creating homesteads, up to the elimination of pastures and forests. Land is almost not for sale, and only small areas change hands through the market mechanism.

The policy of extending the cultivated area in some countries did not stop at the frontier of the country. Export-import of agricultural produce — i.e., extending the domestic territory by acquiring foreign territories and so expanding to other countries, through the medium of the market mechanism, or through a system of colonization — is a further method of extending the cultivated area.

The SECOND stage is reached when extension of agricultural lands is no longer possible to any significant extent, i.e., when the 'frontier' is reached and the pioneering age is over.

In this situation the main concern of agricultural policy turns to land redistribution. The differentiation in the village between the small and the large proprietor becomes the stumbling block of agricultural policy. Lack of capital to improve production in order to satisfy increased demand creates further need for agricultural credit where livestock and equipment procurement become more important than the purchase of land. Property changes take place within the village, and land becomes marketable. Institutional measures regulating land use become the most important instruments of policy. The problems of economic development are no longer linked to expansion of land but to problems of land redistribution by sale and purchase, by law or by spoils. One of the main concerns of developmental policy becomes that of satisfying the wants of those who work on land; land therefore gets into the hands of those who for reasons of thrifty subsistence, of political pressure, or of better husbandry, can gain most from it.

The most common mechanism of land redistribution is the formation of a market for land, which is to an ever greater extent drawn into commerce. It is bought and sold like any other commodity at commercial prices, which depend in principle on returns from capital invested in land. To this commerce problems of agricultural credit, especially of mortgage loans, are added as an important instrument of mobilizing land transfers. Land reform occupies an important place as a real redistribution of land and instrument of policy. Consolidation of farms and rememberment at village level, limitation by law of the size of holdings and estates, prohibition of further dismemberment of agricultural plots, and imposing by law the minimum indivisible size of holdings, are the most frequent measures.

Obstacles to trading in land are gradually removed, the security of land ownership is reinforced and freed, so as to enable it to be traded from the less to the more successful agricultural operators. Therefore contracts on farming the land are relieved of the remains of the past and made as commercial and binding as possible. In some socialist countries collectivization of land took place as the main instrument of agricultural policy.[13]

In the third situation, that of reducing the cultivated area and increasing the volume of production at the same time, the main policy is that of intensification of agriculture by capital investment. Submarginal land is abandoned because of its low fertility or high costs of production or because of inaccessibility or distance. Capital substitutes for land as the

[13] Cf. R. Bićanić, "Problems of Socialist Agriculture", *Indian Journal of Agricultural Economics*, Silver Jubilee Number (Bombay, 1964).

dominant factor of production and, for reasons of more favorable opportunity costs, becomes the main concern of agricultural policy. Extension of the area under cultivation is no longer pushed, reallocation of land becomes of secondary importance, because it is not of much use to cultivate it on a competitive basis. The technique of development is such that increased demand can be satisfactorily met by ever progressing technical improvement which, with less labor and less land, delivers more goods and services for an ever greater number of consumers. Land now begins to follow labor in acquiring a negative power in the production function. In some countries further increase of agricultural areas is actually discouraged by government policy (soil bank practice, agricultural tourism, extension of national parks, conservation of forests, guarding of mountain landscapes, etc.). The area under forests does not contain reserves for expanding cultivated areas, and forests or what is left of them are carefully conserved.

Thus comparative advantages in agriculture and from agriculture, are carefully weighed against other competitive investments; practice of landless agriculture and livestock breeding is put into operation, hydroponics are carefully studied, etc.[14]

3. CAPITAL

In dealing with capital in agricultural development we wish to emphasize two things. First, we do NOT include land as such in capital. Second, capital is a very heterogeneous category with regard to its productivity and shows partial capital output coefficients which move from 0.5 to 33.[15] There is a heavy capital coefficient in land reclamation (irrigation, drainage, terracing), water supply, flood control and erosion, and also in setting up of vineyards, olive groves, and arboriculture. Buildings and construction of roads, etc., also have a heavy capital coefficient. The medium capital coefficient shows in livestock and machinery investment

[14] This situation has induced the French rural sociologist Mendras to speak of a landless agriculture ('agriculture sans terre'). Cf. Henri Mendras, *L'Agriculture et l'avenir de la société rurale*, and the commentaires in *Bulletin SEDEIS, Futuribles* No. 905 and 911 (Paris, December 20, 1964, and February 20, 1965).

[15] M. Cépède gave the following partial macroeconomic capital coefficients for French agriculture: water works 2.7, road building 4.2, farm consolidation 0.5, building construction 33, electricity 7.7, agricultural machinery 12.5, total agriculture 6.4.

For Yugoslavia the partial capital output ratios in the period 1957-1962 were: crop farming 4.7, animal husbandry 2.6, vineyards and arboriculture 12.4, overall agricultural capital coefficient 5.7 (Institute of Agricultural Economics, Belgrade).

CHART VI

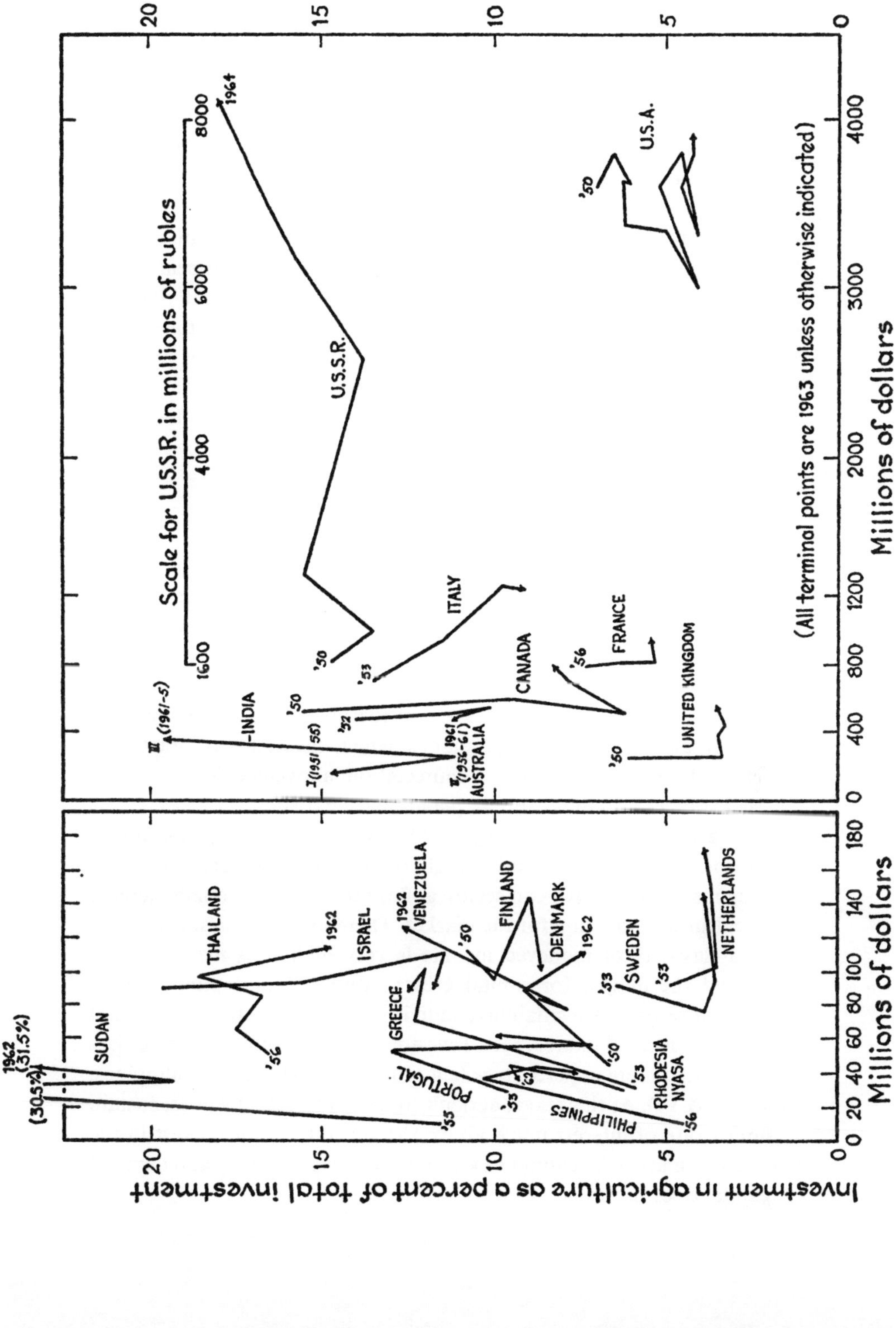

Investment in agriculture as a percent of total investment
Millions of dollars
Scale for U.S.S.R. in millions of rubles
(All terminal points are 1963 unless otherwise indicated)
U.S.S.R.
U.S.A.
ITALY
FRANCE
CANADA
UNITED KINGDOM
INDIA
AUSTRALIA
SUDAN
THAILAND
ISRAEL
VENEZUELA
FINLAND
DENMARK
SWEDEN
NETHERLANDS
GREECE
PORTUGAL
PHILIPPINES
RHODESIA NYASA

for services, use of fertilizers, and various kinds of inventory. Therefore the assessment of the role of capital in agricultural development will not lead us far if we measure it in terms of a homogenized quantity, i.e., in financial terms. We have to distinguish clearly its longevity, the various combinations of the physical capital-mix of different partial capital coefficients, and, most important, the changes in the quality of capital due to technical progress.

Taking capital as an independent variable we can logically distinguish three different stages in agricultural development. The first appears when capital is scarce and becomes the limiting factor in economic development. The second is when captial is available for agriculture at the general rate of interest and is invested according to the profit it makes possible. The third stage is created when capital decreases in financial terms and even begins to decrease in quantity because of the great influence of technical progress. (Chart IV, Table V.)

A. *Capital as a limiting factor*

From the capital supply point of view the starting point in agricultural development is the auto-reproductive process in which internal physical capital formation prevails over external (seeds from own harvest, animals bred and manure produced from own herd, tools to a great extent home made, farmhouse built from domestic material by family labor, etc.). Natural risks and capital losses are considerable (fire, floods, erosion, animal diseases, drought, etc.), aganist which insurance is practically non-existent and for which no depreciation allowance is calculated. External sources of capital supply play a marginal role.

Starting from this situation agricultural development depends on an increase in external capital goods bought on the market (cattle, machinery, building materials), which can secure a more than proportionate increase in agricultural production for the market. Therefore the marginal capital-demand elasticity of moneyed income is very high; this makes capital scarce and the hunger for capital great; saturation of capital demand depends more on the availability, indivisibility, and mobility of capital than on the financial interest rate. Investment in agriculture increases less in millions and more in percentage (e.g., Indonesia, Thailand, Philippines, India, Chart VI). At this stage, agriculture can, and actually does, sustain a usurer's rate of interest much above the general rate of interest in the economy. A market for capital based on the display of supply and demand for capital does not exist.

Therefore the financial rate of interest cannot be used to measure real demand for capital in agriculture. This situation brings about simultaneously a hunger for capital and overcapitalization in production; overindebtedness and squandering of windfall gains; compulsory capital accumulation and exorbitant rates of interest. To counteract this, agricultural policy aims at the organization of a specific capital market for agricultural investment (predominantly out of public funds fed by taxing the very same agricultural population: redistribution by exploitation).

In the course of development the capital coefficient increases and the capital burden becomes heavier. The increasing capital coefficient requires ever more capital investment per unit of product while passing over the threshold of development.[16]

The incremental capital output ratio (ICOR)[17] in European agriculture in the decade 1949-1959 was in the less developed countries: Greece 0.9, Spain 1.7, Turkey 1.8, Yugoslavia 2.5, Italy 3.2, and Portugal 3.7. The more developed European countries have the heavier ICOR. In West Germany, the Netherlands, Finland, United Kingdom, it was around 7, and in Belgium and Austria it moved between 9 and 20. A heavy capital coefficient operated in the United States (17.6) and Canada (12.2), while in Norway it reached 31.4.

In the course of general development agricultural investment takes an ever smaller share of the national capital although it increases in absolute quantity (e.g., Greece, Denmark, Italy, the Netherlands in Chart No. III). This increases the possibility of draining some capital back into agriculture by private or public channels. The availability of capital from savings both inside and outside agriculture makes intensive agricultural development possible and brings the rate of interest in agriculture closer to the general rate.

Long-term capital formation in agriculture (secular trend) falls constantly in relative terms, which means that other sectors grow faster. From 1800 to 1927 farm capital in the United Kingdom decreased steadily from 19.3 to 2.4 per cent of the national wealth. The net fixed capital formation in Swedish agriculture fell in one hundred years (1861-1962) from 33.2 to 3.6 per cent, and in Norway (1865-1962) from 34 to 7.3 per cent. In the U.S.A. in the period 1880-1958 the addition to agricultural product fell from 26.2 to 3.6 per cent of the total addition. From 1861 to 1880 Australia increased her capital formation in agriculture from 15.6 to 32 per cent; after that period it fell to 6.2 in 1930-1939 while the

[16] Cf. R. Bićanić, "The Threshold of Economic Growth", *Kyklos*, No. 1 (Basel, 1962).
[17] U.N.-E.C.E., *Some Factors in Economic Growth in Europe in 1950s*, III, 28.

agricultural share of the national income remained the same (23 per cent). Argentina's gross fixed capital formation in agriculture moved from the beginning to the mid-twentieth century from 23.8 to 5.3 per cent of the total capital formation.[18]

B. *Turning Point*

When there is a downward movement in agricultural investment in a relative sense, and almost a stagnation in the increase of such investment in absolute sums, this means that the turning point is approaching (e.g., in Israel, Canada, Australia, France, Finland in Chart III). The turning point in capital investment occurs when capital supply becomes available at the general rate of interest, and gain from investment in agriculture is nearly proportionate to the amount of capital invested. Income in cash greatly prevails over income in kind and the total income elasticity of demand for capital moves between small coefficients. Agriculture is treated the same way as are other branches of production, and investment criteria are set following the same evaluation. In such a situation reasons for the existence of a special capital market for agriculture gradually disappear or remain as a historical left-over. Capital is no longer a limiting factor in the development of agriculture.

The financial decision as to whether or not to invest no longer depends on capital availability at any cost but on the rate of interest: does it pay or not? Therefore substitution of land and labor by capital, and above all substitution of capital of a low productivity by capital of a higher productivity, takes place.[19] The natural risk of capital loss is decreased but commercial risk is greatly increased because of the heavy proportion of fixed assets.

The exigencies of the market are so pressing and the capital investment so heavy that the producer is forced into a position where he will seek to be relieved from the risks of the market, be it by government policy or by contract farming or by economic planning, so that he is able and indeed pressed to concentrate on problems of production technique and

[18] S. Kuznets, "Quantitative Aspects of Long Term Growth of Nations, VI. Long Term Trends in Capital Formation Proportion" (*Economic Development and Cultural Change*, July 1961, Part II. Appendix.)

[19] The position of British agriculture is characterized by a decline of 500,000 acres of agricultural land over a decade or 50 to 60,000 acres p.a. mainly for building development. The labor force declined by 200,000 in agriculture in the same decade, or 20,000 a year. The annual productivity of labor has increased by 4 per cent from 1954 to 1960, and by 6 per cent from 1960 to 1965.

management of cost reduction. An extensive service supplies him with all the necessary information and technical, financial and other resources. Thus the tendency towards monopoly of production is overpowered by the tendency towards monopsony.

When the domestic consumer is satisfied to the level of saturation, the production drive is transformed and further increase in the volume of production is discouraged (U.S.A., Sweden, even Finland), so that the attention of the producers is focused on the quality and processing of agricultural products. The closing of the market to agricultural imports becomes more a safeguard of income policy than a question of competitive costs. The agricultural operator assumes the role of *entrepreneur* weighing profits and losses, which influence his investment decisions. This means that capital frequently changes form. The entrepreneurial decisions are mainly concerned to combine factors of production which will give optimal results in terms of return to global financial capital invested, which also means a reduction in the capital coefficient by a better combination of its component parts. This optimal capital-mix is rather empirical, finding its limits in ecological and technical conditions (crop rotation, animal life cycle, vegetation period, humus preservation).[20] It is also limited by the institutional framework such as family size, property relations, managerial skill, legal regulations, etc.

Managerial skill acquires such importance that it is separated from the providing of capital and treated as a special factor in production (A Marshallian fourth factor of production). Those who cannot invest, or do not do it in a successful way, are doomed and their lands and capital taken over by more skilful 'capital-mixers'.

C. *Capital Decrease*

There are signs in some countries that the peak has been reached and that they are approaching the stage in development of agriculture where capital will tend to decrease. This decrease is now taking place at an accelerated pace in a relative sense in the fast declining share of agricul-

[20] The new British National Plan gave the following assessment of agricultural development in Britain: there is no technical limit to rapid expansion of production of poultry meat, pig meat and eggs. Production of beef meat and milk can have a relatively slow technical expansion. Crops, especially cereals, would be limited both in acreage and yield, encountering both technical and economic limitations. In production of fruit and vegetables the prospects are mixed; one limiting factor is the time required to grow fruit and another mainly the cost of establishing new green houses. Production of sugar depends on very heavy investment in sugar refineries. H.M.S.O., *The National Plan*, p. 138-139.

tural capital in the global national wealth. And one should also expect, in spite of the steadily increasing volume of production, a decline in the absolute quantity of capital engaged in agriculture.

Yearly gross capital investment in agriculture in the U.S.A., France, and Sweden did not increase to any significant extent in the years 1953-1962. It increased somewhat in Sweden and slightly in the U.S.A. and France (from 3,600 to 3.800 million dollars in the U.S.A., and in France from 800 million dollars in 1953 to 820 million in 1958 and 1962 at market prices), which means a decline in net capital formation. Capital investment in agriculture fell considerably in relative terms, from 6.6 per cent to 3.6 per cent in Sweden, from 7.1 per cent to 4.4 per cent in the U.S.A., and in France from 7.4 to 5.4 per cent[21] (Chart No. VI). This trend is now manifest in the policy of limitation in agricultural production in several countries, because of the saturation of demand or the general low income elasticity of demand for agricultural products. In others it leads to pressure for an almost complete overhaul of agricultural policy. We interpret these signs to indicate the following:

(a) The tendency to change the capital-mix in such a way that the average capital coefficient becomes lighter, i.e., the productivity of capital per unit of product greater. This results from the fact that the main capital investment requiring heavy capital coefficient, such as land reclamation and building of infrastructure, is already accomplished; cultivation of submarginal lands is abandoned; building construction by farm operators is decreasing because of population decline;[22] structural

[21] During the same period Italy, Portugal, Greece, Denmark, Ireland, witnessed a considerable increase in capital investment in absolute terms, while a decline in relative terms took place (e.g., in the United Kingdom from 6.2 in 1950 to 3.6 per cent, in Finland from 16.3 to 8.5, in Italy from 13.6 to 9.8). The absolute sums and the percentages increased in Ireland, Denmark, and Greece, which still show a considerable distance from the turning point. The investment in agriculture in Britain is planned at an increase of 16 per cent in five years over the existing (1964) investment level which is only 29 million pounds more (181 to 210). The total investment in the Five-Year Plan amounts to more than 8 billion pounds or an increase of 41 per cent, so that the investment in agriculture will fall from a 3.12 per cent to a mere 2.62 per cent of total investment p.a. (H.M.S.O., *The National Plan*, p. 57.) (Computed from the *U.N. Yearbook of National Accounts Statistics* for 1963; for rates of exchange Table 3B was used.) Another source indicates that agricultural investment in the 1950's increased in West Germany, France, Switzerland, Austria, the United Kingdom, the Netherlands, Norway, Israel, Italy, Poland, and Portugal. The decline in absolute terms took place in Finland, Sweden, Belgium, Ireland and Denmark. U.N.-E.C.E.-F.A.O., *Towards Intensive Agriculture* (Geneva, 1961), Table XII.

[22] In France the number of farms declined in the years 1954-1963 from 2,284,000 to 1,900,000 or by 384,000 which means a reduction of 17 per cent in a decade. (*Etudes et Conjunctures*, Paris, June 1965, p. 712.)

investment in machinery has been mainly achieved and only maintenance and replacement are required.[23]

(b) Great technological progress in agriculture is such that the productivity of capital invested is ever increasing. This is particularly so where chemical (fertilizers, insecticides, pesticides) and biotechnical (artificial insemination, antibiotics, hybrid plants, and other uses of genetics, etc.) investments are concerned, which again require less than proportionate capital investment per unit of product and give an increasing return.

(c) Increased specialization of production requires less capital per unit of production than in mixed farming. Overcapitalization is greatly liquidated and idle capital put into operation. There are signs of financial dis-investment in agriculture due to specialization, such as cutting of vineyards, orchards and forests, liquidation of some herds and abandon-

In the U.S. the Economic Report of the President of 1966 stated: "The decrease in the total number of farms between 1960 and 1965 is estimated at 573,000. ... Many of these small units disappeared through consolidation with other farms. ... This trend of declining numbers of small farms is expected to continue" (p. 33).

[23] The physical assets in American agriculture showed the following movement: Livestock reached its peak in 1952 at 19.5 billion dollars and fell till 1964 by 5.1 billion. The peak figure of crops value kept on farms (or held off farm by farmers as security for Commercial Credit Corporation) increased from 8.8 in 1952 to 9.8 billion dollars in 1964. Household furnishings and equipment moved from the peak year 1956 at 10.5 billion dollars to the 1965 8.8 billion figure. Only the machinery and motor vehicles show a steady and continuous increase. In the last ten years the increase amounted to 5.9 billion dollars. And the perspective in this group of assets is no longer so much on the increasing side (*Economic Report of the President*, 1966, p. 298). The yearly increase of tractors in the U.S.A. in 1950 amounted to 8 per cent or 270 thousand and in 1960 only to 0.4 per cent (20 thousand), with the prospective annual increase till 1980 of 50,000 tractors per year. The corresponding numbers for grain combines were 13.2 and 0.5 per cent and for corn pickers 18.5 and 2.6 per cent. Demand moved from structural growth to functional replacement.

This point has not yet been reached in Europe. Between 1950 and 1959 the number of tractors in the E.E.C. countries increased five times, of milking machinery six times, and combined harvesters twelve times. Landsberg, *et al.*, *Resources in America's Future* (Johns Hopkins U. Press, 1963), pp. 776-777; U.N.-E.E.C., *Some Factors in Economic Growth in Europe in 1950s* (1964), Ch. III, p. 27. Nevertheless, in France, which in 1945 had no more than 35,000 tractors, the number of tractors increased in twenty years almost to the saturation point. In 1939 there was one tractor per 600 ha., or per 200 agriculturally active people. In 1954 the number reached 230,000 and in 1965 one million. The expected number for 1970 is 1.2 million, which will saturate the demand. While in 1957 100,000 tractors were bought, for 1970 the expected demand is not bigger than 70,000-80,000, which represents the replacement market (M. Gervais, C. Servolain, J. Weil, *Une France sans paysans*, Seuil, 1965, pp. 48, 50, 58. Also, *Christian Science Monitor*, Oct. 12, 1965). Colin Clark spoke about oversaturation with tractors in the U.K. as long ago as 1955 (*Manchester Guardian*, May 25, 1955).

ment of stables, and generally less investment in construction than hitherto because of the greatly decreased number of farms.

(d) Indirect agricultural investment is directed to extra services, enabling the agricultural operator to get activities performed for him. On a microlevel he can purchase services which earlier required his own capital investment and the keeping of greater inventory supplies. On a macroeconomic scale such investments can be supplied by more rational utilization of capital than on an individual basis (e.g., fertilizers and oil supply).

Moreover, a considerable amount of capital hitherto counted as investment in agriculture has been transferred to services supplied by many branches of manufacturing industry, commerce, and transport, and is therefore statistically excluded from the agricultural sector.

The farmer's activity is based to an ever greater extent on scientific research offered to him by public extension services as well as by commercial and other industrial vertical organizations in 'agribusiness'. This decreases his commercial risks, and leads on one hand to a government policy protective towards agriculture, and on the other hand to contract farming. Both factors have greatly rationalized the commercial and financial risk for capital investment previously undertaken on the empirical trial and error (i.e., 'free market') basis. They also require a lesser amount of capital and secure a more orderly flow of goods and services. At the same time such development reduces the function of the agricultural entrepreneur to the role of technical manager, and TECHNICAL PARITY becomes the main concern of agricultural policy.

Technical progress — jointly with land, labor, capital, and managerial activity — thus becomes the fifth independent variable in agricultural development. Its application increases the interdependence of agriculture within the global economy so that the operation of the market mechanism, and partial uses of a command mechanism, do not provide adequate services. There is, therefore, an ever growing opening for contract economy and use of the planning mechanism, and this all the more as agriculture is increasingly integrated into the process of economic development.

APPENDIX I: THE AGRICULTURAL POPULATION TURNING POINT AND THE DEMOGRAPHIC FACTOR

There is little doubt that the increase of agricultural population in absolute figures is predominantly influenced by the demographic factor of population increase, particularly so because of the comparatively small mobility of agricultural population and of its greater fertility. This is not so when the decline of agricultural population, especially of its active part, is analyzed. Here the demographic forces compete with other factors which sometimes influence the agricultural population to a much greater degree than the population factor. Thus there is not necessarily a positive correlation between the decrease of the active agricultural population and the changes in the natural growth of the total population.

For measure we shall take the year of the beginning of the third stage of the population cycle. That is the period when the birth rate of population begins to fall at an accelerated pace while the death rate declines slowly or stops falling so that the rate of the natural increase of the population shows a significant fall. We shall also introduce a lag of 20 years as we assume that this much time is necessary for the decline in the birth rate to produce a visible influence on population movement, i.e., that people will have grown up enough to be able to decide whether they want to move out of agriculture.

In Table No. VI we have, for a number of countries, put the years in which the birth rate began to fall at an accelerated pace, and the years of turning points in the movement of the active agricultural population. These countries can be classified into three groups (taking into account the lag of 20 years): (a) when the turning point of the agricultural active population occurs well BEFORE the fall in the birth rate; (b) when both years happen almost in the same time period, or within a lapse of 10 years on one side or the other, and (c) when the turning point takes place well AFTER the beginning of the third phase of the population cycle.

In the first group are countries which had the turning point at least 10 years before the fall in the birth rate could be significantly felt. In our sample this group includes countries like the United Kingdom, Switzerland, the United States, Austria and Yugoslavia. In this group the demographic factor did not have a predominant effect on the decline of agricultural population, as the active agricultural population began to decline long before the birth rate began to slow down. This can be interpreted as follows: the population factor influenced the fall in the number of agricultural active population less than did other factors (industrialization, emigration, etc.). The pull-out forces were stronger and acted faster than the push-out forces of population growth.

The second group is composed of countries in which the turning point occurred almost at the same time as the slowing down of the population increase, i.e., within $\pm$ 10 years' difference. This happened in the following countries: Italy, Portugal, Greece, Sweden, Norway, and Japan. In these countries the population factor was the dominant influence on the movement of agricultural population; the other push and pull factors kept each other almost in balance and the demographic factor played the predominant role.

The third group is formed of countries which achieved the turning point long (at least 10 years) AFTER the beginning of the general decline of the birth rate. These countries are: France, Germany, Denmark, Netherlands, Spain. Here again the demographic factor exerted its full influence, acting as a pull in force, because of the general decline in the population growth. The pull-in forces were stronger than the push-out forces, but other pull-in forces were stronger than the pull-in force of the declining population factor, and they kept the agricultural population on land longer than the fall in the birth rate would allow. This retention lasted for 10 to 50 years longer than might be nationally expected.

APPENDIX II: TURNING POINTS AND ECONOMIC DEVELOPMENT

Is there any relation between the turning point of the agricultural population and the level of economic growth? If we look at the country and year at which the turning points were reached in our Chart No. V, we can notice at first glance a positive correlation between them and the developmental level of different countries. The historical sequence in turning points of various countries as shown in Table I (p. 184) clearly demonstrates this tendency. The sequence in reaching the turning point was as follows: the U.K. in 1820, Switzerland in 1850, Belgium before 1856, Sweden in 1880, France in 1900, the U.S.A. in 1910, Italy in 1920, Germany in 1925, Denmark and Finland in 1940, Yugoslavia in 1948, Spain and Portugal in 1950, and Greece in 1960, which shows a remarkable relationship between economic growth and the agricultural population turning points. Thus we can say: the more developed a country, the earlier in its history this turning point takes place. This is the first rule. Evidently there is a positive correlation between economic development measured by the real national income per head and the turning point of the active agricultural population.

Turning points in active agricultural population and economic development:

Country	*Year of Turning Point*
United Kingdom	1820
Switzerland	1850

CHART VII

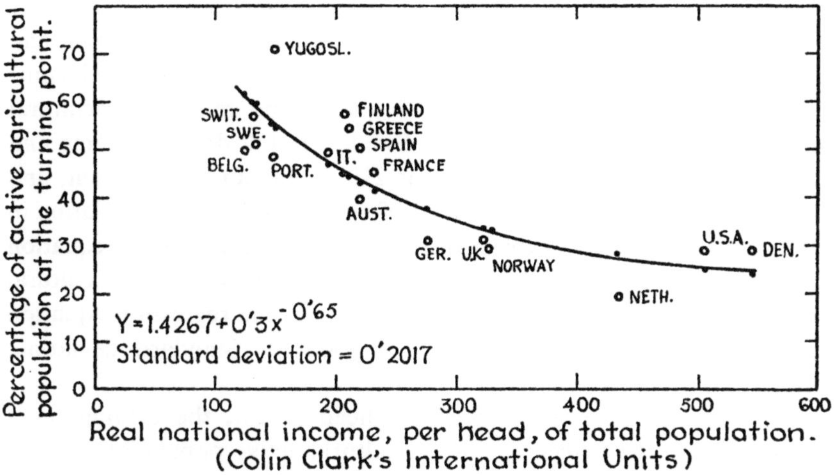

Country	*Year of Turning Point*
Belgium	1856
Sweden	1880
France	1900
U.S.A.	1910
Italy	1920
Germany	1925
Norway	1930
Austria	1939
Denmark	1940
Finland	1940
Netherlands	1947
Yugoslavia	1948
Spain	1950
Japan	1950
Portugal	1950
Greece	1960

Nevertheless, the connection is not simple. The data show that the turning point did not occur in all countries at the same level of economic development. On the contrary, it occurred in different countries at very different levels of total real national income per head. Neither did it occur at the same stage of the national division of labor as expressed by the relative number of agricultural or non-agricultural population. For instance, the turning point happened in the U.K. when the real national income per head was 325 dollars[24] and agricultural active population at 31 per cent. In the U.S. the turning point was reached when the level was already 508 dollars and the population in agriculture at 28 per cent, and in Denmark at 545 dollars and 28 per cent. Italy had it when the income per head was not more than at 177 dollars and relative agricultural population was still at 52 per cent, Sweden at 132 dollars income and 51 per cent of population, Finland at 210 dollars and 60 per cent, and Greece at 212 dollars and 59 per cent of agricultural active population in total active population (Table VII, Chart VII). The regression equation shows a negative slope. Taking Y as the percentage of active agricultural population and X as the real income per head, the regression equation is: $Y = 1.467\,x^{-0.65}$ and it shows a good fit (Standard deviation, $S = 0.20$).

In countries where the income per head is low, the turning point occurred when the percentage of agricultural active population in total active population was still high. Thus, we can propose a second rule: the lower the level of development, the higher the percentage of agricultural active population at which the turning point takes place.

Agriculture was not able to maintain the previous number of active population and therefore precipitated it even before the division of labor attracted it to other activities; thus the percentage of non-agricultural occupations was very low (about 30 per cent); therefore, the high percentage of agricultural population at which the turning point takes place. In this way an urban subproletariat was created in many countries (Southern Italy, Middle East, South East Asia). In other countries there was a strong tendency to emigrate overseas (Italy, Yugoslavia, Greece). The endogenous push-out forces in agriculture were stronger than the non-agricultural pull-out forces. This situation ended in a turning point of absolute agricultural population before the division of labor significantly increased.

In countries at a high level of development and a pronounced division of labor, development has created conditions where the agricultural pull-in (attractive) forces operated with greater strength than the agricultural push-out (expulsive) forces. But this can occur only when a comparatively high general level of development is reached and more

[24] There is a very limited number of internationally comparable historical series of national income per head. We have taken Colin Clark's figures of real International Units as given in the 1957 edition of *Conditions of Economic Progress* for the above countries (pp. 18, 88-196). The International Unit equals the purchasing power of one U.S. dollar in the decade 1925-1934.

opportunities for jobs are created, which means that a decrease in percentage of agricultural population is attained, and the agricultural population starts to decrease at a lower percentage of active population.

In the bottom half of the observed countries, the absolute decline of agriculturally active population took place when the relative number of this population was around 57 per cent and the average income per head was 166 dollars. This led some authors to generalize that the absolute decline 'normally' takes place when the agriculturally active population equals the non-agricultural one. But the empirical data show that the top half of the observed countries had reached that stage long after relative population engaged in agriculture fell well below 50 per cent and reached an average of 33 per cent. The percentage of agriculturally active population was between 45 and only 19 per cent when it began to decrease in absolute numbers. This happened at the 342 dollars per head level of development.

The delay in the decline of absolute numbers of agricultural population may be caused by many factors, such as resistance of family farm population to change and keeping more people than necessary on the land because of family ties; another is protective legislation which for many reasons — political (vote-catching), military (manpower increase), social (preservation of the peasant way of life), etc. — develops a postponing action. But the main reason is the fast division of labor and the development of the market for agricultural products which absorb the surplus but keep the rest steadily on land, the high level of development enabling them to do so.

Sources to Table I

National Statistical Yearbook; F.A.O. Yearbooks; data refer to the year as indicated in the Table or to the closest year to the decade.

For Norway:
G. S. Lellenstrom and G. Skancke, *The Economically Active Population in Norway, 1895-1960, and Forecasts up to 1970 (=Artikler fra Statistisk Sentralbyro,* Nr. 10., Vol. 1964), pp. 14, 15.

For Sweden:
Historical Statistics, F.A.O. Yearbooks, I.

For Switzerland:
W. Gasser Stäger, *Strukturwandlungen in der Schweizerischen Landwirtschaft seit den 19. Jahrhundert.*

For the U.S.A.:
Historical Statistics of U.S., I ed.

Note:
Absolute figures in thousands. Relative figures as percentages of total active population.

Source:
National Statistics, nearest to the year. F.A.O. Yearbook.

Country		1800	1810	1820	1830	1840	1850	1860	1870	1880	1890	19
U.K.	000 %		4.390 35	*4.772* 33	4.613 28	 23	3.518 27.6	3.149 23.2	2.809 19.1	2.561 16.3	2.405 14.3	2. 3
Switzerland	000 %	500 66		555 62			*620* 57			558 42	488 37	481 3
Belgium	000 %							*1055* 45		8.07 29	649 22	697 2
Norway	000 %								*348* 47.3		330 42.1	311 3
Sweden	000 %								*2.153* 51.6			
France	000 %						8319 53		8535 51	7890 45		*8.* 4
U.S.A.	000 %			2.071 71.9	2.773 70.4	3.718 68.6	4.965 64.5	6.287 59.7	6.850 53.4	8.585 49.4	9.938 42.6	10. 3
Italy	000 %							8300 58	8700 58	8600 57		944 5
Germany	000 %									7.135 42.3	7.184 36.4	
Denmark	000 %								499 51.2	509 48.9	512 45.4	525 4
U.S.S.R.	000 %											
Portugal	000 %										1683 65	
Finland	000 %											
Puerto Rico	000 %											
Australia	000 %											
New Zealand	000 %											
S. Africa	000 %											
Netherlands	000 %											606 3
Austria	000 %											
Yugoslavia	000 %											
Japan	000 %											
Chile	000 %											
Spain	000 %										4848 69	471 6
Greece	000 %											
U.A.R.	000 %											
Venezuela	000 %											
Mexico	000 %											320 6
Turkey	000 %											
India	000 %											
Indonesia	000 %											

population

…10	1920	1925	1930	1935	1940	1945	1950	1955	1960	1961	1962	Country
83 .8	2.235 10.5		1.478 6.8				1.116 4.9	1.052 4.6				U.K.
	483 26		413 22		415 21		355 17		292 12			Switzerland
	604 18		630				412 12		349 9.4			Belgium
.5	336 31.4		336 28.9			334 24.4	290 20.9		220 15.6			Norway
)16	1058 41		943 33			615 21	632 20		448 14			Sweden
77 .8		8200 36	7.704 35.8	7.012 37.0	7.204 36.0	7.480 36.5		5.137 24	5.039 26		3.908 20	France
92 .0	11.449 27.0		10.472 21.4		9.004 17.6		7.138 13.0			5.723 8.6		U.S.A.
	10.264 56		9.356 51	8843 48			8060 41		6320 30		5341 26	Italy
57 .0		*9.763* 30.5		9.343 28.9	8.934 25.5			7.200 21.0	6.000 18.0	4.943 12.5		Germany
	577 38.2	*630* 35.9	619 33.2	599 30.2	560 26.6		496 23.5	489 23.0	366 27			Denmark
		71.735 87			39.477 50			38.426 39			33.000	U.S.S.R.
			1897 51		1488 49		1590 48		1448 42			Portugal
	1032 69		1107 64		*1157* 57		912 46		721 35			Finland
			364 52				250 39				168 24	Puerto Rico
					548 19	498 16		498 13		459 11		Australia
					150 23	119 20		132 16		129 14		New Zealand
					3395 64	2418 47	1509 33		1698 30			S. Africa
		642 24	655 21			*747* 20			447 11			Netherlands
	984 32			976 31			*1080* 32			769 23		Austria
	4750 81		5083 78				*7148* 75	5240 67		4748 57		Yugoslavia
	14.287		14.131 48				*16.132* 45.3		14.326 33.0			Japan
				529 36			*648* 30		648 28			Chile
		4538 56		3732 46	4718 52		*5730* 50		4803 31			Spain
	338 46	926 50	1476 54			1502 61			1962 54			Greece
				4308 71		4126 64			*4403* 57			U.A.R.
					626 50		705 41				*774* 32	Venezuela
	3.500 71.0		3.605 67		3.803 65	6.050 58			*6.145* 54.0			Mexico
			5.579 85		6.460 82	5.724 76	8.200 80	9.318 77	*9.737* 75			Turkey
			94.749 66						130.992 70	131.143 70		India
			13.795 66								*25.516* 72	Indonesia

TABLE II

Turning points in land utilization, 1910 to 1962
Index numbers — 1952 = 100

Agricultural Area

Country	1910	1927	1938	1952	1958	1962
Kazakstan	44	—	71	100	297	*322*
U.S.S.R.	75	72	96	100	125	*138*
Ukraine	90	—	100	100	105	*111*
Greece	—	—	93	100	102	*108*
Japan	—	—	104	100	114	*120*
Canada	—	—	—	100	104	*107*
India	87	83	87	100	106	*106*
Kenya	—	—	—	100	97	*106*
Spain	—	—	93	100	104	*104*
Finland	72	85	97	100	98	*102*
Italy	—	97	104	100	102	101
U.A.R.	—	—	91	100	107	105
Yugoslavia	—	101	107	100	*108*	106
Switzerland	—	94	100	100	*108*	98
Venezuela	—	—	—	100	*109*	93
U.S.A.	76	—	82	*100*	96	—
Armenia	67	—	84	*100*	80	84
Netherlands	90	94	98	*100*	99	95
Estonia	78	—	*100*	100	82	85
Austria	109	108	*110*	100	101	99
Hungary	100	101	101	100	100	97
Denmark	*102*	101	102	100	97	97
Ireland	*105*	105	100	100	100	—
Sweden	*107*	106	103	100	100	96
Norway	*107*	99	100	100	98	—
United Kingdom	*110*	105	102	100	100	101
W. Germany	*112*	108	104	100	101	98
Czechoslovakia	*112*	107	103	100	98	98
Belgium	110	*113*	105	100	97	90
France	*118*	110	105	100	101	101

Source: U.N.-E.C.E.-F.A.O. European Agriculture (1954), p. 13; F.A.O. Yearbooks; Narodnoe Hozjajstvo S.S.S.R. v (1963) (Godu, Moscow, 1964).

TABLE III

Change from the peak year in land area

Arable land						
Peak Year			Decreased		Increased	
Before 1924	1924-1963	Exp. after 1963	More than 10%	Less than 10%	Less than 10%	More than 10%
	Austria 1938		Austria			
Belgium 1866			Belgium			
		Bulgaria				Bulgaria
Czecho-slovakia			Czecho-slovakia			
	Denmark 1958			Denmark		
		Finland				Finland
France 1862				France		
		Greece				Greece
	Hungary 1947			Hungary		
	Italy 1954			Italy		
	Netherl. 1947			Netherlands		
		Norway				Norway
		Spain				Spain
Sweden 1920			Sweden			
Switzerland			Switzerland			
U.K. 1869			U.K.			
		Yugoslavia				Yugoslavia
		Canada				Canada
		Argentina				Argentina
		Brazil				Brazil
		Peru				Peru
	Venezuela 1956		Venezuela			
Japan 1924			Japan			
		Philippines				Philippines
		Syria				Syria
		Turkey				Turkey
		Australia				Australia
	N.-Zealand 1945		N.-Zealand			
		S. Africa				S. Africa
		Tunisia				Tunesia
	U.A.R. 1954			U.A.R.		
		India				India
	U.S.A. 1935			U.S.A.		
		U.S.S.R.				U.S.S.R.

Source: International Yearbook of Agricultural Statistics for 1924-1925, 1938-1939; F.A.O. Yearbooks 1950-1964.

Cultivated land						
Peak Year			Decreased		Increased	
Before 1924	1924-1963	Exp. after 1963	More than 10%	Less than 10%	Less than 10%	More than 10%
Austria			Austria			
Belgium 1880			Belgium			
		Bulgaria				Bulgaria
Czecho-slovakia			Czecho-slovakia			
	Denmark 1958			Denmark		
	Finland 1938			Finland		
France 1910			France			
		Greece			Greece	
	Hungary 1938			Hungary		
	Italy 1938			Italy		
	Netherlands 1947			Netherlands		
	Norway 1947			Norway		
		Spain			Spain	
Sweden 1915			Sweden			
	Switzerland 1938			Switzerland		
U.K. 1891			U.K.			
	Yugoslavia 1958			Yugoslavia		
		Canada			Canada	
		Argentina		Argentina		
		Peru				Peru
	Venezuela			Venezuela		
		Japan			Japan	
		Philippines				Philippines
		Syria				Syria
	Turkey 1938			Turkey		
		Australia				Australia
		N.-Zealand				N.-Zealand
		S. Africa				S. Africa
		Tunisia				Tunisia
		India				India
	U.S.A. 1950			U.S.A.		
		U.S.S.R.				U.S.S.R.

TABLE IV

Land utilization — Historical series for selected countries in thousands of hectares in percentages of total surface of the state

Country	Year	Arable land	% of total	Cultivated land	% of total	Country	Year
France round	1790	33,094	—	—	—	Sweden	1800
	1821	25,500	48.9	34,106	65.4		1850
	1840	25,227	47.6	31,397	59.2		1865
	1852	26,139	49.3	33,688	63.5		1875
	1862	26,589	48.9	34,413	63.4		1885
	1883	25,588	48.4	34,594	65.4		1895
	1892	25,387	48.0	34,429	65.1		1905
	1910	23,679	44.7	36,789	69.4		1915
	1920	22,590	41.5	36,219	66.6		1920
	1930	21,791	40.0	34,666	63.7		1938
	1940	18,511	34.5	32,872	61.3		1952
	1947	18,643	33.7	30,435	52.7		1958
	1958	21,436	40.2	34,614	64.5		1963
	1961	19,007	35.7	34,530	64.4		
	1963	21,241	39.8	34,354	64.2	U.S.A.	1850
							1860
Belgium		Arable land		Agricultural land		000 acres	1870
							1880
	1856	—	—	1,831	60.6		1890
	1866	1,601	53.5	1,967	65.6		1900
	1880	—	—	1,983	66.4		1910
	1895	1,472	49.6	1,916	64.4		1920
	1910	—	—	1,956	66.2		1930
	1929	1,128	37.0	1,907	62.5		1935
	1938	1,044	34.2	—	—		1940
	1952	1,008	33.0	1,799	59.0		1950
	1959	946	31.0	1,713	56.1		1959
	1963	946	31.0	1,685	55.2		
						Austria	1924
U.K.		Cropland		Cultivated			1938
							1947
000 acres	1886	13,837	24.3	28,680	50.3		1954
	1869	14,155	24.9	30,339	53.3		1963
	1881	13,226	23.3	32,212	56.7		
	1891	11,768	20.8	32,919	58.0	U.S.S.R.	1913
	1911	10,528	18.5	32.095	57.2		1928
	1922	10,835	19.1	30,751	54.1		1937
	1932	8,491	15.1	29,828	53.0		1950
	1947	12,247	21.5	28,740	50.6		1955
	1954	11,379	20.0	28,094	50.9		1960
	1961	10,475	18.6	28,702	51.1		1963
	1964	11,112	19.8	28,683	51.0		1964
						Ukraine	
							1913
							1928
							1937
							1950
							1955
							1960
							1963
							1964

Cropland	% of total	Cultivated land	% of total	Country	Year	Cropland	% of total
850	2.1	—	—	Kazakstan	1913	4,170	1.5
2,025	4.9	—	—		1928	4,230	1.5
2,333	5.7	4,279	10.4		1937	5,810	2.1
2,737	6.7	4,795	11.4		1950	7,760	2.8
3,079	7.5	4,913	11.9		1955	20,630	7.6
3,424	8.3	4,952	11.9		1960	28,430	10.4
3,593	8.7	5,028	12.1		1963	32,630	12.0
3,723	9.1	5,068	12.3		1964	30,790	11.3
3,820	9.4	5,793	11.6				
3,742	9.1	4,865	11.9	Armenia	1913	346	11.6
3,498	8.5	4,440	10.8		1928	332	11.1
3,666	8.9	4,350	10.6		1937	437	14.7
3,342	8.1	3,867	9.4		1950	471	15.8
					1952	546	18.3
45,000	4.7	—	—		1955	481	16.1
67,000	8.8	—	—		1960	415	13.9
76,000	9.9	—	—		1963	417	14.6
75,000	9.9	124,000	16.3		1964	415	13.9
99,000	13.0	157,000	20.6				
127,000	16.8	237,000	31.3	Estonia	1913	697	15.4
139,000	18.3	251,000	33.2		1940	918	20.3
161,000	22.1	292,000	38.4		1950	812	18.0
165,000	21.7	316,000	41.6		1952	888	19.6
166,000	21.9				1960	762	16.8
159,000	21.0	343,000	45.2		1963	783	17.4
164,000	21.5	358,000	47.1		1964	777	17.2
157,000	20.8	369,000	48.8				
Arable land							
1,878	22.4	4,327	50.4				
1,972	23.6	4,218	51.9				
1,840	22.0	4,156	49.8				
1,768	21.2	4,083	48.7				
1,721	20.6	3,990	47.6				
Sown area							
18,200							
113,000							
135,300							
146,300	4.1						
185,800	5.8						
203,000	5.7						
218,500	6.1						
212,800	6.0						
28,000							
25,400							
25,900							
30,700	51.2						
32,900	54.9						
33,500	56.0						
34,500	57.5						
34,100	56.9						

TABLE V

Gross domestic capital formation in agriculture of selected countries (in millions of domestic currency and in millions of U.S. dollars).

Country	Year	Millions of local currency	Millions of U.S. dollars	Percentage of total gross capital formations
United States	1950	3,600	3,600	7.1
	1953	3,600	3,600	6.2
	1958	3,600	3,600	5.5
	1962	3,800	3,800	4.4
	1963	3,900	3,900	4.3
Italy	1953	310,000	700	13.6
	1958	414,000	935	11.6
	1962	597,000	1,270	9.8
	1963	614,000	1,240	9.1
France	1953	2,800	800	7.4
	1958	3,400	820	6.6
	1962	4,000	820	5.4
	1963	4,400	950	5.4
Canada	1950	507	507	15.8
	1953	580	580	9.4
	1958	498	498	6.2
	1962	701	701	7.6
	1963	804	781	8.3
United Kingdom	1950	93	260	6.2
	1953	94	260	3.4
	1958	134	370	3.7
	1962	161	450	3.6
	1963	179	551	3.6
Australia	1956	190	490	14.2
	1958	197	510	11.8
	1960	213	550	10.5
	1961	192	472	11.2
Netherlands	1953	244	95	5.0
	1958	290	103	3.6
	1962	440	152	3.7
	1963	520	172	3.9
Sweden	1953	497	96	6.6
	1958	393	77	3.9
	1962	497	96	3.6
	1963	719	146	3.9
Denmark	1950	310	45	6.8
	1953	410	59	7.7
	1958	530	90	9.2
	1962	735	112	7.4
Venezuela	1953	417	82	8.7
	1958	392	78	7.8
	1962	580	126	12.6

Source: The countries are ranked according to the sum invested expressed in U.S. dollars. Data are taken from the *U.N. Yearbook of National Accounts Statistics*, for 1963 and 1964. The conversion rate from the local currency into U.S. dollars is taken from the Tables 3B and 6B of the *Yearbooks* for 1963 and 1964, i.e., expressed in terms of relative prices.

Country	Year	Millions of local currency	Millions of U.S. dollars	Percentage of total gross capital formation
Thailand	1956	932	51	16.7
	1958	1,268	66	17.5
	1960	1,642	85	16.8
	1961	1,842	95	18.7
	1962	2,120	114	14.7
Finland	1950	—	—	16.3
	1953	266	111	11.8
	1958	303	95	10.0
	1962	461	144	9.0
	1963	457	100	8.6
Greece	1950	534	—	8.7
	1953	425	16	5.8
	1958	2,179	70	12.4
	1962	3,189	101	12.0
	1963	2,900	91	12.5
Israel	1955	118	90	19.7
	1958	157	93	15.7
	1962	222	111	11.3
	1963	264	88	11.8
Portugal	1953	762	31	9.6
	1950	1,229	53	13.0
	1962	1,095	48	7.2
	1963	1,389	61	9.9
Philippines	1956	51	14	5.8
	1958	40	11	4.5
	1960	125	35	10.4
	1962	168	45	8.7
	1963	172	42	7.5
Rhodesia-Nyassa	1956	9.6	32	6.2
	1958	9.8	36	7.0
	1960	12.7	45	9.5
	1962	10.0	34	9.3
Sudan	1955	1.8	4	11.5
	1958	10.7	25	30.5
	1961	15.7	35	19.3
	1962	20.9	51	31.5
U.S.S.R.	1950	1,661	—	15.0
	1952	1,933	—	13.7
	1958	4,728	—	15.8
	1960	5,172	—	14.1
	1962	6,316	—	15.7
	1963	6,983	—	16.5
	1964	8,242	—	18.0

TABLE VI

Agricultural population turning point and birth-rate changes

Country	Year around which the birth rate began to fall	Year around which the birth rate stopped falling	Year of the agriculturally active population turning point	Difference between the year of the falling birth rate and the turning points: (1)-(3)	Difference: Diminished by 20-yr lag
	(1)	(2)	(3)	(4)	(5)
U.K.	1875	1930	1820	+55	+75
Switzerland	1925	1957	1850	+75	+95
Sweden	1855	1930	1880	−25	− 5
France	1825	1940	1900	−75	−55
U.S.A.	1928	1945	1910	+18	+38
Italy	(1908)	1951	1920	−12	+ 8
Germany	1875	1930	1925	−50	−30
Denmark	1870	1930	1925	−55	−35
Norway	1901	1930	1947	−46	−16
Portugal	1920	1940	1930	−10	+10
Austria	1930	1955	1939	− 9	+11
Finland	1930	...	1940	−10	+10
Yugoslavia	1957	...	1948	+ 9	+29
Spain	1903	1950	1950	−47	−27
Japan	1930	1955	1950	−20	0
Netherlands	1901	1930	1947	−46	−16
Greece	1930	1950	1960	−30	−10

TABLE VII

Turning point in agricultural active population and economic development

Country	Year of Turning Point	Real Nat. Income per Head I.U.	Percentage of Active Agr. Population		± Δ
			Observed	Computed	
		x	y		
Denmark	1940	545	28	23.72	− 4.28
U.S.A.	1910	508	28	24.83	− 3.17
Netherlands	1947	434	19	27.51	+ 6.10
Norway	1930	327	29	33.06	+ 4.06
United Kingdom	1820	325	31	33.20	− 2.20
Germany	1925	274	31	37.09	+ 6.09
France	1900	231	45	41.45	− 3.55
Austria	1939	220	39	42.78	− 3.78
Spain	1950	220	50	42.78	+ 7.22
Greece	1960	212	54	43.84	+10.16
Finland	1940	210	57	44.10	+13.90
Japan	1950	194	49	46.45	+ 2.56
Yugoslavia	1948	150	71	54.88	+17.12
Portugal	1950	148	48	55.36	− 7.36
Sweden	1880	132	51	59.64	− 8.64
Switzerland	1850	130	57	60.23	− 3.23
Belgium	1856	125	50	61.79	−11.19

VIII

THREE CONCEPTS OF AGRICULTURAL OVER-POPULATION

From being regarded as a problem of under-developed countries only, agricultural over-population has now become a common problem in most countries, affecting many fields of agricultural policy — from price policy to structural changes. It has attracted the attention of students of agrarian policy ever since the first number of the *International Journal of Agrarian Affairs* in 1938 was entirely devoted to it.

In most studies of this phenomenon at least three main concepts can be distinguished: those of consumption, those of production, and those of mobility of population.

1. THE CONSUMPTION APPROACH

From the consumption point of view agricultural over-population may be said to depend on what size of agricultural population an area can support at a certain standard of personal consumption (f_o). The positive surplus above this number we shall consider as agricultural over-population (V). In connection with this we also use the term population pressure (g) which is a relation between the actual number of agricultural population (A) and the standard number of this population (A_o). Thus we get:

$$V = A - A_o \tag{1.1}$$

$$g = \frac{A}{A_o} \tag{1.2}$$

The standard population figure is arrived at by dividing the available aggregate consumption fund by the standard consumption per head.[1]

$$A_o = \frac{F}{f_o} \tag{1.3}$$

[1] We make a distinction here between the level of living and the standard of living in the U.N.O. terminology sense.

$$g = \frac{A}{F} \cdot f_o \tag{1.4}$$

Thus the surplus of agricultural population is expressed by the following formula:

$$V = A - A_o = A - \frac{F}{f_o} \tag{1.5}$$

The agricultural population pressure is greater the larger the absolute figure of that population, and the smaller the aggregate consumption fund put at its disposal, and the larger the standard of personal consumption per head. Thus, if the agricultural population in a country increases, or if its aggregate consumption fund decreases, then agricultural over-population increases too. If in a country the consumption standard of the agricultural population increases, the agricultural population pressure also increases in a positive correlation.

This consumption concept of agricultural over-population is the basis of the whole approach to economic development when it deals with an increase of the standard of living, which is hampered by an increase of population which cannot be matched by an adequate increase of food production. All discussions dealing with the maximum or optimum carrying capacity of an area, a country, or the Earth itself, are linked to this concept of over-population as are also the problems of the population explosion, the hunger line, etc. Maximization of product per hectare is the main policy target.

This kind of pressure of agricultural population can also be considered an indicator of many other social phenomena, from the decomposition of the institutional framework in which the agricultural population lives, up to political revolts and agrarian revolutions which occur when a level of irreducible consumption is approached which cannot be countered by economic means.

To determine the magnitude of agricultural over-population in connection with this first concept, three sets of problems have to be elaborated. The first is to define the agricultural population. Here we are taking into consideration the TOTAL agricultural population. The distinction between the terms 'rural spatial' and 'agricultural occupational' is important. It opens up a whole set of questions, especially in countries in which agriculture is not only an occupation but still a way of life; where it comprises a great number of additional and auxiliary activities, and other multi-functional family services connected with life on the family holding either as main or accessory occupations.

The second set of problems is concerned with the aggregate consumption fund. At first this fund was assumed to be evenly distributed and proportionate to the agricultural land, and the problem was to find out how much land was necessary to support one person living by agriculture or one consumption unit. As land proved to be an unreliable indicator, the next step was to take volume of production in physical terms (in kind, or food production per head) as a standard measurement of agricultural over-population. The problem of minimum subsistence level (calories, kg., etc.) is the expression of this kind of problem. The next stage was to move from volume to aggregate income in cash and kind, conceiving over-population in terms of average income from agriculture per head of agricultural population. The problem of parity of income between non-agricultural and agricultural population arose as a measurement of living standards.[2]

Further refinement of the over-population concept led to the regional analysis of population distribution, moving also from regional to communal, local or village over-population figures so as to remove the semblance of equal distribution of population over wide areas, thus evening out the surpluses with the vacuums.[3]

A switch from the spatial to the institutional dimension was the next natural step. Agricultural over-population came to be defined according to size of holding assuming the number of people in an area to vary according to the size of the holding, the smaller ones being overcrowded, and the larger ones sparsely populated. The problem became linked with land reform policy bringing about a redistribution of land both locally and regionally, leading to internal migration. External colonization was the obvious extension of this problem.

Soon the concept of over-population by size of holding was replaced by a more accurate standard, that of the size of the income from agriculture per holding per head. Instead of the spatial, the money dimension was adopted, measuring the number of people living on agricultural holdings according to the income distribution. Another variant of this

[2] J. D. Black as far back as 1938 set the following standard (his second) for agricultural over-population: "... population in agriculture which is able to obtain the same returns from its labour and content of living as comparable social classes can obtain in other industries. ..." "The Problem of Agricultural Overpopulation", *International Journal of Agrarian Affairs*, Vol. 1 (1939), p. 10.

[3] The assumption is still made that income at the personal disposal of the agricultural population is evenly distributed. A more accurate measurement of the total disposable consumption fund would be found by deducting expenditure, i.e., according to the real burden of direct and indirect taxes, debts and other tranfers, rent, investments, etc.

concept defined by income standards is the distinction between the internal income achieved on the holding and the off-holding income which again can be intra-local and extra-local. In a stricter sense only internal income, earned on the holding, could be included when counting agricultural over-population. But as the definition of agriculture itself has not only technological elements (raising crops and animals), but also institutional ones (auxiliary and additional activities), the off-holding activities are not easily isolated from the internal ones. In defining agricultural over-population, therefore, the technological factor cannot be separated from the institutional. Here sociology mixes with economics. Therefore, in measuring the subsistence standard it is not only the size of the agricultural income that matters but the number of people supported by the holding, which depends on socio-economic ties, unpaid family labor being more strongly linked to an agricultural holding than is hired labor. In this way agricultural over-population was conceived in several different forms. The division between family farms and commercial farms in the United States of America is one example. Distinction between those who own land *in absentia* and those who live and work on farms is another example. A third is the problem of peasant labor forces working on *latifundia* and living on *minifundia* in Latin America, giving agricultural over-population a specific semi-feudal and seasonal note.

Thus the problem had to be treated not only from the point of view of economic policy but also from that of social policy. Different measures of protection (customs, price policy, homestead, or direct and indirect subsidies) enable the peasant population to remain on land for lack of other opportunities of earning their livelihood where economic considerations alone would not justify their staying. In this respect the family peasant holding plays the role of an institutional reservoir for giving subsistence to marginal agricultural over-population. In the Soviet Union this role is partly played by another institutional form, the *kolkhozes* as opposed to the *sovkhozes*.[4] The most articulate socio-economic distinction in analyzing agricultural over-population has been made by G. Orlando,[5] who distinguishes over-population according to

[4] Explaining why the time used to produce 100 kg. of grain is 1.8 hours in the *sovkhozes* and 7.3 hours in the *kolkhozes*, Khrushchev said: "... In the *kolkhozes*, parallel to the problem of achieving a high productivity of labour, is the problem of securing work for all members of the collective and achieving incomes under the same conditions of equal effort and input of labour as in the social economy. ... The *sovkhozes* are a different affair", *Izvestia* (Dec. 16th, 1958).

[5] G. Orlando, "Metodi di Accertamento Della Disoccupazione Agricola. Italiana", *Rivista di Economia Agraria*, 3 (Roma, 1952).

type of holding: people on family holdings, share croppers, proprietor-workers, operators, part-time workers, and labor on capitalist estates.

The third set of problems is that of the standard of consumption (f_o). This represents a constant magnitude, specially defined. Although in reality it depends on the kind and absolute magnitude of the aggregate consumption fund, for the purpose of the study of over-population it has to be conceived, conceptually, as a constant. Various methods have been used to define such standards of consumption per head or per consumption unit. It was defined either in physical or in money units (income per head), as an empirically or scientifically devised norm, physiological minimum, the hunger line, minimum of existence, number of calories, physical units of food or textiles, etc.

This standard of consumption has been set also in relative terms in relation to the consumption of a previously taken basis, or compared with another country or economic region.[6]

2. THE PRODUCTION APPROACH

From the point of view of production, agricultural over-population can be defined as the number of people in excess of a standard number of producers required for agricultural production in a certain area. In this concept only the economically active agricultural population is taken into account (A_e). Maximization of production per producer is its main target.

Of course the most appropriate criterion would be the optimum number of economically active members of the population. But as optima are often difficult to define or even to assess, it is more convenient to adopt other standards.

A. *Level of Production*

The standard agricultural population (A_{eo}) is the active agricultural population of a standard productivity necessary to achieve a given volume of production in a certain agricultural area.

$$V_e = A_e - A_{eo} \tag{2.1}$$

$$g_e = \frac{A_e}{A_{eo}} \tag{2.2}$$

[6] The concealed assumptions in this concept are homogeneity of consumption over time, the continuous flow of income and expenditure, etc.

$$A_{eo} = \frac{Z}{z_o} \tag{2.3}$$

$$A_e = \frac{Z}{z} \tag{2.4}$$

In this case V_e is agricultural over-population, and g_e is population pressure. Z indicates aggregate volume of production, z stands for actual agricultural productivity of the active agricultural population, while z_o represents standard agricultural productivity per head (or unit) of such population.

When the first studies of agricultural over-population from the production point of view were undertaken, the density of agricultural population on a certain area (P) used to be taken as the measure of over-population (say 1 person per ha. of land). This involved so many concealed assumptions — e.g. that labor requirements are proportionate to the agricultural area — that more precise measurements were soon seen to be necessary. First the agricultural area under various crops (arable land, gardens, meadows, orchards, vineyards, or pastures) was converted into a homogeneous average or standard agricultural area (Q, arable equivalent) by using different factors of conversion (k) for different crops in order to show the distribution of land by the intensity of cultivation.[7] Next the fertility of land and the intensity of production were added as a specific factor[8] expressed in physical terms (harvest units). A further development was to represent the natural indices of production computed by F.A.O. on the natural unit basis. Colin Clark introduced multiple harvest and the irrigation factor[9] for a (wet or dry) cultivated area.

If we put all these factors together we can develop the following formulas:

$$Q = kP \tag{2.5}$$

$$Z = qQ = qkP \tag{2.6}$$

$$V_e = A_e - A_{eo} = A_e - \frac{qk}{z}P \tag{2.7}$$

$$g_e = \frac{A_e}{A_{eo}} = \frac{A_e}{Z} z_o = \frac{A_{eo}}{qkP} \cdot z_o \tag{2.8}$$

[7] J. Poniatowski, "Le Problème du Surpeuplement dans l'Agriculture Polonaise", *L'Est Européen Agricole* (1936), pp. 21-60.

[8] Wilbert Moore, *Economic Demography of Eastern and South Eastern Europe* (League of Nations, 1945).

[9] Colin Clark, *Conditions of Economic Progress* (London, 1953).

Following these formulas, agricultural over-population, defined from the point of view of production, is proportionate to the following factors: the larger the numbers of the economically active population; the smaller the agricultural area; the lesser the intensity of crops; the smaller the yield per hectare; and the greater the productivity of labor corresponding to the standard use of the labor force.

It must be emphasized that the pressure of agricultural population increases as labor productivity increases, thus the greater the productivity of agricultural labor, the greater the over-population. On the other hand, such factors as an increase of the intensity of agriculture and increase of yields, as well as an increase of agricultural area, ease the population pressure and reduce agricultural over-population.

B. *Number of People*

Labor productivity in this case has been measured as real product per head of persons active in agriculture. But as the population is not homogeneous the next step was to convert it into labor units of equal productivity, bringing women and young and old people to the average working productivity of men.[10] A further step was to take into account not the number of persons, but their working time, thus the personal dimension was transposed into the time dimension.[11] The average working time in terms of work hours then had to be included in the concept of over-population. In this way labor requirements were taken as the standard labor demand, and labor working time at full employment level as the total labor supply. It should be noted that potential, not actual, working time is taken as a measure.

The outcome is that the formula has been transformed from a personal dimension into labor-time supply and demand, i.e. into the maximum capacity of supply, and the standard demand of labor-time. Divided by a standard working day or year the average number of agricultural working population was obtained:

$$V_e = w \cdot a \cdot A_e - w_o A_{eo} \qquad (2.9)$$

$$g_{ew} = \frac{w \cdot a \cdot A_e}{w_o A_{eo}} \qquad (2.10)$$

Here a stands for the conversion factor from the actual number of

[10] Here again the skill of an agricultural labor unit is still considered as homogeneous, a rather gross assumption.

[11] This conversion has to be done with caution, not overlooking the indivisibility of the factor 'human being', or the relative indivisibility of the agricultural family.

persons economically active in agriculture into a standard number of homogeneous personal labor units; w stands for the number of working hours at full capacity, and w_o for the requirements of labor hours per person in the same period of time (a year).[12]

The difference between the number of working hours at full employment level and the actual working hours measures the efficiency of labor utilization, which must be taken as a factor in assessing the surplus of agricultural labor. In other words, if labor is used less efficiently, then this means concealed unemployment and is not a method of solving the problem of surplus population in agriculture.

Here we come up against the problem of what the full employment of labor is. In order to avoid the complicated question of optimum or maximum use, most students of this problem use relative measures which can be called standard use of labor capacity and may mean anything from conventional to comparative measurement, e.g. a standard work day of 8 or 10 hours; a yearly number of work hours, say 1500, 2500, or 3000 hours per person (with deductions made for holidays and bad weather); or a standard volume of production per head per year, etc.[13]

An improvement over this method — closer to the reality of labor requirements — is to take into account seasonal or surplus requirements over peak seasons of agricultural activity, a demand for labor which, though sometimes of short duration, is nevertheless indispensable. It can be alleviated partly by working harder and longer hours in the peak period; by using the labor of housewives, children, old people, soldiers home on leave, and help from relations in non-agricultural occupations; or by stretching the peaks over longer time periods.[14] But basically the problem of peak labor requirements is one of the main problems of agricultural over-population as it involves the problem of the employment of the unused labor force in inter-seasonal gaps. With regard to this problem some authors distinguish between seasonal and chronic surplus agricultural population.[15] In the slack seasons there may be quite

[12] The most complete list of labor intensity coefficients or labor inputs on an international scale is given by F. Dovring, who quotes 19 countries: F. Dovring, *Land and Labour in Europe, 1900-1950* (The Hague, 1956), pp. 398-418.

[13] F. Dovring, *op. cit.*, pp. 84-98. The level of employment in different European countries varies from 78 per cent to 50 per cent. If the American standard of employment is used, the span of employment levels moves from 14 to 50 per cent only.

[14] P. N. Rosenstein-Rodan, "Disguised Unemployment and Underemployment in Agriculture" (Mimeo., Centre for International Studies, Massachusetts Institute of Technology, Cambridge, Mass., 1956).

[15] A. Pepelasis and P. A. Yotopulos, *Surplus Labour in Greek Agriculture 1953-1960* (Athens, 1962), pp. 126-138.

a large surplus of labor which none the less may be strained in the peak season so that at times there may even be a deficiency of labor in agriculturally over-populated districts. This must be distinguished from a chronic labor surplus representing the long term (more than a year) surplus spread over all seasons.

Our formula for over-population changes when both notions of surplus labor are taken into account as follows:

$$V'_e = A_e - A_{eo} \pm A'_e \tag{2.11}$$

$$V'_{we} = w\,A_e - (A_{eo} \pm A'_e)\,(1 \pm a')\,(w_o \pm w') \tag{2.12}$$

Here A' stands for the additional number of persons, a' for the change in the conversion factor from physical to standard labor units, and w' for hours of additional work done in peak seasons. In slack seasons the sign of additions is negative and the labor surplus is increased.

Thus there is a seasonal change in the numbers of the agriculturally active population, a change in the conversion of persons into labor units, and a change in work hours.

The seasonal surplus is based on the assumption of the functional indivisibility of agricultural labor at certain periods. But underlying this, there is another concealed assumption: that of the indivisibility of some other factors of production (machines, work animals, size of plots, or irrigation schemes).[16]

C. *Capital in Use*

The capital factor in agriculture, which so far has appeared in our analysis only as a concealed assumption that the volume of production is proportional to the capital used, now has to be taken into account. The capital dimension can be included in two different ways: as the intensity of capital (quantity) and the productivity of capital (quality).

By the coefficient of productivity of capital in agriculture we understand the ratio of agricultural product (Z) to agricultural capital (K), i.e. how many units of product correspond to one unit of capital:

$$m = \frac{Z}{K} \tag{2.13}$$

[16] This point has been brought into the open by Tarlogh Singh in his concept of a 'work unit' as the minimum size of family holding for India, dependent on the largest instrument of production (an ox-drawn plough) which occupies 1.5 men. T. Singh, *Poverty and Social Change*, Ch. V (1945). For further development of this concept see: Government of India, *Third Five-Year Plan* (1961), pp. 229-238.

For capital intensity coefficient we take capital per head of the actually economically active population:

$$n = \frac{K}{A_e} \qquad n_o = \frac{K}{A_{eo}} \tag{2.14, 2.15}$$

From the known formula of labor productivity we can deduct expressions of both capital productivity and capital intensity by extending the formula:

$$z = \frac{Z}{A_e} = \frac{Z}{K} \cdot \frac{K}{A_e} = m \cdot n \tag{2.16}$$

$$z_o = \frac{Z}{A_{eo}} = \frac{Z}{K} \cdot \frac{K}{A_{eo}} = m \cdot n_o \tag{2.17}$$

Thus labor productivity in agriculture is the product of the coefficients of capital productivity and capital intensity in agriculture.

We shall call the optimum productivity of capital that capital which is necessary to employ optimally one unit of the economically active population. The capital intensity corresponding to this capital productivity is the optimal capital intensity (n_o).

If in our formulas we now substitute capital productivity and capital intensity for labor productivity, we arrive at the following formula of agricultural over-population and its pressure:

$$g_e = \frac{A_e}{gkP} \cdot z_o = \frac{A_e}{gkP} m \cdot n_o \tag{2.18}$$

$$V_e = A_e - A_o = A_e - \frac{gkP}{m \cdot n_o} \tag{2.19}$$

Thus the greater are the agricultural population, the productivity of capital and the intensity of capital, the greater is the population pressure.[17]

[17] Taking 1920 as 100, the active agricultural population decreased in the United States until in 1960 it had fallen to index 53; at the same time the gross product increased to 140, but the cultivated area fell to 90. In the same period the volume of production rose to 151, and the capital to 159. Intensity of capital per man showed an increase of 300, while labor productivity in agriculture increased up to 270. The productivity of capital fell from coefficient 0.38 to 0.34. The density of the active agricultural population fell from 3.7 to 2.2 per 100 ha. Nevertheless the population pressure showed an increase from 2.22 to 3.16 (index 142).

In the U.S.S.R. the active agricultural population fell from 100 in 1939 to 78 in 1959, the gross product increased to 159, the area under cultivation to 131, and the capital invested to 208. The index of the productivity of capital reached 75, the density of active population decreased to index 60, the population pressure rising to 120.

We reach the conclusion that agricultural over-population from the point of view of production increases with the productivity of labor, i.e. the greater the amount of real capital used per worker, and the greater the productivity of this capital. Thus economic development and technical progress in agriculture do not eliminate, but increase agricultural population pressure.

Let us elaborate this point a little further. Capital intensity (*n*) depends on the quantity of capital and on the number of economically active agricultural persons. But factor *m*, representing the quality of capital, does not depend on the number of persons at all. This factor is brought into the production process from outside, and represents an exogenous and autonomous factor of production.

Productivity of capital determining the quality of aggregate real capital depends on three things: (1) the substitution of labor by capital (labor-saving investment); (2) the capital mix which itself depends on the variety of partial capital productivity coefficients[18] making up the structure of the aggregate agricultural capital; and (3) technical progress itself. Measurements taken of the quality of capital have shown that this first factor of the substitution as such, i.e. replacement of labor by capital, assuming the same volume of production, is of limited importance. The second plays a considerable role particularly from the point of view of short-term changes. But in long-term comparisons technical progress is the most important.[19]

The quality of capital is defined as the ratio of the agricultural output to real capital. Technical improvement of machinery, reduction in costs of building and improved quality of livestock are obvious cases. But real capital can be misleading. One is struck by the fact that a decrease in real capital is followed by a considerable increase in production, depending on the change of the biological structure of real capital. For example, artificial insemination has decreased the number of bulls but greatly improved the quality of livestock production. The cultivation of hybrid corn implied a small increase in cost out of proportion to the increase

[18] Professor M. Cépède has quoted in his very interesting article on French agriculture the following computed coefficients of productivity of capital investments in agriculture in macro-economic terms: water economy 0.37, building of roads 0.24, consolidation of holdings 2.0, buildings 0.03, electricity 0.13, agricultural machinery 0.08, total 0.16. M. Cépède, "Frankreich", *Berichte über Landwirtschaft*, Sonderheft 175, p. 113.

[19] Further development and bibliographical references concerning these problems are dealt with in my article on "Threshold of Economic Development", *Kyklos*, No.I (Basel, 1962).

in production. Vaccination has increased production of all sorts of livestock; the use of pesticides has had a similar effect on crops.

The next step in clarifying the effect of capital on agricultural over-population would be to distinguish between labor-saving and labor-spending capital investments.

3. THE MOBILITY CONCEPT

Agricultural over-population can be conceived also from the point of view of the mobility of the agricultural population. Agricultural over-population in this concept is defined as the number of people whose productivity of labor is nil, i.e. they could be removed from agriculture in a certain area without lowering the level of production there.[20] The fact that the population is removable is stressed. But the emphasis should really be on the other aspect, i.e. that the population is REMOVABLE BUT DOES NOT MOVE. This raises the questions: Why do people not move to other occupations and places? What are the forces which keep them on the spot? When we ask these questions we are linking agricultural over-population with a whole chain of other economic and extra-economic factors which reveal this phenomenon in its great complexity. This concept is linked to a varied set of problems ranging from seasonal and additional wage employment in villages, community development schemes, and co-operative movement, to the conservatism of unmovable peasants and lack of institutional flexibility. Industrialization, building of infrastructure, alternative or heterogeneous occupations, problems of opportunity costs, etc. are added to the CLASSICAL dilemmas of agricultural policies of protection or exploitation, co-operation or commercialization, and conservatism or structural changes in agriculture.[21]

The factors causing agricultural over-population to exist at a certain

[20] One of the more recent definitions of agricultural over-population which could be classified under this concept is: "The amount of agricultural labour which could have been removed from farms for at least a complete year without any reduction in total agricultural output, taking techniques, crop-mix and the quantities of the other factors of production at their historically given levels (with the exception of a routine reorganization of work force)." The other assumption is that "all labour in excess of peak labour employment can be withdrawn without violating the static conditions … … [it is] reasonable to expect that the remaining working people will do more work after the change." A. Pepelassis and P. A. Yotopulos, *Surplus Labour in Greek Agriculture, 1953-1960* (Athens, 1962), p. 30.

[21] For recent data covering most European countries, Cf. European Society of Rural Sociology, *Changing Pattern of Rural Organization* (Oslo, 1961).

place and in a certain time can be divided into two main groups: the expulsive and the attractive factors (push and pull factors). Each of these groups of factors can again be divided into two sub-groups according to whether they operate within or outside the observed area, i.e. are endogenous or exogenous factors.

These are the four cases of over-population mobility:

(1) Attractive endogenous factors (pull-in)

$$(g_1 - \Delta g_1) < g_2 \qquad (3.1)$$

$$\frac{A_1}{A_{o1}} - \Delta\left(\frac{A_1}{A_{o1}}\right) < \frac{A_2}{A_{o2}} \qquad (3.2)$$

(2) Attractive exogenous factors (pull-out)

$$g_1 < (g_2 + \Delta g_2) \qquad (3.3)$$

$$\frac{A_1}{A_{o1}} < \frac{A_2}{A_{o2}} + \Delta\left(\frac{A_2}{A_{o2}}\right) \qquad (3.4)$$

(3) Expulsive endogenous factors (push-out)

$$(g_1 + \Delta g_1) > g_2 \qquad (3.5)$$

$$\frac{A_1}{A_{o1}} + \Delta\left(\frac{A_1}{A_{o1}}\right) > \frac{A_2}{A_{o2}} \qquad (3.6)$$

(4) Expulsive exogenous factors (push-in)

$$g_1 > (g_2 + \Delta g_2) \qquad (3.7)$$

$$\frac{A_1}{A_{o1}} > \frac{A_2}{A_{o2}} + \Delta\left(\frac{A_2}{A_{o2}}\right) \qquad (3.8)$$

If agricultural over-population exists, it means that there is a balance between attractive and expulsive factors (the endogenous and the exogenous). Agricultural population is not on the move — a state of over-population remains. Of course, this state of rest does not mean that varied forces are not in action or that there is no tension among them. What is commonly called the conservatism of the peasants is in fact a state of equilibrium which may have been brought about by many different forces straining and checking each other.

If the pressure of the agricultural population of a certain area is marked by g_1 and the pressure outside the area by g_2, then the agricultural over-population situation is expressed by:

$$g_1 = g_2 \qquad (3.9)$$

$$\frac{g_1}{g_2} = 1 \qquad (3.10)$$

We can take any of the formulas of the first two concepts of agricultural over-population and compare the corresponding pressures between two areas.[22]

When the equilibrium is upset, movement of population takes place from an area of stronger pressure to one of lesser pressure in the horizontal or vertical sense, thus decreasing agricultural over-populaton.

There are many varied dimensions in which the factors causing the mobility of population can be classified. We have classified them in four groups according to the above factors and to the following dimensions: demographic, national wealth, capital, employment, income, consumption (standard of living), institutional factors, level of economic development, and productivity of labor.[23]

As an example of an attractive exogenous (pull-out) factor we take the movement of population caused by the low price of land, or of better land in an area other than that observed. This has an attractive influence, pulling the agricultural population out from the observed area. On the contrary, if the price of land outside the area is high, the population will not move. The price of land in over-populated districts depends much more on population pressure than on any other factor, including the fertility of the land. Opportunity of employment for the agricultural population in manufacturing industries will also operate as an attractive exogenous factor. Such movement will cease when the differences in the incomes of agricultural and non-agricultural occupations are levelled out, taking all other factors as unchanged.

As an example of attractive endogenous (pull-in) factors, we may take any increase of cultivable area (land reclamation, etc.) which will act as a pull-in factor based on changes within the observed area attracting people from outside to move in. A similar effect will be caused by a decrease of population, or by increases of agricultural incomes, or wages caused by better cultivation, or more favorable prices of agricultural products. In order to stop population movement under the influence of these factors, other factors would have to be put into operation. These could be: increased costs of removal, increased taxes or customs duties, greater security of income on the spot, etc.

[22] The general formula used in this concept is:

$$(g_1 \pm \Delta g_1) \gtreqless (g_2 \pm \Delta g_2)$$

[23] The most comprehensive description of factors causing mobility of agricultura population is the publication of the International Labour Office: *Pourquoi les travailleurs abandonnent la terre* (Génève, 1960).

As expulsive endogenous (push-out) factors, the following can be mentioned: increase in agricultural population, natural calamities (floods, erosion), or decrease in the volume of production. Among expulsive endogenous factors there is technical progress, i.e. mechanization causing decrease in the demand for labor; increased productivity of labor because of greater skill among workers; and insecurity of income from agriculture.

Some exogenous expulsive (push in) factors impelling people into an area or compelling them not to abandon agricultural occupation are: compulsory or induced agrarian land settlement, vocational training in agriculture, compulsory transfer of workers, compulsory delivery of agricultural products, heavy investment in indivisible fixed capital, heavy indebtedness, etc. All these factors prevent the surplus agricultural population in an area from abandoning it.

It may be asked whether it is rational to expect peasants to work under conditions of marginal productivity equal to zero. One explanation of the fact that they do so is the high rate of irrationality (ignorance, pressure of family and village customs, etc.) which means that the inelastic demand for agricultural produce is matched by an inelastic supply of labor effort. Various group loyalties must also be taken into account (family allegiance, paternalism, collective solidarity of *kolkhoz* members, etc.). Another approach is to treat labor in agriculture not as a function of wages, or profit, or income, but as a resource. Lack of personal incentive to push out others may be due to semi-feudal exploitation. But there are economic reasons as well. Sometimes in research into economically rational behavior it is overlooked that comparative, not absolute, advantages of labor are among the main incentives to work. What may be zero in absolute cost terms, may not be zero in comparative cost terms. Peasant logic may be different from economists' logistics.

IX

PROBLEMS OF SOCIALIST AGRICULTURE

1. QUESTIONS

There is no country in the modern world where agriculture, or shall we say that economic activity which is usually called agriculture, is not a problem.[1] Members of the European Economic Community encountered a major stumbling block when they came to deal with the problem of agricultural prices and production within the Common Market area. Their negotiations with the U.K. and the latter's relations with the Commonwealth again faltered in the field of agriculture. Even in these highly developed countries of Europe agriculture is actually accused of being inefficient by modern standards.

In the under-developed countries the main problem of development is agriculture. Its increase lags behind the population increase, and agricultural prices show adverse terms of trade with regard to industry, thus leading to both stagnation and poverty.

In the U.S.A. the problem of agriculture is how to deal with surplus production; attempts are made to solve this by putting brakes on the production of unsaleable surpluses, thus each day widening the gap between the growing capacity to produce and the reduced volume of actual production.[2]

Agriculture in socialist countries is a problem of a different kind. In the U.S.S.R. we have a position where, to put it simply, agricultural production is striving to catch up with the U.S.A. The East European countries are faced with similar problems of small productivity and insufficient production. China, with its communes, planned a great leap

[1] The definition of 'agriculture' consists of technological elements (raising of crops and animals) as well as of institutional elements (auxiliary and complementary services), and therefore its content changes with the change of the institutional set-up.

[2] Similar problems of how to stop agricultural production from further growth are occupying the agricultural policy makers of other developed countries (e.g., Sweden and Finland).

forward which turned into a back-somersault. In all socialist countries recent crises caused by wheat shortages have made it evident that the forces of nature are still much stronger than the powers of man.

If in this short article we cannot offer answers, at least we can try to clarify questions. Why is it that agriculture is such a problem thoughout the socialist countries? To be precise, this question should be broken down into three specific queries:

(1) What is the role of agriculture in a socialist economic system?
(2) What is the role of socialism in agriculture?
(3) Can agricultural problems be solved better within a socialist than a capitalist system and if so, what ways are used in socialist countries to achieve this solution?

There are three main ways in which the problems of agriculture in socialist countries differ from those in other countries: in objectives, in methods, and in pace of growth. First come differences in OBJECTIVES. Agricultural policy in socialist countries aims in principle at disallowing growth of agricultural production in the private sector and forcing growth in the socialist sector. Secondly, socialist collectivization is opposed to capitalist concentration in the METHODS it uses to achieve agricultural progress. Thirdly, as to PACE the intention is to achieve agricultural growth with the same technical methods but in a shorter time.

2. APPROACHES

When analyzing the role of agriculture in a socialist economic system we have found four different approaches:

One is to consider agriculture as an end in itself which the socialist system must serve. The second is the reverse, where the socialist system is an end in itself which agriculture must serve. The third approach is to consider socialist agriculture as competing with capitalist agriculture in order to achieve a faster growth of the socialist economy than of the capitalist system. The fourth takes socialist agriculture as an integral part of the socialist economy, an outcome of the growth of forces of production which develop at a different intensity and speed, i.e. different in agriculture than in industries, different in crop raising than in livestock breeding.

(1.) The first approach, where agriculture stands as an end in itself which the socialist economic system must promote, we may call an agrarian socialist approach. In this case agriculture as a whole has priority over the non-agricultural socialist system, which is treated as complementary, residual or marginal to agriculture. The development of agricultural production FORCES comes before socialist production relations. There are several aims of this agricultural mode of production which are used to justify the high priority given to agriculture.

(a) One is the consideration of agricultural occupation as a way of life, almost sacred; this is commonly called the conservation of traditional peasant culture. Speaking in more precise terms, it means the preservation of multifunctional services linked to existing institutions of agricultural production units.

(b) High priority is given to agriculture for defense reasons and its task is to assure the highest possible degree of national self-subsistence in food and raw materials in case of war.

(c) Agriculture is given precedence for demographic reasons as a national breeding pool, a prolific nursery of the best human stock.

(d) A high priority is granted to agriculture also for political institutional reasons, such as preservation of a nation; agricultural population representing the majority of people; yielding to pressure groups in a vote-catching democratic electoral system, etc.

In all these cases agriculture plays the role of an independent variable, and the non-agrarian socialist system is considered as a function dependent on this independent variable.

(2) The second approach, where socialism is the end which agriculture has to serve, we might call the socialist sectoral approach. In this case the building of socialism, i.e. the creation of socialist institutional relations, comes before the balanced development of production forces. Socialism is considered an extra-agricultural system (Industrialization!) using the existing agricultural population, the 'backward' peasants, as an object of exploitation to serve other more 'advanced' purposes. Moreover agriculture as a whole is neglected, with regard to investment, price policy, etc.

In the primitive, crude form of this approach agriculture provides the means for primitive socialist accumulation; it is subjected to such policy instruments as: compulsory deliveries in kind extracted until the peasant population reaches minimum existence; procurement of agricultural products at government-controlled prices which are below costs of production; progressive income tax with the very low income bracket taxed, making all saving in agriculture impossible.

In a more subtle form this approach gives agriculture a subordinate role in economics as supplier of food for the non-agricultural population, as provider of raw materials for manufacturing industries, and as producer of exports to pay for imports of machinery for industries. It is almost irrelevant what happens to the residual part of agriculture and its population once the targets of the above three objectives have been attained according to plan.

The main care of the central planners is to secure deliveries for non-agricultural purposes only, and the interests of agriculture play a complementary and marginal role.

In this case the non-agrarian socialist sector is the independent variable and agriculture a dependent one.

(3) The third approach is based on the idea of competition between the socialist and the capitalist systems. The socialist countries started from a lower level and are endeavoring to reach and overstep the capitalist countries in agricultural development. This main objective is to be attained by an accelerated pace of economic growth. The extent to which the absolute goal of socialism — to develop the production forces to the maximum without exploitation of man by man — has been reached is gauged by measuring progress in a relative sense against the development of those forces which at a given historical moment happen to exist in the most developed country, at present the United States of America.

This rather quantitative approach leads on to a further question, that of quality, i.e. whether modern agricultural progress can be achieved better in the socialist or in the capitalist economy.[3] This demands the question what is a progressive economy and what is 'better' in concrete relations where different elements of the past are mixed with those modern ones which are of such great importance in agriculture. Is the most progressive economy that which can most quickly dispense with the traditional elements? And if so at what expense, and at whose expense? Or do other, e.g. human, values have to be taken into account as well? Another question is that of tendencies in the development of both systems. Are they diverging or converging under the pressure of the modern technical developments influencing both of them?

These problems go beyond the purpose of this article as they are problems of a comparison and not of socialist agriculture in the proper sense.

[3] Over-emphasizing the qualitative incommensurable difference between the socialist and capitalist economies to a great extent made a comparison of the two systems impossible, particularly where such a comparison was not to the advantage of socialist agriculture. This feeling of insecurity has been largely overcome.

(4) The fourth approach is socio-economic — that of the integration of agriculture with other branches of economic activity into one integrated socialist economic system, resulting from the process of economic growth. It could be given the name of a socialist integrative approach to agricultural problems.

Agriculture is here considered an integral part of the socialist economy, treated on an equal footing with other kinds of economic activity, and even enjoying protection, subsidies, and special attention when it is necessary in the interests of the economy as a whole. How long it takes before such policy becomes imperative in a socialist country depends on the pressures of disproportions developed in the course of building socialism, such as:

(a) when shortage of food appears due to lagging of neglected agricultural production, and imports of agricultural products become so heavy and costly that they are almost prohibitive, e.g. Yugoslavia, Poland;

(b) when production organized in the socialist agricultural sector appears to be more expensive than in the non-socialized agricultural sector because of over-capitalization and under-employment in the former, and expenses that cannot be transferred to other sectors because they are too large;

(c) when shortage of labor in agriculture occurs, due either to the greater attractiveness (pull) of non-agricultural employment or to the push-out forces caused by the subordinate position of agriculture (e.g. East Germany, Czechoslovakia, northern Yugoslavia).

The objective process of the growth of the forces of production in agriculture leads to vertical and horizontal integration. The level at which such a development takes place in agriculture brings forward the following problems which have to be solved:

(1) the conflict between modern technique and the institutional set-up (traditional, both capitalist and socialist), requiring mutual adjustment of the existing institutions to the demands of technique. But to a certain extent the reverse is also the case, requiring adaptation of the technique to the existing institutions; (2) the management and use of the capital-mix in proportions which permit the optimal size of the largest indivisible means of production, thus forming different collective units concurrent and co-existent according to the different optima of different capital units; (3) management by the direct producers in modern agriculture, requiring a great number of decisions on the spot when complex factors of production are used — this as opposed to the monopolistic or monopsonistic decisions of the few, be they bureaucrats or technocrats; (4) the

tension between ever increasing specialization of production and diversification of consumption in agriculture, driving toward a higher standard of living which means specialization of agricultural production that serves diversified consumption; (5) abolishment of contradictions between the interests of town and country, agriculture and industry, physical and intellectual labor, leading in turn to equal treatment in parity of prices, parity of incomes and parity of opportunity.

3. SOLUTIONS

The solutions so far proposed to solve the problem of agriculture in the socialist economic system relate to changes in the structure of agriculture. These structural changes concern institutional change, technological change, managerial change and change in the market structure.

A. *Institutional change*

Institutional change in socialist agriculture starts with land reforms, be they the abolition of feudal or semi-feudal rent or the real division of land. The next step is collectivization by changing land ownership and by increasing the area of cultivated land to form large production units. There are different forms of action: merging peasant family holdings of a village area into a *kolkhoze* (collective estate); creating communes; forming very large *sovhozes* (state farms) and socialist agricultural estates; transforming *kolkhozes* into *sovhozes*, or attempting to form *agrogorods* (agrocities), etc. The basic underlying idea is that economy of scale will solve the main problems of agriculture and at the same time relieve abundant labor force for industry, and achieve a better, greater and cheaper production of agricultural products. Another purpose of collectivization is to use economic dependence in order to establish political control over the peasants.

(1) Economies of scale in the process of collectivization have proved to be largely offset by other factors. The great number of managerial decisions required for management of large collective units showed clearly how different the optimum sizes of a collectivized unit may be. The size for technological optimum yield for varied crops was quite different from that giving the economic price optimum as determined by the market or deliveries to the supply centers. The instrumental optimum of capital indivisibility differed greatly from the financial optimum based on the maximal return on investment. The optimum use of labor (best

employment ratio) was in conflict with the optimal allocation of crops, while the optimum size of the production unit which a manager was able to control effectively was quite different from the size required by other optimums. There was no market to determine what the *optimum optimorum* was by imposing risks upon those who were neither fortunate nor able enough to find it out at their own expense. This complex problem of economy of scale was simplified by assuming that the greater the size the better the solution for socialist production. Even today the problem of optimalization of socialist production units, although the object of intense research, has not been satisfactorily solved.

Thus collectivization of agriculture as collectivization of land use, which was carried out at great human sacrifices (physical liquidation of millions of peasants) and material losses (decimation of livestock, etc.), had to be abandoned either almost completely — as in Yugoslavia and Poland — or partially, leading to an empirical compromise — as in U.S.S.R., where it developed into the collective production of extensive crops (such as cereals) while intensive agricultural products (such as meat, milk, eggs and vegetables) are supplied largely by the peasants from their individual small plots.

Such are the consequences of the compromise between the principle of socialist collectivization by institutional change as such, and its empirical implementation.

(2) The collective production units of the *kolkhoze* type still perform the role of an instrument of social policy, with the purpose of giving means of livelihood by employment at almost any cost to the village population. A comparison of one institutional form with the other, the *kolkhozes* with the *sovhozes*, in the field of productivity of labor shows in the latter a high retention quota of agricultural labor at a submarginal productivity level over and above the optimum use. In a way, the village communities of the *kolhozes* still perform the same function as the family holdings did at a lower level — that is, first of all, to give means of existence to the population immobilized on land. The technical optimum and economies of scale had to recede in face of the employment problem, thus creating concealed unemployment. Even today after 30 years of experience in most of the *kolkhozes*, the production program is determined by the need for providing employment for a labor force which is earning its means of subsistence. Concealed unemployment in the socialist countries varies between 50 and 39 per cent (in the Soviet Union), and has gone down in some more advanced areas to 12-16 per cent.[4] That

[4] In long-term Soviet planning 1959-1965, it is assumed that the agricultural popula-

agriculture is still considered the reservoir of reserve labor is proved also by the Chinese experience, who sent some 60 million people back to the villages after the 1960's.

(3) When surplus labor is pushed out of agriculture into industry, commerce and administration, it creates an even more difficult problem of surplus population in these branches of economic activity, resulting in still greater effects of concealed unemployment than it did in agriculture (problems of housing, shanty towns, impediment to technical progress because of cheap labor, fall of labor productivity, overburdening of administration costs, etc.).

(4) When the institutional set-up becomes frozen, not flexible enough to be adapted to changes in technology, labor productivity and other factors, reorganization is possible only by administrative acts, which are expensive and almost always follow the rule 'too little and too late'.

(5) Collectivization does not mean only putting plots of land together while the tools are left adjusted to the family-size holding. In such cases collective production is not derived from the economic necessity of using large means of production requiring the joint efforts of a great number of men, but consists only of groups of individual workers lumped together by force of outwardly imposed discipline.

B. *Technological Change*

The introduction of the socialist system in agriculture through technological change means that capital investment has become the main instrument of socialist agricultural policy. Such a policy has two effects: one substitutive and the other additive. The first means that human labor is replaced by capital; also that animal capital (draft animals) is replaced by mechanical traction. The process goes on also in substituting capital goods of higher productivity for capital goods of lower productivity. The second effect is the additive one, increasing the production forces capable of doing better, heavier and faster work in agriculture. It has been proved that the additive effect on agricultural production of technological change is much more important than the substitutive effect.[5]

Technological change also sometimes acquires an ideological side

---

tion will be kept stable until 1970, and that from 1970-1980 the first reduction in absolute figures will take place (i.e. of 10 million fewer people in agriculture in 1980 than in 1970, or 33 per cent of the increase in population).

[5] One has to bear in mind that substitution is almost always combined with an increase in productivity of the capital introduced in the new production process.

which is demonstrated by fetishism of agricultural machinery, e.g. tractors and combines are used little but shown for reasons of prestige on every occasion to visitors, thus getting the character of conspicuous production.

Technological change is also sometimes used to produce political effects, e.g. the introduction of machine tractor stations (MTS) having machinery for servicing *kolkhozes* which were not allowed to have machinery of their own. This monopolistic position in the supply of agricultural machinery was also used for political control by the rulers and at the same time to collect tax in kind from the agricultural producers.

Technological change in socialist agriculture has developed along three main lines: those of mechanization, chemicalization and biochemical fructification.

(1) MECHANIZATION has been the most popular — almost a symbolical form of technological change going from simple tractors to complex mechanization. The maximum level of concentration was reached in the MTS centers. When they were finally dissolved by the Soviet government, the limitations of this instrument of technological change in socialist agriculture were openly seen. The centralization of machinery in the MTS caused partial overcapitalization in some areas due to concentration, and undercapitalization in others because they served too wide an area, causing costly and unproductive journeys. The machines were unused to a great extent because of lack of spare parts, slow repairs, and red-tape in allocation. Their services were expensive because of heavy administration and too elaborate system of payment. The constantly changing personnel consisted of a continuous flow of semi-skilled beginners, as most of the people took this first hasty contact with machinery as a stepping stone towards the factory which they joined at the first opportunity, and where the training process had to start all over again.[6]

These were the reasons which caused the centralization of agricultural mechanization in special MTS to be inoperable; after years of delay they were finally abandoned, and the machines moved closer to the direct producers in smaller but more accessible concentration.

Thus the concentration of agricultural machinery was reduced and brought closer to the level of technological and economic indivisibility which prevailed over administrative and political objectives.

[6] "It takes 3 years of apprenticeship to train a cobbler, and only 30 days to qualify as a tractor driver", complained an agricultural expert.

(2) CHEMICALIZATION. Unlike machinery fertilizers, pesticides, insecticides and other chemicals in agriculture are an almost perfectly divisible means of production. The effect of fertilizers on the size of production units is minimal.[7] On the other hand pesticides, insecticides and veterinary services against infectious diseases in animals can be used effectively over a wide area, but mean little interference with current production. It is almost astonishing what comparatively little use was made of fertilizers in socialist agriculture until recently (1963) when their importance was finally recognized by political factors.

(3) BIOCHEMICAL DISCOVERIES in both animal- and plant-breeding, artificial insemination and hybrid plants, do not require a concentration of agricultural production, but rely on the supply of seeds and insemination services. Moreover, because of the high costs of intensive production, they require highly trained experts, great personal care and continuous calculation of the optimum effects. This attention is difficult to impose by administrative discipline if there is no direct material interest among those engaged in production. On a lower level of agricultural development discipline can yield a certain continuous level of production because of the anxiety of the producers for their physical existence; every higher, i.e. more intensive, level of agricultural development must necessarily lead to material stimulation of agricultural producers.

Technological change has its financial side as well, since investments are the main instruments of policy. In most socialist countries for a long time the financial resources for investment were concentrated in government hands and then administratively allocated. In agriculture this problem is particularly difficult because of a wide territorial scattering of investment goods, the short period of use of agricultural investment goods (seasonal), and the specific problem of quality and of adaptability of such goods to local conditions (livestock, machinery, fertilizers).

As a result, the technical and economic indivisibility of capital raised the problem of different optimum of the cost. In the case of administrative investment decisions only the primary effect was contemplated while multipliers did not operate at all, or at least were not taken into account.

Because the volume of investment was not limited by the risk of the

[7] A witty analyst divided all crops into left-wing crops and right-wing crops. The left-wing ones were those comparatively easy to mechanize, therefore easy to collectivize (e.g., wheat). The others, difficult to mechanize and therefore to collectivize, were called right-wing crops (e.g., maize, livestock). Of course here the question of collectivization was due not to the institutional change but to the technological difference of crops.

producers it was not their responsibility to strive for optimal solutions. It was not until recently that the '*selkhoztechnika*' (the agricultural technique agency) tried to replace administrative allocations by some kind of market of capital good in agriculture.

C. *Changes in managerial structure*

The problem of managerial changes in the process of socialist revolution began with the breaking down of the managerial machinery of the old society. The old managers, politically not trusted but technically competent, were replaced by a new group of managers, politically trusted but with no training and experience in agricultural management, or at least not to a degree satisfactory for the technical level required by the increased concentration of production in agriculture.

As the number of politically trusted managers has usually been very small, the way out was meant to be found in a high concentration of decision-making. The consequence was centralized decisions by central managers far away from the real conditions of the agricultural production units which they had to manage. Such centralized management first led to separation, then to isolation, and finally to sterilization of the decision-making process.

Since this happened in all socialist countries during revolutionary process, exaggerations and excesses took place which put the experts in a position where either they had no part in the process of managerial decision-making and their field of action was restrained to technical routine, or there was steady political interference from either the new bureaucracy or the party bosses, imposing decisions in an arbitrary manner from afar. Thus the responsibility for decisions was often shifted onto them, and they in turn became the whipping boys for the inefficiency of the political leaders in the first line. In other words, before the political personnel were called to task by their superiors they tried to offer up the experts as sacrifice for their own mistakes. Decision-making is a time-consuming process still going on until the responsibilities are sorted out and properly assigned. This general phenomenon is particularly significant in agriculture for the following reasons: serious natural uncertainties and economic risks of production; the magnitude of the complex task of creating and managing large collective enterprises; and the growing function in number, importance, intensity, effectiveness and scientific precision of the managerial decisions that have to be made when dealing with modern agriculture.

For these reasons a great number of trained agricultural experts prefer to find a safe shelter in administrative offices and unproductive institutes, preferring to plough the desks and harvest the statistical forms than to take operational responsibilities.

It must be emphasized that the problem of management of socialist agricultural estates is in essence different from that of running large peasant family-holdings. It is not a matter of the same thing on a larger scale, but rather a different quality and kind of managerial decision which the village peasant-producer is not competent to make, be he politically reliable or not, be he a good husbandman in his village or not.

The simple system of commandeering some several tens of thousands of political workers from the towns and putting them into the posts of *kolkhoz* chairmen, as has so often been the practice in some socialist countries, simply will not do in modern agriculture.

Thus there is a double shift required in the course of socialist development; one is functional, the other personal. The first is to bring the decision-making process from the heights of the central offices dealing with statistical averages down to the firm ground of production units coping with real complex problems. The second shift involves not only an institutional change but also a personnel change, replacing the trusted but inefficient political managers by trained experts in modern agriculture. Moreover a climate has to be created which gives the expert stimulation to develop his initiative and also to bear responsibility. He must not be frightened away from taking decisions but encouraged by making it worth his while. This means both legal security and material stimulation.

This, of course, is not an easy task if the burden of responsibility is left on the thin layer of managerial experts. Therefore it has to be deepened and extended into a workers' management in which the fruits of labor are shared to each according to his labor, and the responsibility for failures jointly borne by each according to his capability.

D. *Change in market structure*

Socialist agriculture has usually involved a change in the market mechanism, which has meant socialization of trade of agricultural products on both retail and wholesale level and of internal as well as foreign trade. Indeed the market mechanism was meant to be replaced by a planned exchange of agricultural products where central planners would strike the balance between planned resources and requirements by setting up planned targets. This centrally planned exchange can be compared in principle to a monocentric (monopolistic-monopsonistic) market. This mechanism was so inelastic that prices were separated from the cost of production, volume of exchange isolated from prices, and prices made independent from consumer demand.

(1) The separation of prices from the costs of agricultural production led to a situation where the delivery of agricultural products to the state had to be made at a price below the level of the cost of production. One can understand this impossible situation lasting for one year or two until the internal reserves were exhausted, but it can hardly be explained when lasting for over twenty years unless one bears in mind two compensatory devices: (a) a part of what was left to the producers in kind for their subsistence was sold by them on the tolerated (gray) market at much higher than official procurement prices, and (b) the harvest that grew on the fields and that amount which appeared in reports to the authorities varied, thus securing to the producers a much greater quantity than the central planners realized.

(2) The separation of the volume of deliveries to the state from the fixed, planned prices meant that prices were no longer a stimulation to increase the volume of production.

As deliveries were fixed in quantities per hectare or proportionate to the estimates of the harvest in the field (the biological harvest), risks fell upon the agricultural producers so that in certain cases, e.g. meat and butter, some producers (*kolkhozes*) had to buy agricultural products on the 'gray' or even black market at high prices in order to meet the compulsory deliveries.

Central planning reached as far as it could stretch its authority; in fact, planning of agricultural products turned into planning the delivery of agricultural products to the state agencies. This was true also for the cooperative *kolkhozes* and, to a lesser extent, for the state farms.

(3) The separation of prices from consumer demand also put the consumer in an unfavorable position. The initial period of rationing was developed later into unequal distribution depending on the classification of shops in which certain classes of consumers were allowed to buy agricultural products.

This centralized type of planning turned supply into state procurement and demand into administrative requirement; incentive by economic interest was replaced by force, or fear of force, of the administrative machinery.

The administrative maximum and forced procurement of agricultural products were far from the economic optimum of production.

On the other hand, leakages in the system and an overgrowth of all sorts of middlemen profiting from rigid central administrative planning, led to the flourishing of black and 'gray' markets to which not only the consumers had to resort but also the state factories, state farms and above all the *kolkhozes*, if they wanted to get some additional consumption and sometimes even to fulfill the plans prescribed for them.

This untenable position acted as a brake on development of production, which showed a spectacular rise when the prices of agricultural products were increased and central planning decentralized. This meant also that the market became less rigid on both the demand and supply sides; prices came closer to costs, and the volume of deliveries to prices. This change was not due to a change of the ideology of the system or the organization of the government administration in agriculture. It came from changes in material production which required structural changes in the market as well.

On the supply side, a higher level of agricultural production involves a greater number of factors in a greater variety of combinations. Thus decisions made on the spot were more effective than those in government offices, which means a demand for freeing agricultural producers from administrative control and their adaptation to the requirements of the market: a more elastic price mechanism taking the risk of new combinations of factors, and direct producers materially stimulated to search for such combinations and bear the risk for them.

This level of production has to take into account consumer demand as well. In an economy of scarcity the consumer has little to say, whereas in an economy of abundance the consumer is the master and his choice is of predominant influence. This applies to socialist economies as well.[8] No wonder that nowadays economists in socialist countries are preoccupied with market research and with the problems of the consumer function as the basis for socialist planning. Agricultural prices were so far removed from the real costs of production that today great efforts are necessary to bring them back from administrative arbritrariness to economic reality.[9]

[8] It is not correct to call a capitalist system a consumers', and a socialist system a producers' economy. There are many socialist economists who would strongly object to such a worn-out classification.

[9] This is also true on the international scale where one of the greatest obstacles to international trade among socialist countries themselves is the non-existence of a common denominator, i.e. a socialist market price.

4. CONCLUSION

As we have seen, there are many reasons why socialist countries had such difficulties when dealing with problems of agricultural policy, despite the evidence of considerable technical progress.

If one had to point out one single reason, among many, as the most important for this state of affairs, I would say that it is the effort always to attain the maximum instead of the optimum. To maximize the general policy line means to play safe, and makes the existent agricultural policy a fetish which must be followed without rational examination of the degree of its usefulness and the rationality of its effectiveness.

The underlying theoretical assumption of this political attitude in agriculture is the negation of the law of diminishing (or of changing) returns.

As a theoretical justification for this attitude, Lenin is quoted as saying that the law of diminishing returns does not operate because accumulated capital changes its technological composition and therefore alters the returns. No reasonable person would deny this, but neither is it possible to deny that the law operates, all other things being equal.

In our opinion this idea expressed by Lenin in one of his earliest works was used in the Stalinist period to impose upon the administrative machinery unquestioning obedience to follow the party line to the extreme without examining the rationality of agricultural policy. Thus solutions to the problems of agriculture in socialist countries, even after the most severe criticism in official assemblies, were sought in the reorganization of the administrative apparatus of the ministry of agriculture.

Today the increasing emphasis on the search for optima in agricultural policy is a sign that times have changed. To search for an optimum solution means to examine, individually and on the spot, the effectiveness of measures of agricultural policy and to assess the turning points at which they become less effective. This means competence, freedom of judgment, creative thinking, personal responsibility and individual security from arbitrariness, and it means managers not only stimulated by material compensation but also working within the community of the producers themselves as one of them in the management of common resources.

The purpose of this article is to draw attention to the fact that problems of agriculture in socialist countries have been approached in different ways not only on the level of technical application of policy measures but also on a much higher level of abstraction. Not one single proposition could be considered as a panacea for structural changes in socialist agriculture, and none would operate once for all. On the contrary, there are changes and turning points in agricultural policy in the course of socialist development which create new problems and therefore have to be solved by different methods and varying instruments.

YUGOSLAVIA

X

ECONOMICS OF SOCIALISM IN JUGOSLAVIA: THE THIRD STAGE — THE REFORM*

1

What is happening in the political and economic arena in Yugoslavia today should not be haughtily dismissed as the result of disruptive ideological disagreement among self-righteous Marxist factions. Nor is it a reflection of the evil influence of foreign propaganda, Communist or anti-Communist. Nor has it grown out of mischievous activity of reactionary forces eager to achieve the restoration of the old régime.

Some of the problems facing Yugoslavia are peculiar to Yugoslavia, and in them history and geography speak. But many of the most pressing are those which every community of nations is experiencing today in both East and West, problems of international regionalism or of supranational centralism. Other countries, too, face problems such as inflation versus stability; maximizing growth or the standard of living; authoritarian discipline as a convenience of the few or democratic self-government as the responsibility of the many. And there also are many other problems which are specifically socialist. All the complexities of the modern world are bound to take a special form in a multinational commonwealth of 20,000,000 people seeking to build socialism beyond the present level of $ 500 national income per head per year.

The casual observer is often puzzled. Only a few years ago Yugoslavia was presented as an example of a country with one of the highest growth rates in the world; now the foremost aim of economic policy is to reduce investment. For more than a decade the socialist economy struggled against bureaucratic command; now an administrative price freeze has had to be introduced. Yugoslavia was the first country in the world to initiate workers' management in factories and business enterprises and to abolish the wage system; now there is division about whether this

* This article was printed in *Foreign Affairs* (July 1966) under the title: "Economics of Socialism in a Developed Country".

means too much or too little democracy. The 1963 Constitution formally declared a one-party state; yet the top political leaders now emphatically demand that the economy be de-politicized. National problems were said to have been solved; and now the country is pregnant with increased tensions among the constituent nations, tensions newly created and socialist in origin. Efforts to find solutions to all these problems are now concentrated into two words: THE REFORM.[1]

It has been said by highly responsible people that this Reform has very great significance, greater even than the introduction of workers' management which has so far been considered the most original contribution made by the Yugoslav brand of socialism. The new policy became possible only when a major political battle between those favoring centralist solutions and those in favor of self-government had cleared the way. First, in 1963, a new Constitution was adopted which confirmed the principles and enlarged the legal framework of self-government, further decentralized the country along federal lines and enhanced democracy within the socialist system. It took two years of inside discussions before the Constitution was adopted. Then, in 1964, at the Eighth Congress of the League of Communists the same policy was restated in clear political terms, as issues became more polarized and clarified. Finally, in 1965, the federal parliament decided that the Reform should be carried out, which meant putting the third stage of socialist development into operation.

The immediate purposes of the Reform were to combat an increasing pace of inflation, to remove a deficit in the balance of payments, to get idle capacity in industry going, to reverse the increase in unemployment, to raise a standard of living so unfavorably low compared to neighboring countries in the West, and to find a form of government able to give the country a consistent economic policy. These short-term objectives were necessarily linked to some longer-term measures of structural change in the economy such as: to overhaul the whole price system; to revise growth and investment policies; to put the productivity of the economy on an internationally competitive level; and to liberalize foreign trade in order to remove the structural causes of its continual deficit. The whole economic system introduced in 1954 had become obsolete, and the new Constitution of 1963 laid down new principles for the economic and political system, the main aim of which could be described as to base the whole economy and society on workers' management. Thus the Reform

[1] One of the most systematic and comprehensive presentations of the causes of the Reform and of the measures taken in it can be found in K. Džeba-M. Beslač, "Privredna reforma. Sto i zašto se mijenja" (Zagreb, Stvarnost, 1965).

is an integration of short-term and long-term economic objectives and the implementation of the 1963 Constitution.

To make clear what this means we must review the development of the Yugoslav economic system in the two previous stages. First came administrative socialism of the Stalinist type from 1945 to 1952, inaugurated in the Constitution of January 1946. This was followed by what was known as the 'New System' of 1953 to 1964, given legal blessing in the constitutional reform law of 1953. The third stage was formulated in the new Constitution of 1963.

2

A. *The Mechanism of Social Control*

In the Stalinist centralized type of economic system, government machinery was completely merged with party organization and business management into one monolithic system, run by authoritarian, centralized command through the medium of directives. That is, orders issued from those above to those below in the hierarchical system were not binding on those above, but had to be implemented without question by those below. This inefficient system blocked initiative from underneath and placed responsibility for numerous operational decisions — and mistakes — on top party leaders. It was finally discontinued at the end of 1952.

Under the decentralized New System the government apparatus was separated from business management, and workers' management was introduced into business organizations, which were authorized to run current operations. In the government, the bureaucratic element was separated from the political party organization, and ultimately the position of the top party functionaries was separated from that of the head of the government. Ministries were abolished and only a small number of administrative state secretaries remained. Instead of being subordinated to ministries, the socialist enterprises formed their branch associations, federated into business chambers, to organize coöperation and represent their interests. Parliament, although consisting of Communist Party members only, nevertheless became less and less a rubber stamp. In this tripartite ramification the position of the party organization was that of arbiter, without formal responsibility for running current affairs; this made criticism and even personal changes in government possible without directly engaging the authority of the Party. In spite of this, however, the *de facto* influence of party officials remained great, and this led to a split between the real decision-makers and those who had to bear the responsibility for implementing decisions.

The Reform emphasized the fight against government bureaucracy, which continued to wield great influence at all levels, notwithstanding the self-management legislation. Moreover, a further division in the mechanism of social control was taking place. The aim now was to de-politicize decision-making in business management, not only in regard to current operations but also in the field of investment and with regard to branch size, location and financing.[2]

The main criticism of the politically minded was that they pushed their special interests with no regard for economic optimums; interfered in the selection of top personnel of business enterprises, taking political reliability as a justification for promotion in spite of managerial incapacity; and put pressure on enterprises, demanding expenditure beyond what the law ordered for extra-economic funds and fiscal benefits. The federal authorities were not immune to criticism either.

Those who oppose de-politicization claim that it is a sign of the decomposition of Communist control. Its supporters claim it is a prerequisite of the increased division of social functions necessary in a developed society.

B. *Property Relations*

In the centralized system all business organizations, industries, banking, transport, commerce, mining, building — everything except small-scale handicrafts employing up to five persons — became state property. A drive to nationalize agriculture also took place at an accelerated rate.

In the decentralized system, all nationalized property remained, but its character changed from state to 'social' property, which meant that management was taken out of the hands of the state administration and (in 1950) given over to the workers' councils, whose power gradually

[2] Tito said, "It is my opinion that we must absolutely discontinue the practice of political people deciding where and what should be built, and how much. This is something the enterprises and factories should decide. ... The building of new factories will also be decided upon through the intermediary of the banks. But political factors should keep out. We political people can give only general lines of an investment policy; you must make the decisions" (*Borba*, December 31, 1965). Vladimir Bakarić, former President of the Assembly of the People's Republic of Croatia, stated explicitly that, before the Reform, "Power in Yugoslavia was in the hands of quite a social segment ranging from party to leading business officials (*rukovodilaca*): all these lost their power when self-management was introduced in factories and enterprises" (*Borba*, March 6, 1966).

increased. In 1959 nationalization of houses and building sites took place, but the forcible collectivization of peasant property was discontinued in 1953, and only purchase or economic coöperation was used to increase further the socialist sector in agriculture. The basic fact was that, with the two exceptions of peasant holdings (limited to 10 hectares) and small handicrafts (limited to five workers), it was no longer possible to increase the size of the socialist sector by expropriation, but only by savings from the income produced by the workers themselves within the socialist sector.

The Reform faced the following situation: The rural exodus had increased more quickly than the effective demand for labor in the socialist sector, which led to considerable unemployment, a reduction in labor productivity and an increase in the cost of housing and communal services in towns. Ever-increasing imports of food for the growing industrial population and for millions of foreign tourists increased the demand for agricultural products which the socialist agricultural sector and existing peasant production were not in a position to satisfy. Prices of agricultural products therefore rose and a change in the policy toward the unused capacity of peasant holdings became necessary. The growing tourist business argued in favor of further use of the private sector in the catering trade.

C. *The Position of the Enterprise*

Under administrative socialism, enterprises were totally smothered by state administration. All materials were supplied to them, prices and costs were determined by ministries, sales were transformed into allocation orders, all profits anticipated were paid into — and consequently all deficits covered by — the state budget. The enterprise became a technical unit of government administration.

In the decentralized system, socialist enterprises were free to operate their current activities according to their own decisions and at their own risk. They sold their products on the market, bought raw materials, decided on the employment of personnel, contracted loans and made their own annual plans. They had to cover costs by proceeds from the market, and shared the benefits with the social community (federation, republic and commune). This sharing underwent several changes, from profit sharing to income sharing, until finally the wage system was abolished and instead the workers' councils were given the right to dispose of part of the income of the enterprise allocated to its funds, while another part of the income was allocated to the workers as their personal income. This distribution was, on an average, as follows: 60 per cent of the income of the enterprise went to the social community, 27 per cent to the workers, and 13 per cent to the funds for self-financing. But investment resources remained centralized, and so did decisions regarding the founding of new enterprises — a matter left to the political authorities.

Under the Reform a much bigger share of the income was allocated to the enterprise — i.e. 70 per cent for investment and workers' personal income. The fiscal burden on the enterprises was diminished: the income tax on enterprises was abolished, the capital tax was reduced from 6 to 4 per cent of working capital, the turnover tax, hitherto paid by producers, was changed into a consumers' sales tax collected by the retail trade. The workers' councils were left to decide what proportions of the income at their disposal should go to the self-investment fund and to workers' personal income. Only 30 per cent of the net income, instead of 60, was to be taken by the social community. This was to satisfy a long-standing complaint of the enterprises that those which had proved they were able to earn were punished by having their income taken away, while those incapable of making an income were rewarded by being given investment funds and subsidies from the central funds.

Whether enterprises are going concerns must be tested on the market. Prices are to be those of the world market, and enterprises which cannot stand such competition, with normal customs protection, will have to make efforts to do so, and reorganize, or close their doors. Because many industrial enterprises were built on too small a scale and below minimum technological standards, and suffer from lagging production or incompetent management, this requirement of the Reform means a major structural change. No doubt the final responsibility will rest with the workers' councils, but a great deal of research, help and advice will be necessary; the workers' councils cannot be burdened with something which they are not capable of doing.

D. *Savings and Investment Policy*

In the system of administrative socialism all savings were incorporated into the overall state budget, and investment decisions were made by the top political bodies in the centralized plan.

The main innovation of the New System was the separation of investment funds from the state budget, i.e. the bulk of the investment savings was collected into a general investment fund by the central Investment

Bank, which made microeconomic decisions regarding their distribution upon request of the individual enterprises, while macroeconomic decisions (how much for which sector and branch of industry) were made by the annual Social Plans. Thus some decision was shifted from the state bureaucracy to the bank bureaucracy, and the procedure became so complicated that in the end the decisions were guided by political factors.

As we have already said, the Reform demands that investment decisions be left to the enterprises. The free funds are concentrated and credits given by the banks on business principles. Therefore the General Investment Fund and other funds were discontinued in 1965, and their function taken over by the investment banks.

E. *Consumption and the Standard of Living*

The centralized system put standards of living and personal consumption on a very low level of priority. Administrative planning, low wages, moral stimulation rather than economic incentive for productivity, and a small span between the wages for skilled and unskilled labor — these were the main characteristics of the system. Only one exception must be emphasized: enlarged care for education and health, and an expansion of social insurance.

The decentralized system gave greater attention to consumption, which doubled from 1953 to 1963. Beginning in 1954, competition increased the choice and variety of goods, and this, plus the fact that imported goods were available, acted as a stimulus to employees to work more in order to be able to buy more. The stimulation of production by workers' management, income sharing, market economy and consumer credits also contributed to the increase in the consumption level. Changes took place among the consumers themselves. Over a million people shifted to towns and became urban consumers; a cultural revolution increased the level of education and stimulated new wants. The influx of foreign tourists and the large number of workers abroad (over 200,000) had their effect too.

The general line of policy was to stimulate production and productivity by higher incomes; this was counteracted from below by demands for equalization of income.

The Reform's main task was to link the level of living to that of productivity, and to raise both. These aspirations had to be suppressed temporarily because of the price increases of some agricultural products (meat, milk); the reduction of imports and forced exports of certain consumer goods; limitations on the disposable income in enterprises; and the pursuit of a deflationary policy. Compensation proposed by the Reform to offset income reduction had to be paid from the funds of the enterprises. All these measures intensified the problem of raising the level of consumption and increased pressure to carry out the Reform faster.

F. *Economic Growth Policy*

The centralized system had just one objective: to maximize investment while fixing an order of priority for the means of production over consumption, heavy industry over light, industry over agriculture. The rule was stiff: maximize growth at any cost, with no regard for optimization.

This obsession with growth continued in the decentralized stage of Yugoslav socialism. The rate of growth in the manufacturing industries was one of the highest in the world. Growth was still based on compulsory saving, with a threefold burden on existing fixed capital (i.e. on developed sectors): centralization of funds for depreciation, capital tax (6 per cent) and the interest rate on long-term capital loans. The order of priorities, however, changed. After 1955, priority was given to those industries which could accumulate the greatest savings in the shortest time, mainly light and consumer goods industries. Decentralization of industries took place so that in each administrative district ('a little to everyone') industry had to accomplish a triple purpose: to create a working class or enlarge it; to provide fiscal income for the local administration; and to increase production. This led to the creation of a number of small and inefficient 'political factories', built with credits provided from centralized funds — i.e. with other people's money. Thus the building of the 'political factories' was the end result of the centralized investment fund. Had the investors had to do it from their own resources, they would have thought it over twice. Integration became the slogan of the next phase, but it, too, met with many obstacles, some subjective (i.e. resistance of the managers and local politicians). The merger of healthy and sick enterprises was often carried out for political reasons, regardless of reasons that were stronger.

The Reform demands that an end be put to this overall maximization of growth, and advances instead the principle of selective growth. Formerly the rate of industrial growth was 15 per cent; the presently planned rates are between 7 and 10 per cent, which is still very high. Many grandiose investment projects have been abandoned, and the whole federal investment commitment, which already centralized 80 per cent of all available funds for the next five years, is being revised.

G. *The Price System and Stabilization Policy*

Low prices for capital goods, raw materials and food, high prices (increased by the turnover tax) for consumer goods, both imposed by the central government — such was the main policy of prices and income during the first period. This meant a régime of fixed, low wages which in turn provided labor services of low productivity; and yet because labor was cheap there was little incentive to substitute for it capital of higher productivity. Technical improvement was a matter of automonous decision, not induced by production costs. Thus in spite of heavy outlays for costly equipment and machines, often paid for with precious foreign currency, they frequently lay idle in sheds and fields because the system made them more expensive to use than labor.

In the decentralized system macro-income distribution was altered and market prices replaced fixed prices imposed by the government. Agricultural prices remained low and so did those of raw materials, semi-finished goods, power and transport. This was to stimulate industrialization and also to prevent abuse of the monopolistic position of these sectors. Other prices increased. The share of the gross national product taken for investment remained high (33.4 per cent in 1964) and decisions to invest greatly surpassed the volume of production of investment goods, so that the prices of these increased 50 per cent more than the general price index. Therefore, as early as 1957 limited price control was introduced. Inflationary pressure, caused by ever-increasing demand, had increased to such an extent by 1964 that galloping inflation threatened unless measures to stem it were taken and a stabilization policy introduced, curtailing, in the first place, investments.[3]

The Reform introduced a stabilization policy which explicitly deflated bank credits, reduced consumer credits, strengthened price control and severely curtailed spending (particularly on investment) at all levels of government — federal, republic and communal.

Planning also had to be changed. The decentralized system had reversed central, authoritarian state planning and introduced combined macro-microeconomic planning by annual and five-year federal, republic and communal social plans. The Reform abolished yearly social plans altogether, kept five-year plans as 'moral and political commitments' and relied primarily on enterprise plans.

[3] In 1965 the effect of the Reform was to reduce the investment share in the G.N.P. to 27.6 per cent (*Borba*, February 4, 1966).

H. *Foreign Trade and the Balance of Payments*

From a complete state monopoly of foreign trade, the Yugoslav system moved to an open economy in three stages.

The centralized system was autarchic; it looked on foreign imports as a necessary evil to provide capital goods for which it had to pay with exports. The main interest was in amassing foreign currency; the domestic planned system of exchange of goods and of prices was considered completely divorced from the outside world. The decentralized system introduced first the commercial independence of enterprises on foreign markets. Foreign trading enterprises had to cover their expenses by their proceeds. At the same time, the volume of foreign trade began to increase rapidly. The idea that industrialization would make the country independent of foreign countries in the sense of less trade was seen to be erroneous; imports increased, not balanced by adequate exports. Multiple rates of exchange were introduced to cover the gap. But all these manipulated rates proved in the end to be ineffective and foreign debts increased rapidly.

Trading with Western countries was of vital interest for Yugoslav industries and for the food supply, to which the United States and other foreign aid and commercial credits, West and East, made significant contributions. The balance-of-payments deficit was to a great extent covered by foreign credits, international and commercial. Exports did not expand because of increased demand on the home market, lack of agricultural products and the level of prices abroad which made it difficult for Yugoslav exporters to compete. The centralized accumulation of foreign currency did not stimulate increased exports.

The Reform introduced the following changes. First, the multiple exchange rate has been replaced by a uniform rate based on 1,250 old dinars to the dollar. Reorganization will make possible trade based on world market prices.[4] In foreign commerce, the main stress is now on liberalization. All quantitative restrictions will be removed. Customs duties, reduced from 23 to 11 per cent, will remain as the chief form of domestic protection against foreign competition. A reserve fund of foreign currency

[4] The use of world market prices for international trade among socialist countries is not a new one. The Eastern bloc (C.E.M.A.) took world prices as a basis for exchange. The difference between the C.E.M.A. and the Yugoslav system is that the former uses average prices of some past years while the latter takes actual world market prices. The Yugoslav Reform takes them as a measure for domestic prices as well, while other socialist countries stick to their domestic planned prices, each of them having a different structure from the others so that they cannot be brought under a common denominator.

will gradually have to be built up to $ 500,000,000 and then free convertibility will be introduced. In 1965, for the first time since 1945, Yugoslavia had an active current balance of payments. There was a satisfactory increase in invisible exports, especially from the tourist trade, the merchant fleet and remittances of workers from abroad.

It has now been recognized that the main Yugoslav economic problems cannot be solved within the country. This means completely abandoning any idea of autarchy and accepting a policy of long-term structural integration of the Yugoslav economy into the world division of labor in place of merely short-term commercial operations. Instead of fear of competition, there will be a more self-confident policy of competitive interdependence which will pull the Yugoslav economy the hard but rewarding way toward progress.

3.

To sum up, the Reform intends to achieve far-reaching results indeed. Its aim is no less than to build a model of a socialist system for a developed country, one which will be able to stand the competition of other developed countries and progress on its own merits, without the constant tutelage of government machinery. This is to be achieved by a process of what I would call the four Ds: De-centralization, De-étatization, Depoliticization and De-mocratization. The process has been begun within the framework of a Communist ideology and a one-party system, but it would not be objective to deny that it has an effectively liberalizing and progressively humanizing character.[5]

How might the Reform affect other socialist countries? Looking at the problem, one could say with a considerable amount of bold generalization that the European socialist countries are now entering the second stage, building a decentralized New System of the kind that Yugoslavia is just abandoning. The basic features of this process are: the reintroduc-

[5] The concept greatly differs from that of the welfare state. The essence of the welfare state is to leave the production machine capitalist, with some marginal intervention in the public sector, and, by state taxation, to redistribute the income taken from the richer to the poorer consumers. The Reform in Yugoslavia denies this role of redistribution to the state (even to a socialist one) and endeavors to organize production on the basis of workers' self-management, in order to eliminate the roots of exploitation of man by man through income redistribution. It leaves decisions on income distribution to the workers who produce the income (on enterprise, local, regional, state and international levels), but takes the world level of productivity as the objective measurement.

tion of market prices; gradual emancipation of the socialist business enterprises from the state administration; the introduction of commercial criteria into foreign trade; disbelief in the omniscient and infallible central planner; material stimulation of the workers' productivity. They still remain firm on certain principles: predominance of the political factor in economic decisions; priority of production over consumption; disbelief in workers' self-government; and belief that the process of de-étatization and democratization represents a danger for socialism.

The Reform in Yugoslavia is overcoming these past postulates of socialist policy. There are not many rational elements to aid one in forecasting how long it will take other socialist countries to gain the experience which Yugoslavia has paid for very dearly; but my guess would be that it will depend on the pace and level of their development, and on the pressure of technical progress due to international competition. The new Yugoslav model may provide some stimulating ideas to socialist and Communist parties in developed countries; and developing countries — particularly those which have decided to build socialism — may become aware of some pitfalls in developmental policies.

Yugoslavia's acceptance of a model of a developed country, after hitherto presenting its economic system as an example for under-developed countries, is a big step, one that would be likely to meet with opposition in any country, let alone in such a complicated multinational state as Yugoslavia.[6] Opposition to the Reform would logically be expected from those who are least developed, who have to work most and longest to cross the borderline and achieve the level of developed lands; from those who used to get more from the central moneybag than they put into it; and from those who gained more from their political influence than from their industrial skill. The greatest advocates of the Reform would be those who are most developed, who put more into the central bag than they got out of it, and whose economic strength was greater than their political influence.

These logical expectations correspond to reality. The first advocates of the Reform and the spearhead of it were the Slovene Communists. They were joined by the Croats; the two now march together, and with them the Serbs of Croatia. The Reform's strongest opponents came from

[6] In the 1961 population census, 7,800,000 people declared themselves as Serbs (41.6 per cent), 4,300,000 as Croats (23.4 per cent), 1,600,000 as Slovenes (8.8 per cent) and 1,046,000 as Macedonians (5.3 per cent). The Montenegrins numbered 514,000 (2.8 per cent), the Moslems 973,000 (5 per cent), and those who declared themselves just Jugoslavs 317,000. The Albanians numbered 915,000 and the Hungarians 504,000.

Serbia. The Communists from other Republics took varied attitudes, probably not feeling strong enough to compete with the larger Republics and expecting in the end to find their interests taken into account by either side.[7]

Yugoslavia has just reached the level of $ 500 annual income per head, which many economists consider to be the demarcation line between developed and undeveloped countries. So the model for under-developed societies would no longer work; it would pull the economy backward. The difference in the level of development in the 1960's shows that the average national income per head in the most advanced Republic, Slovenia, amounted to $ 935; in Croatia it was some 20 per cent more than the Yugoslav average of $ 605. In Serbia it was $ 480, Bosnia $ 348, Macedonia $ 339 and Montenegro $ 330. These differences, taken objectively, would not be of such economic importance if it were not for the following reason: The two most developed Republics have crossed the threshold of development, while the others have not. This aggravates the psychological tension.

On the basis of this situation, there developed two opposite concepts, indeed two models of economic policy, both Marxist, both socialist; but one crystallized into an ideal type of a Communist recipe for an under-developed economy,[8] and the other into an ideal type for a developed socialist economic system.

UNDER-DEVELOPED MODEL	DEVELOPED MODEL
Maximization of growth (no constraint)	Optimization of growth under constraint of profitableness
Autonomous investments decided by central planner	Induced investments decided by enterprises
Priority of production over consumption	Priority of consumption over production
Planned administrative prices	Market prices
Monocentric planning	Polycentric planning
Inflationary tendency	Deflationary tendency
National income redistribution by the state	National income redistribution by the producers themselves

[7] The Constitution of 1963 created a special federal fund to assist underdeveloped areas.

[8] Many of the articles printed in the edition "Yugoslav Economists on Problems of a Socialist Economy", *Eastern European Economics* (New York, I.A.S.P., Fall-Winter, 1963-1964), express the views of this group of economists.

Administrative direction of flow of goods, labor and capital	Flow of goods, labor and capital by economic interest
Autarchy in foreign trade	Integration in the international division of labor

A second source of discontent arises from psychological attitudes, aspirations and expectations more than from objective conditions. In areas that are less developed there can easily arise an exaggerated sense of poverty, frustration and injustice, resulting in impatient demands for compensation from the Federation in the form of grandiose projects of development. Among the more developed, on the other hand, a sense takes hold that they are giving much more than they are getting (exploitation), a fear that there will be a repetition of past oppression by the center, and — most sensitive of all — that their progress is being hampered by the less developed areas.

Now dress these collective and real interests in national symbols, put this new content into historical perspective, make it an emotional appeal for political action, and you have raised nationality feelings to a high state of tension. Socialism in Yugoslavia is not being built in a historical vacuum, and the Federation consists of fully developed nations which have cultural individuality and rich political traditions. This was fully recognized in 1946 and reconfirmed in 1963 by all the constitutions of New Yugoslavia. These nations have a constitutional 'right to self-determination, including the right to secession' (Constitution of 1963, Principles, I) as the Leninist formula goes, and this is a condition *sine qua non* of the existence of Yugoslavia.[9]

When Yugoslavia was created in 1918 as a union of lesser-developed Serbia and Montenegro and the more economically developed South Slav parts of the Hapsburg Empire, the politically dominant élite of Serbia adopted this political equation: greater political power plus smaller economic wealth equals greater economic wealth plus smaller political power. Thus redistribution of national income by political power was the main function of the state in Yugoslavia between 1918 and 1939; in it, therefore, the various nations could never achieve equal

[9] Here we have to go back somewhat in history. The pre-1918 Kingdom of Serbia was an underdeveloped but homogeneous and centralized country, without a developed capitalist system; the political, economic and cultural élite lived on the state and took the place of a capitalist class. The Croats, Slovenes and those Serbs who belonged to the Hapsburg Empire until 1918 were used to living in a multinational state. But their national aspirations and the development of their individuality had been achieved against the will of the Hapsburg state and in opposition to it. Therefore their élite did not consider it 'normal' that social action should be taken through the state.

political rights. For this reason a doctrine of national unity was created, since in a single nation the ruling élite had no need to justify their refusal to share political power. This same political formula was transferred to new Yugoslavia, but under it the socialist system developed somewhat differently.

The four most important versions of Yugoslav unity are the following:

(1) The romantic idea of Slav unity which will ultimately unite all South Slavs into one Great Nation, as expressed through history by the 'best sons' of all the South Slav peoples, who must put all their resources together, like real brothers, in order to fulfill a great mission which simple uneducated people do not understand. This idea of a Yugoslav super-nation was finally rejected by the Eighth Congress of the Communist League in 1964:

> An expression of nationalism which must be checked is seen ... in the mistaken idea that in our socialist development of society nationalities have been outlived, and that a unified Yugoslav nation should be created. Such beliefs are expressions of bureaucratic centralism and unitarianism and usually manifest themselves in a tendency to ignore the political, social, economic and other functions and responsibilities of republics and autonomous provinces.[10]

(2) Another concept is that of technocratic unity, put forward in the name of science for optimizing technical progress in Yugoslavia as a whole. The decision regarding the optimum should be reached by rational scientific methods, and the state should allocate resources for it. To refute this idea the technocrats were reminded that Yugoslavia is not populated by abstract *homines technologici* or *economici*, but by human beings whose happiness is their own responsibility. Moreover, further objections should be made, as for instance, that in searching for an optimum, why stop at the frontiers of Yugoslavia? Modern technology does not require centralized decision-making; it makes a polycentric system of decision-making not only possible but preferable. The computers are liberalizers, not centralizers. When the question is put, "What price shall we have to pay for federalism?" the echo is, "What have we to pay for centralism?" And the balance is not in favor of the latter. Thus Marshal Tito was right in refusing to identify technical progress with

[10] Resolution of the Congress, *Yugoslav Survey*, No. 20 (January 1965), p. 2909. In his report to the Congress, Tito said: "Some people, even some Communists, think that nationalities have withered away ... they confuse unity of the people with the liquidation of the nations and the creation of something new, something artificial, i.e. one single Yugoslav nation, which is somewhat similar to assimilation and bureaucratic centralism, unitarianism and hegemonism. The Yugoslav socialist integration is a new type of social community, nı which all nations find their common interests." ("Osmi kongres S.K.J.", *Kultura*, Belgrade, 1964, p. 132.)

centralism; and Edward Kardelj, President of the Federal Assembly, refused to put order in opposition to democracy.[11]

(3) The third concept of unity is the policy of equal stomachs. It appealed to socialist solidarity because of the idea that the central authority of the state should take the income and resources from those who 'have' and distribute them among those who 'have not'. The Reform aims at a socialist society where, in order to 'have', people must work and earn their income by their labor. Redistribution of income by the state means to take part of the income earned by one worker or group of workers and give it to another individual or group who has not worked for it. This solidarity may be the basis of a policy of social assistance, but it cannot stand as a basis for a socialist economic system.

(4) The fourth main concept justifying unity is to be found in the field of foreign policy: whatever the internal conditions in Yugoslavia, the supreme interest of relations with the outside world demands unconditional unity; and this is a central function which requires the strengthening of the center.

To this one must reply that the policy of active and peaceful coexistence has eliminated all serious threat to Yugoslavia from abroad. The psychology of the besieged fortress, genuine or staged, is out of place. The real problem is the great difference in the standard of living between Yugoslavia and her western neighbors, or Europe as a whole. To reduce this economic tension, the Reform has undertaken to liberalize foreign trade and to promote the structural integration of the economy into the world division of labor; GATT was joined, a certain coöperation achieved with C.E.M.A. and action taken to work with the European Economic Community and EFTA.

[11] *Borba* (December 31, 1965). Asked whether self-management does not hamper technical progress, Kardelj said that reluctance to accept 'rational' solutions was the result of unhappy experience with strong administrative intervention. He took as an example the problem, long and passionately discussed in parliament, of electric power and its centralization. In refusing to agree that the state should order the centralization of the electricity system into a single unit, Kardelj said that those who use electric power should be responsible for building electric power stations. The Federation of Electrical Enterprises should not be vested with the authority of a government agency. Those who decide to build power stations at greater than optimal cost will have to pay dearly for it and bear the cost themselves.

In the same way as the personal interest of each worker is to be rewarded according to his work so that he is in a position to improve his standard of living and strengthen the material basis of his life, so republics and national interests exist in order to satisfy those wants which can be satisfied only within a local or national community. ... National interests cannot be degraded into regional or statistic ones. (*Borba*, March 3, 1966. Under 'national' Kardelj means the Slovene, Serb, etc., national interests.)

In conclusion — all the above concepts of unity have been used to justify a political distribution of income by an étatistic élite and are therefore not acceptable throughout Yugoslavia, but only at the center, which has always advocated other than democratic procedures.

The national tensions which increased in all the nations of Yugoslavia to such an extent that they became a central problem, first economic and then political,[12] were subject to analysis at the Eighth Congress of the Communist League. The line it took was that if there is a general phenomenon it must have a common cause. It found this cause in the system of bureaucratic centralism against which all the nations were reacting. In order to eliminate national tensions within the country, the first thing to do was to eliminate their common cause. Thus it was that the policy for reducing national conflict became closely linked to the policy of economic reform. The protagonists of the Reform are not provincial anarchists but stand above local nationalism; they are more 'internationally minded' than the autarchic centralists. Their main idea is that the socialist economic integration of Yugoslavia is a long process which started in the liberation struggle of the Second World War, but is not yet accomplished; indeed, that its development depends on the extent to which true socialist relations exist, and on the degree to which the policy inaugurated by the Eighth Congress will be carried out.

It is commonly agreed that the Reform is not progressing at a very satisfactory rate. One of the reasons may be that the Federal Government finds itself in a difficult position, struggling with the overt or covert resistance of the high bureaucracy which on one occasion discreetly puts on the brakes, at another pushes the reform measures to unrealizable and absurd lengths. The heated debates in the federal parliament, exclusively composed of Communists, where bills are passed with a majority of 4 or 6, show how far the process of liberalization has gone. On the other hand, they manifest the strength of the opposition to concrete reform.

One must remember that the Reform is divided into two kinds of measures. First, extensive central control was strengthened (price control, credit restrictions, rate of foreign currency exchange) in order to clear the field for the further liberalizing steps. But since some success was

[12] Asked whether national tension was only question number two in Yugoslavia, Vladimir Bakarić said (*Borba*, March 6, 1966): "Today it is at least question number two. With the battle for the Reform we have to win the battle against nationalism as well. If we don't win this battle, then it might become question number one." He also said that the nationalities problem might even be sharper now because it had not been dealt with in proper time.

achieved in the first stage in relieving the immediate critical situation, a twofold reaction has now set in. This came to the fore in the meeting of the Central Committee in February-March 1966. All participants were for the Reform; but some (mainly from Serbia) praised it and demanded that the first centralizing measures should be further pursued, while others (e.g. from Croatia) asked that more energetic measures be taken in pursuit of the main purpose of the Reform. In the complex tactics of the Reform — "to retreat in order to advance better" — some praised the retreat, others pressed for faster advance. Heed should be paid to the warnings of Boris Kraigher, the operational head of the Reform, that it may last for a long time, perhaps for a decade, and that the most difficult period, that of structural changes in the Yugoslav economy, is still ahead. Speeding up the Reform is of utmost importance. Failure of the Reform would deeply shake the faith of many people that Yugoslavia's problems can be solved by consent.

The two opposing views of the Reform within the Communist League have managed to gather behind them a considerable following outside the Party itself.[13] Will the policy of the League be to institutionalize emotional 'national' appeals, thus fighting the issues of the Reform out in the open and furthering the process of democratization? Or will it close ranks, isolate itself and use its only available instrument, that of bureaucratic centralism, admittedly the cause of the present difficulties, thereby pushing national dissent underground and at the same time destroying the Reform from within? In my opinion there is no 'once and for all' solution. These are problems of long duration and great amplitude. If it is true that the foreign policy of every state reflects its internal relations, then Yugoslavia should adopt the principle of active, peaceful coexistence to solve the problems of her own component nations.

[13] The Croat Communists have to be given credit for leading in the Reform. Nevertheless it seems to me that the handling of the psychological side of Croatian national dissatisfaction is not adequate, as some instances in Croatia have shown. On the other hand, Croatian nationalistic outbursts, staged or spontaneous, would just play into the hands of the anti-reformist centralists. Some Croats should remember the heroic silliness of Eugene Kvaternik whose revolt in 1871 was used as a pretext to prevent the reorganization of the Austrian Empire along federal lines.

XI

SOME ASPECTS OF THE POLICY OF WORKER'S[1] INCOME IN YUGOSLAVIA

The policy of the formation of workers' incomes in Yugoslavia is carried on within a socialist economy of specific characteristics. All industrial enterprises, banking, commerce, transport, etc. are socialized and so is the 20 per cent of agricultural land which is not part of small, private peasant-family holdings. Within this institutional set-up the following characteristic features are found: (a) an accelerated process of industrialization; (b) a high investment quota for the national income (20-27 per cent) and of general government and public consumption (23-13 per cent) with personal consumption at the percentage of 57-52 of the national income; (c) intensive pressure on employment because of the exodus from agriculture by economically active population, the transition from agricultural to non-agricultural occupations proceeding faster than urban concentration of population; (d) high and increasing rate of indirect income through the wide range of social welfare benefits including free education; (e) practically all workers are members of trade unions, and though neither collective bargaining nor strikes are practiced, the workers find other ways to express their dissatisfaction, e.g. dispersed slow-down of work, reduction of productivity, decrease of working discipline, etc.

The consequences of this general situation on the incomes of workers and employees is that they are low not only in absolute but also in relative terms. Therefore most workers' families cannot live from the wage or salary of one wage-earner only, but have to supplement it by having two or more income-earners in one family. Forty per cent of all workers and employees in non-agricultural occupations live on peasant-family holdings. Many workers take complementary second jobs, increasing fringe benefits, working overtime, taking temporary assign-

[1] In Yugoslavia the term 'worker' is used in two different ways: first as a stricter term differentiating those who do physical jobs from white-collar workers; secondly in a wider sense to cover all employees including the top personnel. In a still wider sense all civil servants are also included in the term 'workers'.

ments, etc. in the socialist sector, or private jobs doing repairs, etc.

In the beginning this tendency was encouraged by a government policy in which everyone was urged to work as much as possible. But later it was realized that such efforts by the workers do not simply add to their product but compete with their regular employment. Thus the workers' attention is often divided between two jobs, which most of the time are located in two different sectors, the socialist and the private. The competition is one for working time, for money income, but above all for the energy and physical strength of the workers.

In Yugoslavia the workers' wage-, or rather income-,policy is dominated by the fact that the workers are employed by socialist enterprises. This policy is, therefore, largely part of the policy for distribution of the revenue of socialist enterprises. There are two main periods in which different policies must be distinguished: One is the period of administrative socialism on the Soviet pattern which lasted from 1947-1951; and the second period is that of the specific Yugoslav socialist system, which can be sub-divided into three phases — (a) the wage-bill-saving-and-social-funds rate system; (b) the profit-sharing phase; (c) the income-sharing phase.

1. ADMINISTRATIVE MANAGEMENT OF THE NATIONAL ECONOMY

In the first period (1947-1951) the policy regulating workers' incomes was a comparatively simple one: all wages and salaries were decided and strictly regulated by the State for all branches of industries and all groups of workers and employees. Neither the workers and employees nor the management of the enterprises where they worked had anything to say. In this period of post-war reconstruction of a war-torn country the wage policy was dominated by inexperienced enthusiasm and revolutionary drive in their prime, and material incentives to work were considered counter-revolutionary. Consequently wages were low, hardly enough to meet essential needs. No personal saving was supposed to take place even from earnings from work, and all investment was meant to be confined to compulsory saving through the medium of the overall state budget.

Yet the whole system of rigid, planned proportions, where the wage-level played one of the most important roles, broke down first in the field of wages. Managers of enterprises, anxious to fulfill the plans, and in fear of the consequences if they did not do so, began to compete for skilled labor in short supply, and to pay 'black' wages over and above the stipulated ones. Labor, with no material incentive regimented and regulated by a hastily-formed bureaucracy, decreased productivity the more the difficulties of living became prolonged. In the course of a few years, planned average wages became completely alienated from the realities of economics. This, and the economic blockade of the country ordered by Stalin in 1948, caused the whole system of administrative management to be abandoned and replaced by a new socialist system.

2. THE WAGE-BILL-SAVING-AND-SOCIAL-FUND-RATE SYSTEM (1952-1953)

The NEW ECONOMIC SYSTEM was not established overnight from a ready-made blueprint. It was built in the struggle with day-to-day problems, and with it a renewed ideological outlook was adopted. Gradually prices were freed from government regulations; enterprises came to be managed in a more and more businesslike way — acting autonomously on the market on a profit and loss basis, deciding upon their microeconomic plans within the framework of the macroeconomic social plan, released from operational, administrative management by government departments, and run by workers' councils. Socialist enterprises could increase their sales and increase their returns, but the division of these returns was strictly regulated by law. They could employ labor according to their own decisions, and pay it from income gained by the enterprise itself.

The last elements to be freed from administrative control were wages and salaries. The reasons were, first, that the government did not want to take the risk of letting wages be decided by what were at that time inexperienced workers' councils, and secondly because no workable system had been found which could be trusted with such an important role in what was a new type of socialist economy.

The system of wages and salaries was based on Marx's formula:

$$y = c + v + m$$

Returns equals constant capital, plus variable capital, plus socialized surplus value. This policy transformed into policy measures prescribed the income of the enterprise, gained on the market, to be distributed according to the saving rate imposed by the plan; the residual represented the workers' aggregate wage-fund. This meant that aggregate saving and contributions to the social funds were deducted from the income of the enterprise at a rate determined in advance by the yearly federal plan. This amounted to an overall average of 122 to 597 in manufacturing industries, and for certain enterprises up to 2000 per cent.[2] Nominally the workers' wages were fixed by the tariff of the enterprises but in fact they were decided by the controlling, administrative departments. What was left after deductions represented the wage bill. If this sum was not sufficient to cover a certain level of minimal wages set by the plan, the difference was made up by the government. The plan prescribed the minimum capacity of production for every enterprise. A contribution, at progressive rates, had to be paid into the state budget to drain off most of the income above the level corresponding to this prescribed minimal capacity of production.

This system, called the wage-bill-saving-and-social-funds-rate system, was in existence for only two years. Its main defect was that it concentrated the whole income distribution of the enterprises into one single policy instrument, and if this was wrongly fixed there was no way to compensate for the error by other instruments. In point of fact these saving rates were chosen with little preparation and often very arbitrarily, which greatly distorted the whole economic process. Many changes in the rates, sometimes depending on the 'pull' of the managers and their VIP friends created uncertainty and dissatisfaction. The difference between branches was too big, and the whole system had no upper ceiling to prevent inflation. Progressive rates taxed away all gains from increased productivity. On the other hand, every increase in the workers' wages automatically led to a multiple increase in prices in an economy starved of goods. As the prices of consumer goods were not controllable in the private sector (food), and scarcities of industrial consumer goods prevailed in the socialist sector, workers' wages had to be increased; this led to inflationary pressure.

This system was abolished by the end of 1953, and a new system — that of profit-sharing — introduced in 1954.

3. THE PROFIT-SHARING SYSTEM (1954-1957)

The profits of socialist enterprises were considered to be a result of the institutional set-up of the socialist society, and therefore to belong to Society as a whole. The wage-policy in the profit-sharing system was

[2] In other words, to increase the workers' wages by one dinar, the enterprise had to increase its income by six dinars or more.

based on the partition of workers' wages into two parts, one fixed, the other variable. The fixed or regular wage was meant to cover the essential needs of the worker and his family. Its sum total formed the basic wage-funds of the enterprise. The variable part of the wage was supposed to play the role of a stimulant to the productive efforts of the workers. It was derived from a share in the profits of the enterprise. This share was a percentage of the basic wage-fund decided on by the district social plan. Later the Federal Plan fixed its maximum and minimum rates (8-16 per cent). There was constant competition between the district authority, the enterprise funds and the wage-bill as to who was to get a bigger share in the net profits after deduction of the Federal income. The Federal government secured top priority for its own share, and for the rest played the arbiter between the competitors, protecting the workers' share from the district authority and strengthening the funds of the enterprise against the claims of the workers for bigger shares.

In 1954 the wages were still 'accounted wages', fixed by government orders according to 'classification by skill', and made dependent on the aggregate wage-fund and on the structure of this fund according to the skill and level of the wages of the workers. If, for instance, a manager wanted his salary increased, the workers' council had to raise the whole wage-fund proportionally so that the proportion of the shares of the highly qualified, the skilled and the unskilled workers remained constant. This block system of wage-structure made any increase in the income of higher paid workers and employees more difficult. In practice it unnecessarily increased the number of unskilled workers in the lower pay brackets.

After 1955 wages and salaries were no longer determined by the government. The decision was left to the enterprises themselves. Every enterprise had to evaluate each of the working places in the enterprise in the form of a norm, and include it in a tariff which was part of the statutes of the enterprise. This tariff, on whose composition many workers and experts cooperated, had to be agreed upon by the local trade union council, and confirmed by the District people's committee (= district authority). In principle each enterprise was independent in deciding about the fixed wages, and in this way in establishing the aggregate wage-bill as part of the costs of the enterprise. The net revenue, after deduction of taxes and other contributions to social funds etc., was shared by the Federal government (which took its 50 per cent), the Republics and the District authority. The workers' share amounted, in 1954, to 4.8 per cent of the net profits of the enterprise, and this percentage gradually rose to

9.2 per cent in 1957. In proportion to the workers' fixed wages in the enterprise it amounted mainly to the value of one monthly pay (called the 'thirteenth pay'), sometimes to two, three or even more.

This policy gave the workers' councils a much greater say in the fixing of wages.[3] It was a very considerable improvement over the system of administratively regulated wages. Nevertheless, guidance was given by the trade unions which at that time mainly transmitted the wishes of the government to the workers' councils and worked as equalizing moderators bringing some system into the decisions of particular workers' councils and trying to keep the wages down. To this system of evaluation of the working places, premiums were added for special performances by the workers, and also overtime bonuses, etc.

But the main interest of the workers remained in their variable share of the profit, which, especially in large enterprises, they could not directly influence; they considered it more as a windfall profit, sometimes depending more on the skill of the chief accountant than on their efforts or those of the technical manager or the commercial director. Sometimes temporary results of the year were distributed as interim or anticipated profits, which, once distributed, it was difficult to recover from the workers if the balances of the whole accounting year showed a smaller profit than that expected by part-time balances. In some enterprises enjoying a monopoly on the market, and especially in commercial enterprises, profits rose sky high, and in some cases as many as eight extra monthly wages were paid out. This again contributed to inflationary pressure, which also had some other causes (investment etc.).

Another preoccupation of the wage policy was to stimulate productivity of labor and to prevent further increases in employment, which were encouraged by the way the profit-sharing system operated in practice. The profit-sharing system was altered to a greater or lesser extent every year in a game of hide-and-seek between the Federal government, the local authorities, the managements of the enterprises, the workers' council and the workers themselves all competing as to who was to get better gains from the profit-sharing legislation.[4] The system was finally abandoned in 1958 and the income-sharing system introduced.

[3] In 1957 there were 6,134 workers' councils in enterprises of 30 or more workers. They held 74,391 meetings and the following items appeared on agendas the number of times shown: workers' wage tariffs 16,457, investments 18,377, use of the fund of the enterprise on which workers, council decides 15,476, distribution of profits 11,684.

[4] For an analysis of this game of competition see our article "Interaction of Macro and Micro-economic Decisions in Yugoslavia 1954-1957", *Value and Plan*, ed. G. Grossman (California Univ. Press, 1960), pp. 346-359.

4. INCOME-SHARING (1958-1964)

The basic principle of income-sharing in Yugoslav socialist enterprises is that the workers who run socialized property through workers' councils do not receive wages and salaries, but get their earnings in the form of personal incomes. In other words, the workers are not considered to be hired personnel who have the right to be paid, but get from the enterprises the amount which they have earned by their work. The wage system has been abolished altogether. In this way the workers' earnings do not represent costs of the enterprise. The workers are operators of socialist funds who chose the workers' council and therefore have to carry the risks of management. Thus the workers' wage-policy has become a more general workers' income-policy (concerned with that part of the workers' income derived from work in the enterprise). Thus the workers' personal income is no longer an independent variable, but a function depending on the proceeds, business gains and losses of the enterprise. Their share of the gross REVENUE of the enterprise is calculated after deduction from the total proceeds of all costs of running the enterprise: i.e. costs for raw materials and energy, depreciation allowance, taxes, contribution to the general investment fund (6 per cent of the working capital per year), etc. This may be called the first, or external, distribution of the gross revenue, by which the INCOME of the enterprise is established.

This income is divided between the funds of the enterprise, and the aggregate workers' gross personal income. From this sum (after deduction of the tax, mainly for communal budgets, and contributions to social insurance) the aggregate net personal income of the workers is obtained. This is the second, or the internal, redistribution of the revenue of the enterprise, and is decided by the workers' council. It amounts to roughly 40 per cent of the gross revenue, of which some 25 per cent was allocated for the workers' net personal income and 15 per cent to the funds of the enterprise. The tendency is to bring it to a 28 to 12 per cent (70:30) ratio of the internal income of the enterprise.

In this second redistribution the gross income of the workers is determined as follows:

(1) All working places are internally evaluated by POINTS which show how much a worker's work is worth for the enterprise including assessment of payment by effects of work.[5] These points are counted in money when

[5] As an illustration we give here the points evaluation of a number of workers in a Zagreb textile factory. Points evaluation is given for 440 different jobs.

the final accounts of the business year are closed. In the course of the year the worker gets a monthly advance on his income, depending on the preliminary estimates of the final outcome. In my opinion these points will necessarily develop into some sort of internal money of the enterprise (the 'certificates' of old socialists) having a rate of exchange with the national money, and it will be interesting to follow the effect of changes in the rates;

(2) The second principle is that of ECONOMIC UNITS. In order to secure among the workers more direct interest in the effects of their work, enterprises are divided into economic units either on the technical principle (workshops, plants), or on the functional operational principle (transport department, bookkeeping service, etc.), and the effect of work is calculated not only per individual worker, but also per economic unit as a whole. Each economic unit has, in most cases, its own worker's councils with somewhat limited autonomy. There is a quasi selling and buying of products among economic units within the enterprise, calcu-

	education	ability and experience	management	responsibility	physical effort	mental effort	working conditions	TOTAL POINTS
general manager	100	170	150	190	10	100	10	730
technical manager	100	140	140	160	10	90	10	650
works manager	100	130	100	120	10	90	30	580
foreman	80	60	40	50	10	40	40	320
skilled weaver	50	40	—	40	35	30	40	235
semi-skilled spinner	50	20	—	20	30	10	40	150
sales manager	100	130	100	140	90	10	10	580
book-keeper	100	100	50	90	10	80	10	440
lorry-driver	80	60	—	70	30	40	40	320
cleaner	20	10	—	10	40	10	40	130

There are also premiums for decrease of costs, quality of products, increase in the productivity of labor for economic units measured by actual performance above that planned.

The top personnel get premiums of up to 10 per cent of income by points for successful management.

lating internal costs and benefits. This has greatly increased the interest of the workers in the problems of management.

Collective productivity is further developed into the work of the whole enterprise. Thus there are three levels at which the workers' income is decided: — his personal efforts; the collective effort of the unit; and the efforts of the enterprise as a whole.

(3) The third principle is that concerned with safeguarding a MINIMAL INCOME for the worker. Although it is an accepted principle that the workers must bear the risks of their own work and management, there is nevertheless an underlying basic principle that the worker's and his family's existence depends on his income from work, whatever the outcome of the business success of the enterprise in which he works. Therefore two safeguards have been introduced: a guaranteed personal income level, and a minimum personal income. The first is established by the government on the basis of the last yearly average personal income per employee in the corresponding branch of industry (varying from 17,600 to 23,800 dinars per month). If any enterprise cannot pay the guaranteed minimum, there is a communal reserve fund to which all enterprises contribute and out of which the sum is forwarded to the enterprise to provide the difference. This sum must be returned to the communal fund after the enterprise has improved its position. If the results of the enterprise show no improvement, workers' mangement can be suspended and ultimately the enterprise can go bankrupt and be liquidated. This guaranteed income is distributed within the enterprise according to its own points system. The other safeguard, the minimum personal income, is fixed by law (in 1963, at 12,700 dinars a month) and is the same for all industries and all enterprises. It is paid out of the funds of the Commune if the enterprise has no other resources. There is a special fund in each enterprise called the joint consumption fund, into which a part of the income, allocated by the workers' management, is paid. This fund is used to increase the general welfare of the working collective — e.g. health dispensaries, workers' houses, children's creches, reading rooms, sports clubs, etc.

5. ACTUAL PROBLEMS

There are quite a number of problems in the actual operation of the system described, and in its perspective development. These are partly related to the specific workers' income policy, but to a large extent reflect the effects of general economic policy on workers' income.

(1) In implementing the general socialist principle 'to each according to his work' a difference of opinion arose which became manifest when the new constitution was debated in 1962/1963, and in discussions concerning the causes of the 1961-1962 economic recession. One trend of thought interpreted that in concrete policy 'to each according to his work' should be translated 'to each according to the intensity, effort and sacrifice in his work'. Those holding the other opinion, mainly from the more industrially developed areas, claimed that the principle means 'to each according to the results, i.e. productivity of his work'. The constitution provided a compromise formula by using both subjective and objective interpretations, but present government policy rightly puts weight on productivity, although there are voices representing the other view.

(2) The stimulation of workers is based on the increase of income dependent on increase in productivity, and in a rise in the level of living dependent on the increase of income.[6]

The question arose whether the enterprise returns, and consequently the workers' aggregate income, should be taxed at a flat or a progressive rate. One opinion, mainly from less developed areas, was for the progressive rate, maintaining that the socialist taxation policy had always been progressive rates. The other opinion was based on the fact that stimulation effect on workers is greatly reduced by progressive rates, and that the state would be penalizing the most advanced enterprises and productive workers for the benefit of the least successful. Moreover it was stressed that different principles must be applied under conditions of workers' management of socialist enterprises and income-sharing than under private, or even state-owned, enterprises, where the workers get their wages and salaries as part of the costs of the enterprise. The principle of flat rates has been applied, and the extraordinary contribution to the state budget, which had been based on a kind of progressive tax basis rate, was going to be abolished in 1963.

(3) The different productivity of individual enterprises, and particularly the differential average productivity of labor in different branches of industry and different regions has necessarily led to the problem: from which basis ought the productivity of labor to be calculated.[7] This

[6] The new constitution introduced a 42-hour week instead of 48 hours. Efforts being made to achieve this reduction of the working time under the same system of income-sharing seem to be having success, as there are reserves of working efficiency in many enterprises.

[7] The differences of the net monthly average income of workers varies from 58,000 dinars in maritime transport and 54 000 in construction drafting bureaus to 19,000

problem of the starting basis is still being discussed, and an acceptable solution has not yet been found.

(4) The span between the lowest- and highest-paid workers in the enterprise has also given rise to various difficulties, particularly when all income and direct and indirect benefits are taken into account. As always in a period of inflation there is a tendency to level out the workers' incomes by increasing first those of the lowest paid group. Indeed, the percentage of workers in the lowest paid groups has been halved since 1961, and in other low-income groups greatly reduced. On the other hand some of the managers and highly trained experts won relatively excessive incomes (producing a span of 1:7 between the highest and the lowest group within a single enterprise). Political pressure was exerted to end some excesses, and this was interpreted as a sign for a general movement towards *uravnilovka* (levelling) of all personal incomes in enterprises, hitting the technical experts hardest. This primitive concept of socialism soon showed its negative effects, as many of these experts, always in short supply, moved to better-paid jobs; the tendency was reversed again, but with less excessive claims being made.

(5) There is a steadily felt competition between the share of the revenue which the enterprise can distribute between the workers, as their personal income, and the funds of the enterprise (the working capital fund, including depreciation allowances, the reserve fund and the joint-consumption fund).

In 1962 the workers' councils were given the right to use the net revenue more liberally, which they did by allocating more to workers incomes with no adequate increase in productivity. As prices also began quickly to rise the workers' councils increased the share distributed to the workers at the expense of the funds of the enterprise.[8] Administrative intervention was considered necessary, and indeed government commissions were set up at all administrative levels to advise the enterprises on how to distribute their revenue between the two main purposes. Besides subjective guidance, a formula was prescribed giving the right proportions. This was considered an encroachment on the rights of workers' management, and in 1963 the government set up machinery by which an agreement was reached between the Federal Secretariat of

dinars in the timber industry and 19,800 in the textile industry, the overall average being 25,000 dinars. The average per worker per month in Slovenia is 37,000, in Croatia 30,600, in Serbia 27.300 and in Macedonia only 23,500.

[8] From 1960 to 1961 the share of the net personal income rose from 25.2 to 26.4 per cent, and that of the funds of the enterprises fell from 18.7 to 16.7. In 1962 the corresponding figures were 23.9 and 15.4 per cent.

Labor, the Federation of Trade Unions, and the Business Chamber (economic chamber representing federations of managements of all socialist enterprises) on the indicators to be applied in the internal distribution of that part of the revenue of the enterprise which was left to the workers' councils to distribute.[9] These indicators were not combined into one consistent model, and thus left workers councils to make final decisions using the indicators only as a guide.

This tripartite agreement is the first instance where the Trade Union Federation openly stood as an independent and separate representative of the workers interest side by side with the state authority, and the representatives of the management of socialist enterprises.

(6) Another problem of workers' income policy is the macroeconomic distribution of the national income. The question is asked whether the present generation should carry the main burden of economic development, or whether some of the burden should be left for coming generations. In terms of economic policy it is a question of whether the investment quota of the national income should be increased or made smaller to the benefit of personal consumption. The question used to be discussed in more academic terms, and a step forward was taken in 1956 when the burden of investment was made somewhat lighter. But there was no pressure felt from organized labor, partly because at that time the workers still represented the minor part of the population. But since the 1960's the workers have made up more than 50 per cent of the active population and the macroeconomic proportion affects them more evidently than ever before. Therefore their influence is being felt, and in discussions concerning more recent social plans the Trade Unions Federation is putting more and more stress on the desirability of increasing the percentage of the national income allocated for personal consumption. This is low not only in absolute terms, but also in relative ones, amounting to 52 per cent of the national income, while in 1952 it was 56 per cent. There is a feeling that a general re-examination of the national income-distribution policy is due (1964).

(7) Competition between work in the socialist sector and private, extra work is still a major problem. In order to make workers concentrate their energies in their regular employment, greater stimulation and the possibility of increased earnings are required. This has been partly met

[9] These indicators are combined in 5 groups each consisting of 4 to 6 indicators such as: comparative net product per worker; the rate of saving and of workers' income per head; the used capacity and productivity of capital; gross volume of production per worker; total sales compared to total costs.

by the introduction of a system of stimulative payment by effect. One great problem is that 40 per cent of all workers live in peasant families on holdings which are additional sources of income, and also require additional efforts. Any speed-up of the process of vertical and horizontal mobility is hampered by the fact that the greatest share of the workers' budget is spent on food, expenditure which is greatly saved in the case of the worker-peasants who are supplied by the peasant family holding. This is even more true for rent, as housing is in such short supply that many workers are unable to move to towns and factories even if they want to. Increased building activity since 1958 has not yet been able greatly to improve the situation.

(8) Population pressure and rural exodus was fostered by the government as in favor of their policy of creating a working class in a predominantly peasant society. The indirect consequence of this movement was that it made the policy of low wages possible. What was once surplus agricultural population has now, to a certain extent, been transformed into surplus industrial, commercial and administrative population.

Since the combined effect of the economic recession, the policy of deflation and the increased workers' influence on income-sharing in the enterprises (revealing surplus labor) is being felt, a reversal of policy is beginning to take place. The effect of this policy must necessarily be towards increasing the workers' personal incomes.

(9) Practically the same development is true for the increased, open unemployment into which some agricultural and industrial concealed unemployment has been transformed. When the manufacturing industries were but little developed and on a low level of productivity, unskilled labor was good enough, and with a little training could be turned into semi-skilled. But as the industries have progressed quite a number of unskilled workers have become superfluous, although it has become difficult to meet the need for highly trained personnel. Therefore registered unemployment has risen to 7.5 per cent of all employed. Emigration of labor to some European states has partly eased this pressure. The tendency is to increase the development of services that have so far been poorly equipped in order to employ surplus labor after retraining.

(10) The consequence of inflationary pressure is the lowering of real income. The gap between the nominal and real personal income of workers has been widening again since the beginning of 1961. It looks as if inflation-deflation tendencies affect different sectors of the economy in different ways, and that the workers' income is caught between the

hammer of increased living costs and the anvil of the policy of deflation. Some more energetic measure than hitherto will have to be applied to escape from this situation.

6. CONCLUSIONS

The workers' income policy in Yugoslavia now depends on the workers' management of the socialist enterprises as it operates within the general framework of the economic system and current economic policy.

The effect of workers on management depends on the maturity of the working class and the experience of workers' councils in which up to now more than one third of all workers have taken part over the last twelve years. Maturity grows with responsibility and with growing experience. In the beginning the main interest was centered on personal problems and labor relations. It turned to commercial problems of prices and the quality of products in order to improve sales. This led to investment problems where it was thought that investment would solve all difficulties. But as on one hand public funds were insufficient to cover all claims, and on the other the autonomous funds of the enterprise were increased, so workers' councils had to rely more on their own resources. In 1953 investments out of autonomous enterprise funds amounted to 21 per cent of all investments. In 1962 this figure was 30 per cent. But this increased freedom of action was paid for by increased demand for responsibility and more far-sightedness on the part of workers, especially when decisions posed the dilemma: increase of personal income or increase of enterprise investment funds.

So far it could be said that the result has proved successful. Moreover there are cases where workers have decided temporarily not to take the variable share of their income, but whether they put it partly or wholly for the increase of the local authorities, there is no doubt that the final decision is made by the workers' councils. Their behavior is influenced by two major considerations: (a) the relationship between their nominal and real income which depends on the monetary policy, and the price of agricultural produce in the first place; (b) the equality of treatment in economic policy. Two tendencies are to be felt: one trying to solve all difficulties by demanding exceptions and privileges, thus shifting the burden onto others; the other demanding equality of treatment for all according to certain objective criteria such as productivity of labor and rationality of investment. One could say that the workers' councils follow the principle 'we do as all do'. If there is a feeling that others are being given investment credits out of public funds in an easy or privileged way, then they put forward their claims for getting credits too (not to be left out), without much rational examination. The competitive spirit is a corollary to the willingness to bear sacrifices and to cut down the shares of one's income. Thus decisions made in an authoritarian or arbitrary manner would cause dissatisfaction and a trend toward increase of personal income. If, on the other hand, decisions are made in a democratic way, persuading the participants about the rationality of decisions, then the interdependence is felt more directly, and the growth process is more favorably influenced.

Thus the workers' income-policy in a system like the socialist system of Yugoslavia becomes closely connected with the whole problem of economic growth. Moreover, it becomes the major political issue for which the new constitution has endeavored to provide the basic principles and the political machinery.

Bei Fragen zur Produktsicherheit wenden Sie sich bitte an:
If you have any questions regarding product safety,
please contact:

Walter de Gruyter GmbH
Genthiner Straße 13
10785 Berlin
productsafety@degruyterbrill.com